Jules Gouffe

The Book of Preserves

Jules Gouffe

The Book of Preserves

ISBN/EAN: 9783337294649

Printed in Europe, USA, Canada, Australia, Japan

Cover: Foto ©Lupo / pixelio.de

More available books at **www.hansebooks.com**

THE
BOOK OF PRESERVES

(LE LIVRE DE CONSERVES)

CONTAINING INSTRUCTIONS FOR

PRESERVING MEAT, FISH, VEGETABLES, AND FRUIT

AND FOR THE PREPARATION OF

TERRINES, GALANTINES, LIQUEURS, SYRUPS, PETITS-FOURS, &c.

BY

JULES GOUFFÉ

CHEF OF THE PARIS JOCKEY CLUB; AUTHOR OF 'THE ROYAL COOKERY BOOK'

TRANSLATED FROM THE FRENCH

ALPHONSE GOUFFÉ

HEAD PASTRYCOOK TO HER MAJESTY THE QUEEN

Illustrated with 34 Woodcuts

LONDON
SAMPSON LOW, SON, AND MARSTON
CROWN BUILDINGS, 188 FLEET STREET
1871

PREFACE

THE PRESENT VOLUME lays no claim to being a complete Cookery Book; it is rather the continuation or complement of the one I recently published under the name of the '*Livre de Cuisine*.' *

The work is subdivided into three distinct parts, which retain, however, a certain connection one with the other.

The First part treats of Preserving in all its branches, and illustrates the many advantages to be derived from the permanent preserving of meat, fish, eggs, milk, vegetables, and fruit.

The Second part comprises all that relates to the Confectioner's art; namely, the preparation of *bonbons*, *petits-fours*, candied fruits, and other numerous requisites for balls and parties.

In the Third part, I have collected a number of Recipes,

* 'The Royal Cookery Book.' Sampson Low, Son, & Marston. 1870.

which will be found of special value for the dietary of invalids.

Finally, in the shape of an Appendix, I have given a few hints on the selection of Wines, and their judicious introduction at table.

I trust that my remarks will not be without their use, for they will enable many to prepare, without difficulty, dishes which have hitherto been beyond the reach of their skill or their purse.

The following five hundred and odd recipes should thus tend to supply a want which existed until now.

CONTENTS

PRELIMINARY OBSERVATIONS

UTENSILS AND APPLIANCES

For greater clearness I subjoin a list of the different utensils required for the operations enumerated in each of the following chapters, with their use, and, when necessary, some hints upon their construction.

The first cost of these requisites will soon be covered by the greater facility they will afford in the daily work.

CHAPTER I

SALT AND SMOKED BEEF

For salting, procure a wooden bin, made of 2-inch board, and 2 feet 6 inches square.

This same bin will also be used for salting pork.

Be particular, after each time of using, to scald the salting bin, and to singe it with a handful of lighted shavings to prevent any taint of dampness remaining.

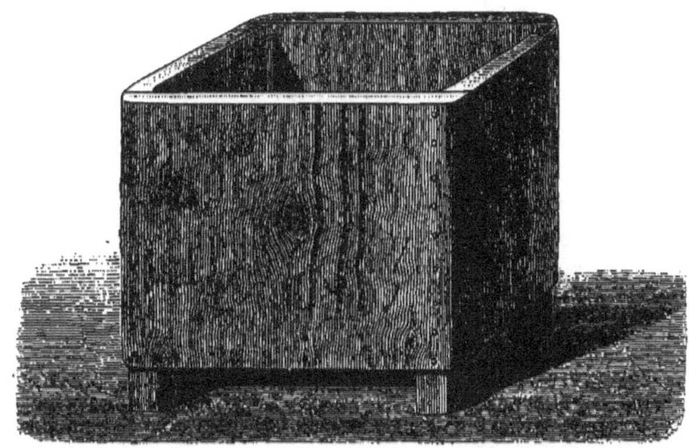

SALTING BIN

CHAPTER II

PORK

For all that relates to the sundry preparations of pork the following will be required :

A pointed pork-butcher's knife,

A knife to scrape and cleanse the inside of the pig,

A chopping knife,

A cleaver,

Two funnels of different sizes for filling sausages,

A funnel for filling up black puddings,

A sausage machine, although not indispensable, is a very desirable acquisition and will soon repay its very moderate cost.

CHAPTER III

FISH SALTED AND SMOKED

To salt fish procure a small salting bin, similar to the one which will be described for salting hams and sides of bacon ;

For the mode of smoking fish refer to the description given of the Smoking-closet, chapter I. p. 11 ;

For marinaded fish small barrels will be necessary ;

For salted oysters and herrings still smaller barrels are generally used ;

Red mullet, fillets of mackerel and of sole are put in barrels similar to those in which Ostend oysters are sold.

CHAPTER IV

POTTED MEATS

The articles enumerated as necessary for the divers preparations of pork will here be sufficient.

The potting pans must be selected of the sizes requisite to suit the several purposes they may be wanted for.

CHAPTER V

PRESERVES IN TIN CASES

Provide yourself with a large boiling pot and tin cases of various sizes according to the purposes in view ;

Place a wicker mat at the bottom of the pot, or a layer of straw 2 inches thick may be substituted ;

The knives, &c., described for chapter II., will answer for the present purpose also.

CHAPTER VI

FISH PRESERVED IN TIN CASES

Use the same utensils and cases as above.

CHAPTER VII

VEGETABLES PICKLED IN VINEGAR

Basins, jars, bottles, and a copper sugar-boiler or preserving pan will be necessary for these operations.

CHAPTER VIII

VEGETABLES PRESERVED IN SALT WATER

For these procure stone jars or small wooden barrels.

CHAPTER IX

CONSOMMÉS, SAUCES AND PUREÉS

Procure some quart and pint tin cases.

CHAPTER X

VEGETABLES PRESERVED BY STEAM OR BOILING WATER

Procure the same tin cases as above, or, preferably, employ glass bottles with a wide neck, in which the preserved vegetables will keep sweeter.

CHAPTER XI

FRUIT PRESERVED IN SYRUP BY STEAM OR BOILING WATER

Fruit is generally preserved in bottles, choose these of different sizes ;

Tin cases may be used, but the bottles are preferable.

CHAPTER XII

FRUIT PURÉES PRESERVED UNCOOKED

Procure a hair sieve and wide-necked bottles.

CHAPTER XIII

FRUIT JELLY PRESERVE

Procure :

A preserving pan,
Basins,
A fine hair-cloth sieve.

CHAPTER XIV

SALADS

Basins,
Salad bowls,
And wooden salad forks and spoons.

CHAPTER XV

SYRUPS

Hair sieves,
Preserving pan,
Copper skimmer.

CHAPTER XVI

VARIOUS RECIPES FOR PARTIES

Different sized kitchen knives,
A Dutch wafer-iron,
An ice wafer-iron,
Copper baking-sheets,
A boxwood rolling pin,
A sugar dredger,
A pestle and mortar,
Copper sugar-boilers,
Preserving pans,
A sugar sifting drum,
Copper whipping bowls and wire whisks,
A small pestle and mortar for grinding colours.

CHAPTER XVII

ICES

A copper freezing case,
Freezing-pots,
Spatulas,
Basins,
Ice pails,
Copper sugar-boilers,
Silk sieves,
Fine hair-cloth sieves.

CHAPTER XVIII

COOLING CUPS, PUNCH, SABAYONS

Copper sugar-boilers,
Sieves,
Basins,
Felt filtering bags,
Chocolate pot with frothing stick.

CHAPTER XIX

FRUIT COMPOTES

Copper sugar-boilers,
Draining sieves,
Purée sieves,
Basins,
Small kitchen knives.

CHAPTER XX

FRUIT GLACÉ AU CARAMEL

Copper sugar-boilers,
Thin wooden skewers,
Flat hair sieves.

CHAPTER XXI

PETITS FOURS

Paper *biscuit* cases,
$1\frac{3}{4}$-inch tartlet moulds,
Sugar dredger,
Sugar-sifting drum,

A candy tin,
Copper baking sheets,
Rolling pin,
Pestle and mortar,
Basins.

CHAPTER XXII

JAMS

Basins,
Pestle and mortar,
Preserving pan,
Copper skimmer,
Untinned copper cullender.

CHAPTER XXIII

PRESERVED FRUIT

Preserving pan,
Sieves,
Draining wires,
Basins,
Glass jars.

CHAPTER XXIV.

BONBONS

Preserving pan,
Different sized copper sugar-boilers,
Pastille sugar-boiler,
Sieves,
Draining wires,
Small wooden trays for starch powder,

Plaster moulds to imprint the starch,
Candy tins,
Wooden spatulas,
Pestle and mortar,
A marble slab,
Plaster moulds for bonbons.

CHAPTER XXV

FRUIT PRESERVED IN BRANDY

Basins,
Glass jars,
Copper sugar-boilers,
Preserving pans,
Draining wires,
Sieves,
Skimmers.

CHAPTER XXVI

LIQUEURS

Preserving pans,
Basins,
Felt filtering bags,
Glass funnels,
Sieves.

OBSERVATION

In many of the chapters the same utensils will be found to recur, which of course will not imply that double sets are necessary ;

Thus one set of preserving pans, sieves, pestle and mortar, &c., will suffice for all purposes; but it will be necessary to have different filtering bags for sweet and savoury preparations.

SEASONING

Spices for the seasoning of meat,
Take:

$\frac{1}{2}$ oz. of thyme,
$\frac{1}{2}$ oz. of bay leaves,
$\frac{1}{2}$ oz. of sage,
$\frac{1}{2}$ oz. of nutmeg,
$\frac{1}{2}$ oz. of cloves,
$\frac{1}{4}$ oz. of marjoram,
$\frac{1}{4}$ oz. of rosemary,
$\frac{3}{4}$ oz. of ground white pepper,
$\frac{1}{2}$ oz. of mace;

put the whole in a paper bag in the hot-closet to dry;

When thoroughly dry, pound and pass the spice through a fine hair sieve, put it by for use in a dry glass bottle kept well corked;

To use: mix one ounce of the spice to a pound of fine salt.

INDIAN CURRY POWDER

Take:

3 oz. of coriander seeds,
$\frac{3}{4}$ oz. of powdered Indian saffron,
$\frac{1}{2}$ oz. of whole white pepper,
$\frac{1}{2}$ oz. of capsicums,
$\frac{1}{2}$ oz. of powdered saffron,
$\frac{1}{2}$ oz. of mace;

Dry the capsicums separately and pound them with the

C

pepper, coriander seeds, and mace; add the powdered saffron;

Sift the whole through a fine hair sieve and keep the curry powder in well corked bottles.

COLOURING FOR BONBONS

CARMINE

Put 1 oz. of lump carmine in a small mortar; moisten it with a few drops of water; grind it with the pestle and add, gradually, sufficient water to form a soft paste;

Add $\frac{1}{2}$ oz. of liquid ammonia and pour the colouring into 3 pints of hot syrup registering 32° on the saccharometer;

Place the vessel containing the syrup (preferably a basin), in water to cool;

When cold put the carmine by, in well corked bottles, for use.

OTHER COLOURS

Yellow and green vegetable colouring being somewhat difficult of preparation, I advise their being purchased ready for use.

For blue colouring use ultra-marine ground with water;

For lilac and violet colouring use a combination of ultra-marine blue and carmine prepared as above; for the first put a larger proportion of carmine and for violet let the blue predominate.

For orange colouring add some carmine to the yellow vegetable colouring.

CHAPTER I

BEEF SALTED AND SMOKED

ROUND OF BEEF

TAKE about 14 lbs. of the *noix* or best part of a round of beef; remove some of the fat.

Pound ½ oz. of saltpetre in a mortar, mix it with ¾ oz. of Lisbon sugar and rub it well into the meat.

Prepare a pickle by boiling sufficient bay-salt in a quantity of water, until it registers 18° on the saccharometer;

Let the pickle get cold;

Place the beef in a large pan and cover it with the pickle;

The following morning, drain the beef, rub in the same quantity of sugar and saltpetre as above, and put it back in the pickle;

Repeat this process for four days, after which, let the meat remain in the pickle for ten days longer, being careful to turn it daily; then drain the beef, tie it with string and hang it in the Smoking-closet.

DESCRIPTION OF THE SMOKING-CLOSET

Have a wooden closet made 3 feet in breadth and depth and 5 feet high (*vide* woodcut).

The closet should be provided with a close-fitting door and lock and lined throughout with thin sheet iron.

A hole 3 inches in diameter should be made in the bottom of the closet to admit the flue of the portable stove.

Towards the top of the closet, fix four iron rods, with moveable hooks to hang the meat upon.

The smoking-closet will require a stand $2\frac{1}{2}$ feet high, to allow room for the stove underneath ;

SMOKING-CLOSET

The stove should be of strong sheet iron 18 inches square and 5 inches deep (with a row of holes round the top to facilitate combustion), and provided with a close-fitting cover terminating in a short flue 3 inches in diameter to fit the hole in the bottom of the closet in such a way as to prevent any escape of smoke;

Fit another flue in the top of the closet to carry off the superfluous smoke into a chimney or the open air.

This smoking-closet will be found much preferable to the old-fashioned way of smoking in a chimney.

For smoking the beef, put some live charcoal or incandescent wood in the stove, cover it with a layer of sawdust 1 inch thick, put thereon:

    4 bay leaves,

    an equal quantity of thyme,

    20 juniper berries;

The meat must be left to smoke thus for eight days, the fire being well kept up and the herbs renewed every other day.

When wanted, boil the salted and smoked beef in water, until the trussing needle enters easily;

Drain the meat, press it, and, when cold, trim and put it on a dish garnished with parsley.

Meat jelly may be substituted for the parsley; in that case the meat should be glazed.

SALTED BRISKET OF BEEF

Take 20 lbs. of brisket of beef, remove the bones and tendons;

Salt it in the same manner as described for the round of beef;

Cook the beef; trim and serve it cold, garnished with parsley.

SALTED OX TONGUE

Take a fresh ox tongue ; trim the root, and salt it in precisely the same manner as directed for salting the round of beef.

SALTED AND SMOKED OX TONGUE

For a smoked tongue, salt it as above without previously trimming the root; smoke it for six days and keep it hung in a dry cool place till wanted. Before cooking steep the tongue in cold water for twenty-four hours, and boil it gently until done ;

Trim the root and remove the skin ;

When cold, trim and glaze the tongue, put it on a dish and garnish with parsley.

SALTED CALF, PIG, AND SHEEP'S TONGUES

These tongues are prepared in the same way as ox tongues, merely salting the two first for eight days and the sheep's tongues for six days only.

CHAPTER II

PORK

WHEN killing a pig the blood should be carefully stirred to prevent its coagulating, and put by to use for black puddings;

PORK BUTCHER'S KNIFE

When the pig is singed, scraped, washed and opened, remove the inside;

Inflate the lights and hang them up;

Thoroughly cleanse the guts to be used for sausages and black puddings;

Spread out the caul to cool;

Cut off the head and feet;

Divide the pig into halves;

Remove the hams and the shoulders;

Cut off the breast to the middle of the rib-bones;

Put by the neck and loin without separating them, to be used as directed hereafter.

BAOYNNE HAMS

Trim the hams, bending the knuckles inwards to give them the round shape, which is characteristic of *Bayonne* hams;

Have a wooden salting trough. six feet long by three feet

wide; made of 1-inch board, with a $2\frac{1}{2}$-inch rim all round and with an opening left at the lower end to allow the melted salt to drain off.

One end of the trough should be slightly raised so that the pickle may run off, as indicated below, into a stone jar placed underneath.

SALTING TROUGH

Put the hams on the trough, rind downwards, and rub in some Lisbon sugar and pounded saltpetre; then cover them with a layer of fine and dry salt $\frac{1}{8}$ inch thick;

Repeat the whole process during three consecutive days; then continue putting on a fresh layer of dry salt daily, for twelve days more; making in all fifteen days salting.

The hams should be pressed by placing on them a board with a light weight on the top, during the whole time of salting.

For a ham weighing 18 lbs. use:

 4 oz. of Lisbon sugar,

 2 oz. of saltpetre,

 $2\frac{1}{2}$ lbs. of salt.

At the end of a fortnight wash the hams in cold water,

dry, trim, and proceed to smoke them as directed for Salted
and Smoked Round of Beef (*vide* page 11).

Should the ham be very fat, it will be well to salt it for
four days more.

LORRAINE HAM

These hams are salted in the pickle drained from the
hams in the preceding recipe, seasoned with herbs;

BRAIZING STEWPAN

Rub the hams with Lisbon sugar and pounded saltpetre
for two days;

Put them in a pickling-tub with a sufficient quantity of
the pickle to cover them; add:

12 bay-leaves,

An equal quantity of sage, thyme, and juniper berries.

Let the hams remain in the pickle for fifteen or twenty
days, according to their fatness; then drain, smoke, and
keep them in a dry place.

In Lorraine these hams are often kept in a dry place

buried in wood ashes ; by which they can be preserved for a long time.

When about to cook the hams, they should be steeped in water for two days, wiped clean, trimmed, and tied in a cloth, and boiled in French white wine.

This method of cooking the hams is not widely known, but it is excellent.

The hams are served hot with Moselle sauce.

BONED HAM (JAMBON DE PAYS)

Take a fresh ham, cut off the knuckle at the joint, and put the ham in pickle for eight days ; then boil it gently in slightly salted water ;

When done, remove the bones and put the ham into a basin, rind downwards ; place on it a plate or round board with a 14-lb. weight on the top ;

When cold, turn the ham out of the basin on to a dish, and garnish round with jelly or parsley.

RHEIMS HAM

Take a fresh shoulder of pork ;

Bone it, and put it in pickle for twenty-four hours ;

Tie it in a cloth, and boil it in salted water, with some thyme, bay-leaf, sage, and onion added ;

When done, take the meat out of the cloth, and put it in a basin, rind downwards, placing on it a plate or board with a 14-lb. weight on the top ;

When cold, turn the meat out of the basin, rub it lightly with a little lard, strew it with raspings, and stick in a bone to imitate the knuckle of a ham, and put a paper frill round the bone ;

Place the ham on a dish, and garnish round with parsley.

This ham should be thoroughly cooked.

STUFFED PIG'S HEAD

Bone a pig's head and put it in pickle for two days;

Make some forcemeat with fresh pork and fat bacon, in the proportion of 1½ lb. of bacon to 2 lbs. of lean pork, and season it with spiced salt.

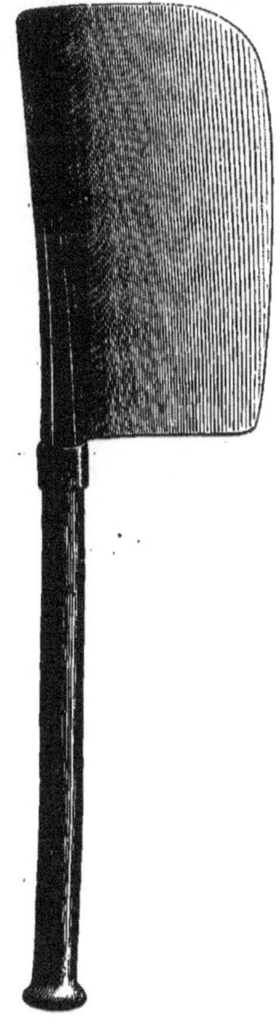

CHOPPING KNIFE

Take the tongue after six days' previous pickling, and cut it lengthwise in eight pieces;

Spread the head out on the table ; sprinkle it with spiced salt ; put on it a layer of forcemeat, and on this place the pieces of tongue and eight similar pieces of fat bacon alternately ;

Put another layer of forcemeat on the top ;

Reshape the head, tie it in a cloth, and boil it in salted water and French white wine, to which should be added :

A faggot of parsley, bay-leaf, thyme and sage,

Some whole pepper,

Two onions,

A clove of unpicked garlic.

At the end of three hours, try the head with a trussing needle, which should enter freely ;

Let the head cool in the liquor for half an hour, take it out of the cloth, and bind it round and round with wide tape, beginning at the snout ;

When quite cold, unbind the head ;

Trim it slightly, rub it over with lard, and strew it with raspings.

Truffles and pistachios may be added to the forcemeat.

STRASBURG BACON

Take the breast of a pig, remove the bones carefully by inserting a knife underneath.

TRIMMING KNIFE

Put the meat in the salting-trough ;

Rub in some Lisbon sugar and pounded saltpetre for four days, and salt it in the way described for Bayonne hams (*vide* page 15) for twenty days, keeping it slightly pressed during the whole time ; then drain and smoke the bacon for eight days.

Hang the bacon in a dark, cool, and dry place.

BACON

Take half the back of a pig ;

Remove the bones, and put the meat in pickle for three months ; then take it out and cover it with coarse salt ;

Put a small weight on it, and turn the bacon every six days, renewing the salt when necessary ;

At the end of three months, hang the bacon up in a dark, cool, and dry place.

If bacon is salted in large quantities, the pieces should be laid one above the other, turned, and fresh salt put on, every six days;

In this case the pieces will be sufficiently pressed by their own weight ; being careful, however, to change their position every now and then.

PIG'S HEAD AND FEET (AU NATUREL)

In small households, while calf's head and feet are frequently employed, there is often a mistaken prejudice against using pig's head or feet, which is to be regretted, as the latter form wholesome, cheap, and palatable dishes.

Bone a pig's head ;

Remove the tongue and the brains, which latter should preferably be used at once ;

Put the head and tongue in a basin, sprinkle with 1 lb. of salt, and let both remain in pickle for two days ;

Put the whole in a stockpot, fill up with water, and add :

    2 onions, with 3 cloves stuck in one,

    A faggot composed of parsley, thyme, and bay-leaf ;

Boil for two hours ;

When done, drain the head and tongue, strip the skin off the latter and cut it in two lengthwise ;

Dress the head and tongue on a dish, garnish round with parsley, and serve with a sauce prepared as follows :

Put in a stewpan :

1 gill of vinegar,

1 pinch of *mignonette* pepper ;

Boil until the vinegar is reduced, and add 1 pint of the liquor in which the head was boiled ; boil for five minutes, and strain through a fine strainer ; add some chopped chervil, chives and tarragon, and serve.

Chopped parsley may be substituted for the herbs.

Proceed in the same way for pig's feet, and serve with the same sauce.

The liquor in which the head or feet have been boiled may be used for vegetable soups by adding an equal quantity of water and no salt.

PIG'S FEET À LA STE. MENEHOULD

Singe and scrape some pigs' feet ;

Cut them in two lengthwise, and tie the two pieces together with string ;

Boil the feet as directed above, and when done, that is, when they become soft to the touch, take the stewpan off the fire and leave the feet in the liquor until nearly cold ;

Drain ; untie and wipe each piece, and, when quite cold, rub them over with a little lard and strew them with breadcrumbs ;

Broil the pieces of feet over a slow fire for four minutes on each side, until they assume a light golden tinge, and serve.

STUFFED PIG'S FEET

Cut and boil 2 pig's feet as directed in the above recipe;

When cooked, bone, and cut each piece in two;

Make 2 lbs. of forcemeat, with equal quantities of lean pork and fat bacon, freed from rind and gristle; season with spiced salt;

Pound the veal and bacon together, adding 1 gill of water;

Cut in slices $\frac{1}{4}$ lb. of cleaned and peeled truffles;

Chop up the trimmings to add to the forcemeat;

Spread out some well steeped pigs' caul on a cloth;

Divide the pig's feet, truffles, and forcemeat into eight equal portions;

Spread half of one of these quantities of forcemeat on to the caul, making the layer the same size as one of the pieces of pig's feet;

Put some slices of truffle on the forcemeat, a piece of pig's feet on these, and cover the whole with the remaining half portion of forcemeat; roll the whole in the caul to an oval shape 2 inches thick, and, when all the portions are prepared in this way, rub them lightly over with lard, strew them with very fine and fresh breadcrumbs, and broil them over a slow fire for fifteen minutes, turning them at the end of seven minutes;

Put the stuffed feet on a hot dish, and serve.

BLACK PUDDINGS

Strain 2 quarts of pigs' blood through a hair sieve;

Peel 1 lb. of onions, remove all the hard part, and cut up the remainder into $\frac{1}{4}$-inch dice;

Blanch the onion in boiling water for five minutes, drain

and put it in a stewpan with ½ oz. of lard, and stir over the fire without colouring it;

Pick 1 lb. of the inside fat of the pig;

Cut it into small dice, put it in a stewpan together with the blood and onions, and season with 1 oz. of spiced salt;

Add ¼ oz. of pounded sugar and 2 eggs beaten up in 3 gills of milk, and stir the whole over the fire until it becomes warm.

FUNNEL FOR FILLING BLACK PUDDINGS

Take some previously salted and well steeped and cleansed skins, tie one end with string, and fill them with the mixture, being careful not to fill the skins too much, to avoid their breaking in the hot water;

Put the puddings in a stewpan of hot water, without boiling them, and let them remain therein until set firm; take them out and hang them to cool.

When wanted the puddings should be cut into 4-inch lengths, and well scored with a knife; broiled over a slow fire for eight minutes, turning the pieces once, and served very hot.

FLAT SAUSAGES, OR CRÉPINETTES

For these sausages the scrag-end of a neck of pork will answer very well.

Free the meat from bones, and add to the lean an equal quantity of fat bacon, or of the inside fat of the pig ;

Chop the lean and fat together, and season with spiced salt, moistening with $\frac{1}{2}$ gill of water to each pound of sausage meat.

Spread out some well steeped pigs' caul on a cloth, put a portion of the sausage meat on it, and wrap it round, so as to form a sausage 3 inches by 2 inches, and $1\frac{1}{2}$ inch thick ;

FUNNEL FOR FILLING SAUSAGES

After all the sausages are thus prepared, broil them over a slow fire, and serve very hot.

The above preparation of sausage meat may, if preferred, be put into skins and some chopped truffles added.

The sausages should be pricked with a fork before broiling, to prevent their breaking.

PIG'S HEAD CHEESE

Bone a pig's head, and put it into pickle for two days only; the tongue, however, will require five days' pickling ;

Boil the head and tongue in salted water, with :

    8 oz. of onions, with 3 cloves stuck in one,

    7 oz. of carrots,

    $\frac{1}{4}$ oz. of whole pepper

and a faggot composed of :

    2 oz. of parsley,

    $\frac{1}{2}$ oz. of sage,

    $\frac{1}{2}$ oz. of bay-leaves,

    $\frac{1}{4}$ oz. of thyme ;

When done, drain the tongue and head, removing the skin of the latter whole ;

Cut up the meat of the head and tongue into pieces ;

Line a plain round mould with the skin of the head, and fill it up with the meat and tongue and with the ears cut into shreds ;

The lean and fat should be well mixed, so that it should look well when cut ;

When the mould is full, place a round board on the meat with a 14-lb. weight on the top, and, when cold, turn the cheese out on to a napkin on a dish.

PIG'S LIVER CHEESE, OR FROMAGE D'ITALIE

Take 2 lbs. of pig's liver and 2 lbs. of the inside fat of the pig ; free the whole of gristle, and cut it into 1-inch dice ;

Put the fat in a large *sauté*-pan over a slow fire, and, when it is melted, add the liver, and season with spiced salt ;

Stir with a wooden spoon over a brisker fire for three minutes, and put the liver and fat in a dish to cool.

Make some panada as follows :

Put in a stewpan :

$\frac{1}{2}$ pint of water,

1 oz. of butter,

a pinch of salt ;

Boil ; and then stir in, off the fire, 7 oz. of flour ; when this is well mixed, put the stewpan on the fire, and stir the panada for a few minutes, to expel all superfluous moisture, being careful not to let the panada burn ; then add 4 eggs, mixing them in one after the other.

Pound the liver and fat in a mortar, and pass it through a tinned-wire sieve ;

Take $\frac{3}{4}$ lb. of fat bacon, free from rind and gristle, boil it in water for half an hour, and, when cold, cut it into ⅜-inch dice;

Put the liver *purée* back into the mortar, mix in the panada, moistening with a wineglassful of double cream, and pound all together until quite smooth;

Taste for seasoning, and mix in the fat bacon, cut in dice.

TINNED WIRE SIEVE

Rub the inside of a plain mould with a little lard, fill it with the above mixture, and cook it *au bain-marie* for two hours;

When quite cold, turn the cheese out on to a napkin on a dish.

This cheese may be prepared without passing the liver and fat through a sieve, but the time taken in the operation is amply compensated by the more successful result.

SALTED AND SMOKED SUCKING PIG

As soon as the pig is killed, put it in hot—but not boiling —water for two or three minutes; then rub off the hairs with a cloth; make a slit down the belly, take out the entrails, and put the pig in pickle for ten days, adding to the ordinary pickle :

4 oz. of sage,

½ oz. of thyme,

½ oz. of bay-leaves ;

Drain ; and hang the pig up in the Smoking-closet until it acquires a light golden colour ; add 1 oz. of sage to the sawdust in the smoking-stove.

When wanted, steep the pig in water for twenty-four hours, and boil it gently in water.

ROAST SUCKING PIG

Clean a pig as above, and put it to steep in cold water for twenty-four hours ;

Drain, and dry it thoroughly with a cloth ;

Prepare some stuffing in the following manner :

Chop a large onion, together with about a dozen sage leaves ; blanch the whole in boiling water for five minutes ;

Drain, and put it in a stewpan with 2 oz. of butter ; stir over the fire, and simmer for ten minutes ; then add 3 oz. of breadcrumbs, season with salt and pepper, mix thoroughly, and fill the inside of the pig with the stuffing, and sew it up with fine twine ;

Truss the legs back, wrap up the ears in well-greased paper, and put the pig to roast before a clear fire, basting it with salad oil ;

When done, serve the pig with sharp or *poivrade* sauces and with a boat of apple sauce.

LYONS SAUSAGE

Take a leg of pork ;

Remove all fat and gristle, and chop the lean to a thoroughly smooth paste ;

For 8 lbs. of this paste add the following seasoning :

 1 oz. of ground white pepper,

 $\frac{1}{4}$ oz. of whole pepper,

 $\frac{1}{4}$ oz. of saltpetre,

 $\frac{1}{2}$ oz. of Cayenne pepper,

 $\frac{1}{4}$ lb. of salt ;

Work the paste well with the hands, to mix thoroughly ; add 2 lbs. of fat bacon, free from all gristle and rind, and cut into $\frac{1}{2}$-inch dice ;

Take some large skins, previously salted for a month and steeped in cold water for twenty-four hours ; before using, dry and tie one end with string, and fill the skins with the sausage meat, pressed well down ;

The firmness due to this pressing is the characteristic of Lyons sausage.

Tie up the end and bind the sausage round and round with string, leaving a $\frac{3}{4}$-inch space between each turn of string ;

Hang the sausages in a dry cold place.

They should not be eaten before at least six weeks' hanging.

SMOKED GERMAN SAUSAGE, OR SAUCISSON

Take a shoulder of pork ;

Remove all fat, skin and sinew, and chop the meat to a smooth paste, as directed above ;

For every pound of the meat take $\frac{1}{2}$ lb. of fat bacon, freed from gristle and coarsely chopped ;

Mix lean and fat in a basin together, seasoning with :

 1 oz of spiced salt,

 a pinch of pounded saltpetre,

 a few grains of whole pepper ;

Take some large skins, previously salted for eight days

and steeped in water for twenty-four hours ; before using, dry them well, and fill them very tightly with the sausage-meat ;

CHOPPING MACHINE

Hang the sausages in the Smoking-closet for three or four days, according to size, and boil them in water.

If the taste be relished, a little garlic may be added to the sausage meat when seasoning.

TRIPE SAUSAGES, OR ANDOUILLETTES

Take a pig's paunch, cleanse it, and steep it for forty-eight hours in plenty of cold water, to be changed every six hours; drain, and cut it into shreds; cut in the same way, ¼ lb. of fat bacon for every pound of paunch, and mix both together, seasoning with ½ oz. of spiced salt to every pound of sausage meat;

Take some large skins, previously salted for a month and steeped in cold water for twenty-four hours; before using, dry and tie one end with string, and fill the skins with the sausage-meat; tie them up tightly, and bind them round with string, as directed for Lyons sausage;

Boil the sausages for one hour in water, with the following proportion of seasoning to every 2 quarts of water;

2 oz. of salt,
2 oz. of parsley,
¼ oz. of whole pepper,
¼ oz. of sage and thyme,
¼ oz. of bay-leaves;

Leave the sausages in the liquor until nearly cold; drain, and press them slightly by placing them between two dishes with a small weight on the top;

When cold, cut the sausages into 5-inch lengths; dip the pieces into some melted lard, score them with a knife, broil them over a slow fire, and serve very hot.

FRESH PORK

Besides what is required for the preparation of the fore-going recipes, the following parts of the pig will still remain for use; namely—

The loin and fillet, which may be roasted or boiled ;

For roasting it should be thickly strewn with salt for two hours ;

For boiling it should first be pickled for eight days.

The neck can be cut into chops or cutlets, breadcrumbed, fried or broiled, and served with sharp sauce and pickles.

The kidneys are cut in thin slices, and cooked in the *sauté*-pan with a little butter.

The lights can be cut up, and stewed with onions and potatoes.

The brains must first be boiled in water, with salt and a dash of vinegar added ; they may then be served with butter, cooked until it acquires a dark brown tinge, and with a little vinegar and pepper added ;

Or, after boiling, they may be left to cool ; then cut in pieces, dipped in frying batter, and fried.

Pig's bladder, when thoroughly cleansed, is used to hold lard, which it will preserve fresh for months.

TURKEY AND CHICKEN SAUSAGE

Draw, pick, and singe a hen turkey ; bone it, and free the meat from skin and gristle ;

Chop and pound it ;

Pound half a pound of fat bacon to every pound of meat ; mix both together to a smooth paste, and season with $\frac{1}{2}$ oz. of spiced salt to every pound of the sausage meat ;

Take some large skins, previously salted for eight days and steeped in cold water for twenty-four hours ; dry them, and tie one end with string ;

Fill the skins very tightly with the sausage meat, and tie them up ;

Break up the bones of the turkey, and put them into a

braizing stewpan, with the rind of the bacon, thoroughly cleansed and cut in pieces;

Add:

A faggot composed of parsley, thyme, and bay leaf,
2 onions, with 3 cloves stuck in one,
1 quart of French white wine,
2 quarts of water;
Season with spiced salt;

Boil for two hours; then put the sausages in the liquor to boil for an hour; when partly cold, drain; and hang them up in a cool place.

Instead of putting the sausage meat into skins, the skin of the turkey may be spread out, the meat put on it, the skin folded over so as to cover it, and the whole tied tightly in a broth napkin, and boiled in the same way;

When partly cold, untie the napkin, tie the sausage up in another, and hang it up until cold.

Untie the sausage when wanted.

Cut truffles or pistachios may be added.

Chicken sausage is prepared in the same way.

Both sausages are much appreciated by travellers and sportsmen.

HARE SAUSAGE

Take a skinned hare;

Bone it, without breaking the second skin; pound the meat, say about 2 lbs. in all, in a mortar, and pass it through a wire sieve into a basin;

Pound 1 lb. of fat bacon, freed from gristle, and add to it the hare in the basin, seasoning with:

$1\frac{1}{2}$ oz. of spiced salt,
$\frac{1}{4}$ oz. of pounded saltpetre,
$\frac{1}{4}$ oz. of whole pepper;

Prepare some skins; and fill them as directed for Turkey Sausage.

Break up the bones of the hare, and boil them for two hours in French white wine and water, with some onions and herbs added;

Boil the sausages in this liquor for an hour; and, when nearly cold, drain, and hang them up.

Instead of putting the meat into skins, the second skin of the hare, which has been reserved, may be wrapped round the meat, as directed in the preceding recipe, finishing and cooking in precisely the same way.

Wild Rabbit Sausage can be prepared in the same way.

WILD BOAR SAUSAGE

Take all the lean of a shoulder of wild boar; free it from skin and gristle, and put the meat for two hours to pickle in a basin, with :

1 oz. of spiced salt,
$\frac{1}{4}$ oz. of pounded saltpetre;

Then chop it very fine, and put it in a basin;

For 2 lbs. of the chopped meat add $\frac{1}{2}$ lb. of fat bacon, freed from gristle, and cut in small dice, and mix both together in the basin;

Take some large skins, which have been eight days in pickle, and afterwards steeped in cold water for twelve hours; dry them, tie the end with string, and fill the skins with the sausage meat, pressing it well down; tie the ends up, and hang the sausages in a dry cool place for two months, when they will be fit to eat.

Observation.— Roebuck and red deer sausages are prepared as directed above, using the shoulder for the former, and the loin for the latter.

All the above sausages may be smoked, if preferred; they should first be hung for three weeks, and smoked for one week, when they will be ready to eat.

WILD BOAR BLACK PUDDINGS

Strain 1 quart of wild boars' blood through a hair sieve into a basin;

Peel and pick 7 oz. of onions; cut them into $\frac{1}{4}$-inch dice, and blanch them for two minutes in boiling water; drain, and put the onion in a stewpan, with 1 oz. of lard, and stir over the fire without colouring it; when cold, add it to the blood, together with 5 oz. of the inside fat of a pig, picked and cut into small dice; season with 1 oz. of spiced salt and $\frac{1}{8}$ oz. of finely chopped sage; and put the whole in a stewpan, and stir over the fire until it becomes warm;

Take some previously salted and well steeped skins; tie one end with string, fill them with the mixture; and tie them up;

When thus tied, put the puddings in a stewpan of hot— but not boiling—water, and let them remain therein until set firm; take them out, and hang them up to cool.

When required, the puddings should be cut into 4-inch lengths, well scored with a knife, broiled over a slow fire, and served very hot.

EEL SAUSAGE

Take a large eel; skin and clean it; steep it in boiling water for three minutes, to be able to rub off with a cloth the second oily skin; pare off the fins from each side of the eel; slit it open down the belly, without severing it, remove the bone entirely, score the fish slightly with a knife, and put it in a basin with some bay salt.

Make some forcemeat as follows:

Put in a mortar, 2 lbs. of pike, whiting, or carp, freed from bones and skin, together with 14 oz. of butter; season with 1 oz. of spiced salt, and pound the whole well together, mixing in three eggs, one after the other, until the forcemeat is quite smooth ; then add 10 oz. of anchovies, previously steeped in cold water, scraped and boned ;

Drain the eel, and wipe it carefully, to take off all the salt ;

Spread it open on a cloth ; place the forcemeat inside the whole length of the eel, and refold the sides so as to enclose the forcemeat ; roll the eel up tightly in a napkin, and tie the ends with string ; tie it across also in three places, to keep it in shape whilst cooking ;

Put the eel sausage in a fish-kettle ; cover it entirely with equal quantities of French white wine and water, adding a faggot, composed of :

 Parsley,

 thyme,

 bay leaf ;

Some salt and pepper, 4 cloves, and some onions and carrots cut in thin slices ;

Boil for one hour, and leave the sausage in the liquor until nearly cold ; then untie it, and retie it more tightly still in a clean napkin, and hang it up in a draught to cool ;

When cold, untie the sausage, take it out of the napkin, and serve.

Observation.—Lamprey and Eelpout sausages are made as directed above ; the liver of the Eelpout should be cut up, and added to the forcemeat.

BOLOGNA SAUSAGE, OR MORTADELLE

Take 6 lbs. of leg of pork, freed from fat, gristle, and skin ; and 1 lb. of well picked inside fat of the pig ;

Chop and pound both together in a mortar to a smooth paste, seasoning with 3 oz. of spiced salt and $\frac{1}{2}$ oz. of powdered saltpetre ;

Take 14 oz. of fat bacon, freed of rind and gristle; cut it into $\frac{1}{2}$-inch dice, and mix it thoroughly with the pounded meat, adding $\frac{1}{2}$ oz. of whole pepper;

Take some pigs' bladders, previously salted and steeped in water; wipe them dry, and fill them with the sausage meat, pressing it well down; tie the bladders up and put them in pickle for eight days; then hang them in the Smoking-Closet for six days, and keep them in a dry place for use.

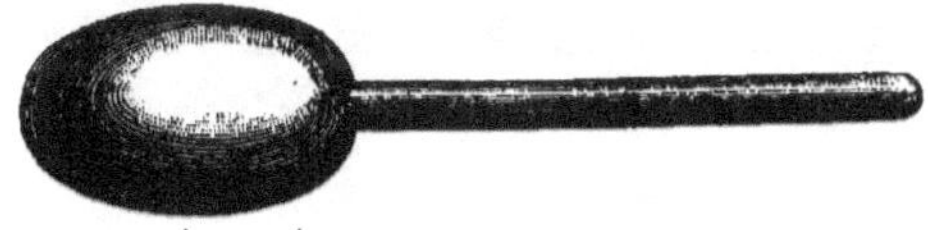

ROUND MALLET

When the sausages are required, tie each bladder up separately in a cloth, binding it round with string, to avoid breaking in the cooking; and boil the sausages in water seasoned with spices and herbs, allowing half an hour's boiling per pound weight of meat;

When cold, untie the sausages, and cut them in very thin slices.

At Bologna the meat is not chopped, but pounded on a board with a round mallet (*vide* woodcut), by which means the sausage meat is smoother, without being as dry as by the process I have indicated, which is, however, the easiest.

WHITE PUDDINGS

Trim sufficient under-fillets of pork to produce 2 lbs. of meat when freed from fat and gristle;

Chop and pound the meat in a mortar, together with 1 lb. of the inside fat of the pig, without skin or gristle; and season with salt and a little nutmeg;

Make some panada as follows:

Put in a stewpan ½ oz. of butter, with 1 gill of milk; boil, and take it off the fire and mix in 2 oz. of flour;

When quite smooth, stir the panada over the fire for two minutes, to reduce it; moisten it with 2 whites of egg, and, when cold, add it to the meat in the mortar;

Mix and pound the whole together, moistening with 1 gill of almond milk, made in the following manner:

Blanch and peel 1 oz. of Jordan almonds; wash, drain, and pound them in a mortar, moistening with ½ pint of milk, and strain it through a broth napkin; add this milk to the forcemeat very gradually, and, when all is absorbed, mix in 3 whipped whites of egg;

Take some skins, previously salted and steeped in cold water, wipe them dry, and tie one end with string;

Fill the skins with the forcemeat, being careful not to over fill them, to avoid breaking in the hot water;

Should the forcemeat be too stiff, add a little more milk; it should be of such a consistence as to run into the skins with a slight pressure;

Tie up the ends of the skins, and tie the puddings into 6-inch lengths;

When thus tied, place the puddings in a stewpan of hot water, slightly salted, without boiling them, and let them remain therein till set firm;

When partly cold, drain the puddings, and let them get quite cold.

When required for use, cut the puddings into lengths, score them with a knife, and broil them over a slow fire, until they assume a light golden tinge, and serve very hot.

When preferred, 3 oz. of onions, previously cut in dice and boiled in salted water, may be added to the forcemeat.

STRASBURG SAUSAGES

Take a sufficient quantity of shoulder of pork to obtain
2 lbs. of meat when trimmed and freed of gristle; chop it
coarsely, together with 1 lb. of fat bacon, seasoning with:

    1 oz. of salt,

    $\frac{1}{4}$ oz. of ground white pepper,

    $\frac{1}{4}$ oz. of grated nutmeg,

    a pinch of pounded saltpetre;

Take some previously salted and steeped skins, 1 inch in
diameter; tie one end with string, and fill them with the
sausage meat; tie the ends up, and divide the sausages into
5-inch lengths;

Hang the sausages in the Smoking-Closet, and let them
remain therein until they become of a golden colour; then
keep them in a cool place;

When required, boil the sausages in salted water for half
an hour.

POLONYS

Trim a sufficient quantity of loin or neck of pork to give
2 lbs. of meat when freed of fat and gristle;

Chop it very fine, together with 1 lb. of the inside fat of
the pig, free from gristle and skin, seasoning with:

    1 oz. of salt,

    $\frac{1}{4}$ oz. of ground white pepper,

    a pinch of pounded saltpetre,

    2 sprigs of thyme,

    2 bay leaves;

Chop the whole until a smooth paste is obtained;

Take some previously salted and steeped skins, $1\frac{1}{4}$ inch in
diameter when filled; tie one end with string, and fill them
with the meat;

Tie and divide the sausages into lengths, as directed in the preceding recipe, and smoke and cook them in the same way.

SPANISH SAUSAGES

Take 1½ lb. of lean leg of pork, freed from gristle, and an equal quantity of fat bacon, previonsly removing the rind and gristle ;

Season with :

    1 oz. of salt,

    ¼ oz. of powdered saffron,

    ½ oz of powdered capsicums,

    a pinch of powdered thyme,

    a small pinch of powdered bay leaf ;

Chop the meat coarsely ;

Take some previously salted and steeped skins, 1¼ inch in diameter ; tie one end with string ;

Work the sasuage-meat with the hands, and fill the skins ; tie the ends up, and divide the sausages into 3-inch lengths ;

Hang them in the Smoking-Closet for four days, and keep them in a dry cool place.

These sausages are used for garnishes to Spanish dishes ; they are also eaten cooked with rice.

LORRAINE TRIPE SAUSAGES

Steep and cleanse 4 lbs. of calf's paunch, and cut it into ¾-inch square pieces ;

Cut 2 lbs. of leg of pork, freed from rind and gristle, in ¾-inch dice ; put it in a basin, together with the cut paunch, and season with 2 oz. of spiced salt ;

Take some large skins prepared as directed for Lyons Sausage (*vide* page 28) ;

Fill and tie the sausages in the same way, and hang them in the Smoking-Closet for eight days.

When required, boil the sausages in salted water; they will be sufficiently cooked when a trussing needle enters easily;

Leave them in the water until nearly cold;

Cut the sausages into 5-inch lengths, score them with a knife, and broil them over a slow fire.

These sausages can be eaten hot or cold, but they are best hot.

MELTING OF THE PIG'S FAT FOR LARD

Chop all the inside fat of the pig, and melt it over a slow fire;

Strain it through a hair sieve into a basin, stirring it occasionally with a wooden spoon, to prevent any lumps forming;

When nearly cold, put the fat into well-cleansed pigs' bladders; tie them up tightly with string, and keep the lard in a cool place.

When very white lard is required, the best fat only should be chopped, and then melted *au bain-marie.*

CHAPTER III

FISH, SALTED AND SMOKED

SMOKED SALMON

TAKE a Salmon weighing about 6 lbs.;

Slit it down the back, without severing it entirely;

Remove the bone, and cleanse the inside;

Wipe it with a cloth, put it on a dish, spread it over with a thick layer of salt, put another dish upon it, with a weight on the top, and press it slightly thus for four days, renewing the salt daily;

Then hang the fish in the Smoking-Closet until it acquires a bright golden colour;

Keep the salmon hung in a dry cool place till wanted.

SMOKED HADDOCK

Take a haddock weighing about 1¼ lb.;

Cut off the head; cleanse, scrape, wash, and wipe the fish;

Slit it down the back, without severing it; strew it with finely pounded salt, and press it between two dishes for four days, renewing the salt daily;

. Smoke the haddock in the Smoking-Closet for four days.

When required, broil it over a slow fire, five minutes on each side, and serve it with fresh butter.

It should be used within a fortnight of its preparation.

Whiting and Mackerel are salted and smoked in the same way.

SMOKED EEL

Skin and clean a large eel;

Steep it in boiling water for two or three minutes, to enable you to rub off the second oily skin with a cloth;

Cut off the head, and pare off the fins from each side of the eel;

Put it for eight days in a salt-water pickle registering 18° on the saccharometer; drain the eel, and put it to smoke for four days in the Smoking-Closet;

Keep the smoked eel for use in a cool dry place;

When wanted, cut it into 3-inch lengths, broil the pieces over the fire for five minutes, turning them once, and serve with fresh butter.

Proceed in the same way for Lampreys and Eelpout.

SALTED HERRINGS

Cleanse and scrape some fresh herrings;

Remove the gills; wash and dry them with a cloth, and place them in layers in a small barrel; covering each layer with pounded salt, a few bay leaves, juniper berries, and grains of whole pepper;

When full, close the barrel hermetically, and leave the herrings to pickle for three weeks.

When wanted, steep the herrings in water for twelve hours, dip them in salad oil, and broil them.

Mackerel are pickled in the same way.

Herrings and Mackerel salted as above may also, after the twelve hours' steeping, be boiled for a quarter of an hour in a Marinade prepared as under, but with the salt omitted.

MARINADE FOR BOILING FISH

Prepare the following:

$\frac{1}{4}$ lb. of onions
$\frac{1}{4}$ lb. of carrots } cut in thin slices,
$\frac{1}{4}$ lb. of shalots,
2 oz. of parsley,
1 oz. of salt,
$\frac{1}{4}$ oz. of bay leaf,
$\frac{1}{4}$ oz. of thyme,
$\frac{1}{4}$ oz. of whole pepper,
4 cloves,
4 cloves of unpicked garlic,
half a nutmeg, grated,
a pinch of Cayenne pepper;

Put in a stewpan $\frac{1}{4}$ lb. of butter and the whole of the above ;

Stir over the fire with a wooden spoon until the vegetables are of a light golden colour; pour in 2 quarts of vinegar and 1 quart of water ;

Boil gently for an hour, and strain the Marinade through a hair sieve into a basin for use.

PICKLED RED MULLET

Remove the gills of 12 red mullet ;

Scrape, cut off the fins, and wipe the fish with a cloth ;

Place them in a deep earthenware pan, and pour in 3 pints of the above Marinade, so as to cover the fish entirely ;

Cover the pan, and put it on the fire, or in the oven, to boil for five minutes ;

Let the fish cool in the Marinade without uncovering the pan ;

Drain; and put the necessary number in a flat china boat
or dish; sprinkle them with chopped chervil, and serve with
oil and vinegar.

Herrings may be pickled in the same way.

PICKLED FILLETS OF MACKEREL

Remove the fillets of 6 mackerel; trim them, and pickle
them as directed above.

PICKLED FILLETS OF SOLE

Take the fillets of 2 large soles;

Cut each fillet in two, and trim each piece to a pear shape;

Place them in an earthenware pan, and finish as directed
for Red Mullet.

All the above pickled fish form excellent *hors-d'œuvre*
dishes; they may be kept for a month by boiling up the
pickle at the end of a fortnight.

PICKLED FILLETS OF EEL

To fill a small barrel, take 3 large eels; skin and cleanse
them, and place them in boiling water for two or three
minutes, to rub off the second skin with a cloth;

Cut off the heads, and cut the eels in two, lengthwise;

Remove all bones, and cut each piece into 3-inch lengths;

Place the pieces of eel in a *sauté*-pan; cover them with
Fish Marinade (*vide* page 44); boil them for a quarter of an
hour, and leave the fish to get nearly cold in the liquor;

Drain; and pack the pieces of eel in a small flat barrel,
such as are used for Dutch herrings; fill up the barrel
with Fish Marinade, and lay six bay leaves on the top;

Close the barrel, and keep it in a cool place.

These pickled fillets form excellent *hors d'œuvre*.

When required for mixing with Russian and other salads they should be cut in small dice.

Fillets of Lampreys are pickled in the same way.

TUNNY PRESERVED IN OIL

Cut up some tunny into pieces weighing from 6 to 10 oz.; remove all the skin and bones, and boil it in salted water;

Drain, and dip each piece into cold water; drain it again, and wipe each piece thoroughly with a cloth;

Place the pieces of tunny in a glass jar, with some whole pepper and bay leaves.

Fill the jar up with salad oil, cover it with a piece of bladder, and keep it in a cool place.

RED HERRINGS PRESERVED IN OIL

Remove the skin and bones of 6 red herrings;

Cut them in strips $\frac{1}{4}$ inch wide and 3 inches long; put these strips in a glass jar, with some whole pepper and bay leaves; fill up the jar with salad oil, cover it with a piece of bladder, and put it by for use.

These fillets are much used for Herring *Canapés*.

PICKLED OYSTERS

Blanch a quantity of large oysters in boiling water for one minute only;

Drain and cool them in cold water;

Drain them again, and wipe them with a cloth;

Pack the oysters in a small barrel;

Boil 1 quart of water with 2 bay leaves, a clove of

unpicked garlic, and sufficient salt to register 16° on the saccharometer;

When this pickle is cold, fill up the barrel with it, close the lid down, and keep the oysters in a cool place.

OYSTERS PRESERVED IN TINS

Blanch, cool, and wipe the oysters as above ;

Pack them in quart tin cases ; fill these up with cold slightly salted water, previously boiled ;

Close the tins by soldering on the covers, and boil them in water for half an hour.

CHAPTER IV

POTTINGS

POULTRY—GAME—FISH

POTTED TURKEY

PICK, draw, singe, and bone a turkey;

To make the forcemeat: chop $1\frac{1}{2}$ lb. of fat bacon, freed from rind and gristle, together with an equal quantity of fillet or cushion of veal, freed from fat and skin; season with 1 oz. of spiced salt, and pound the whole in a mortar, moistening with 1 gill of broth;

Remove all sinew from the legs of the turkey, and lard them and the breast of the turkey with strips of fat bacon, seasoned with a little pepper and salt; these strips should be $\frac{3}{8}$ inch thick $1\frac{1}{2}$ inch long;

Take a potting-pan large enough to hold the turkey; line the bottom with forcemeat;

Spread out the turkey, skin downwards; sprinkle it with 1 oz. of spiced salt; put a layer of forcemeat on the turkey, and fold it over and shape it so as to fit the pan;

Place the turkey in the pan, and cover it with another layer of forcemeat, and with some thin slices of fat bacon and 2 bay leaves on the top;

Place the cover on the pan, and cook the potting in the oven *au bain-marie*; that is, take a stewpan large enough to hold the potting-pan, fill it up one quarter with water, set the pan in this, and put the whole in the oven;

Boil gently, to prevent the water entering the pan.

After three hours' boiling, try the potting with a trussing needle, which should enter easily ;

When done, drain off the gravy from the potting, press it by placing on it a small board, fitting in the pan, with a 4-lb. weight on the top ;

Boil together in some water the bones of the turkey, the trimmings of the veal, and the rind of the bacon thoroughly cleansed ;

Season with spiced salt ; and, after three hours' boiling, ain the broth into another stewpan ; add the gravy drained from the potting ; reduce the whole to a half glaze, and pour it over the potting ;

When cold, cover the potting entirely with a thick layer of poultry dripping or lard ;

Lay a round of paper on the top ; place the cover on the pan, pasting a strip of paper round it to keep it air-tight ; and put it by in a dry cool place.

POTTED POULARD, CAPON, AND GOOSE

All these pottings are prepared as directed above, bearing in mind that, the size of the two former being less, they will not require as much seasoning.

As a general rule, $\frac{1}{2}$ oz. of spiced salt to each pound of the meat and forcemeat together will be found sufficient.

POTTED FOIES-GRAS

Cut $1\frac{1}{2}$ lb. of fat bacon and $1\frac{1}{2}$ lb. of calf's liver into dice; put the bacon in a *sauté*-pan, season with spiced salt, and melt it over a slow fire; when melted, add the liver, and stir over a brisk fire for four minutes ; put the whole in a dish to cool, pound it in a mortar, and pass the forcemeat through a wire sieve.

Take two fine *foies-gras*, and trim off all the part discoloured by the gall ;

Line the bottom of a potting-pan with some of the forcemeat ; on this place the two *foies-gras*, fill up the spaces
with forcemeat, and spread a layer of it over the whole.

Place some thin slices of fat bacon and two bay leaves
on the top, put the cover on the pan, and cook the potting
for an hour and a half *au bain-marie,* as directed for Potted
Turkey.

POTTED PHEASANTS

Pick, draw, singe, and bone two pheasants ; make the
same quantity of forcemeat as indicated for Potted Turkey,
and prepare the potting in the same way.

POTTED PARTRIDGES

Bone 6 partridges ; make the same quantity of forcemeat
as directed for Potted Turkey, and finish in the same way.

If red partridges are used, four will be sufficient to fill the
same sized potting-pan.

POTTED WOODCOCKS

Pick, draw, singe, and bone 6 woodcocks ;

Make some forcemeat as directed for Potted Turkey,
adding the trail of the woodcocks when pounding ;

Spread out the woodcocks, skin downwards, on a cloth ;
put 1 oz. of the forcemeat on each bird, and fold them over
so as to enclose it ;

Line the bottom of a potting-pan with some of the forcemeat ; on this place the woodcocks, sprinkle them with
spiced salt, put another layer of forcemeat over them, and
some thin slices of fat bacon and 2 bay leaves on the top ;

Cover the pan ; cook and finish as directed for Potted Turkey.

Quails, plovers, &c., are potted in the same way.

POTTED SNIPE

Pick, draw, singe and bone 18 snipe;

Make some forcemeat as directed for Potted Turkey, mixing in the trail of the snipe whilst pounding ;

Spread out the snipe, skin downwards, on a cloth ; put a little forcemeat on each bird, and fold them over so as to enclose it ;

Line the bottom of a potting-pan with some forcemeat ; on this place 9 of the snipe; sprinkle them with spiced salt, cover them with a layer of forcemeat, and place the 9 other snipe on it ; spread another layer of forcemeat on the top, and finish the potting as above.

POTTED LARKS

Pick, draw, singe, and bone 36 larks; and prepare the potting as directed for Potted Snipe.

POTTED DUCKS

Pick, draw, singe, and bone 2 ducks;

Make some forcemeat as directed for Potted Turkey, adding the livers of the ducks whilst pounding, and finish the potting in the same way.

Wild ducks are potted similarly.

POTTED HARE OR RABBIT

Skin, empty, and bone a hare;

Remove the shoulders and part of the legs;

For the forcemeat :

Chop 1½ lb. of fat bacon, 1½ lb. of fillet of veal freed from skin and fat, and the shoulders and legs of the hare free of sinew ;

When chopped, pound the whole together in a mortar, moistening with the hare's blood, and seasoning with spiced salt ;

Lard the hare with thin strips of fat bacon, seasoned with a little spiced salt, and fry it for five minutes in a stewpan with a little butter ;

When cold, cut the hare into 12 pieces ;

Line the bottom of a potting-pan with forcemeat ; place 6 pieces of hare on it, sprinkle with spiced salt, and spread in a second layer of forcemeat ; then place in the other 6 pieces of hare, and cover the whole up with the remaining forcemeat ; put some thin slices of fat bacon and 2 bay leaves on the top, and cook and finish as directed for Potted Turkey (*vide* page 48).

For Potted Rabbit proceed as above, taking 2 rabbits for the same quantity of forcemeat.

It will be noticed that I have not made use of the livers in the two foregoing recipes, as I think them unwholesome.

POTTED ROEBUCK

Take 2 legs of roebuck ;

Trim the two *noix* or cushions ; remove all sinew, lard them with seasoned strips of fat bacon, and put them to marinade for twenty-four hours ; drain, and fry them in a stewpan with some butter for twenty minutes, and put them on a dish to cool ;

Chop the trimmings of the *noix*, pound them in a mortar, and pass the meat through a wire sieve ;

Clean the mortar ; put the meat into it again, adding an

equal quantity of chopped fat bacon, and pound both together to a smooth paste, seasoning with spiced salt ;

Line the bottom of a potting-pan with some of the force-meat ;

Cut each *noix* in 4 pieces ; place 4 of these pieces on the forcemeat, sprinkle with spiced salt, and spread another layer of forcemeat on them ; then put in the remaining 4 pieces of rocbuck, and cover the whole with forcemeat, putting some thin slices of fat bacon and 2 bay leaves on the top ;

Cover the pan ; cook; and finish the potting as directed for Potted Turkey (*vide* page 48).

Potted Wild Boar and Red Deer are prepared in precisely the same way.

POTTED FISH

POTTED SALMON

Remove the bones of a sufficient quantity of whiting to produce $1\frac{1}{2}$ lb. of fish when trimmed ; pound it in a mortar, and pass it through a wire sieve ;

Clean the mortar; put the fish back into it, together with 14 oz. of butter and 1 lb. of panada, prepared as directed for Pig's Liver Cheese (*vide* page 26); season with spiced salt, and pound the whole well together, mixing in 3 eggs, one after the other ;

Take 3 lbs. of salmon ; remove the skin and bones, and cut the fish in pieces $1\frac{1}{2}$ inch thick ;

Line a potting-pan with some of the whiting forcemeat; on this make a layer of the pieces of salmon, sprinkle with spiced salt, and spread over a layer of forcemeat ; then another layer of pieces of salmon ; sprinkle these with spiced salt, and cover the whole with a layer of forcemeat, putting 2 bay leaves and a round of buttered paper on the top ;

Place the cover on the pan ; and cook the potting *au bain-marie* for an hour and a half.

When cold, take off the paper, and fill up the pan with clarified butter ; place another round of paper on the top, put the cover on the pan, and keep it in a cool place.

POTTED FILLETS OF SOLES

Make some forcemeat, as directed in the preceding recipe, using :

$1\frac{1}{2}$ lb. of salmon, free from skin and bones,

14 oz. of panada,

14 oz. of butter,

3 eggs ;

Trim the fillets of 4 large soles ;

Fill the potting-pan with alternate layers of forcemeat and pieces of sole, and finish as directed above.

POTTED TUNNY

Make some whiting forcemeat as described for Potted Salmon ;

Take 4 lbs. of tunny, remove all skin and bone, and cut the fish in pieces 2 inches by $1\frac{1}{4}$ inch ;

Blanch the pieces in boiling water ; drain them on a cloth, and season them with spiced salt ;

Fill the pan, and finish the potting as described for Potted Salmon.

All potted fish is prepared in the way indicated for Potted Salmon.

Observation.—To improve the flavour of all the above pottings, 10 oz. of well cleansed and peeled truffles may be added ;

I make a great point of peeling the truffles, as experience has taught me that the full flavour is not obtained when they are used unpeeled.

CHAPTER V

MEAT PRESERVED IN TINS

STEAMED, BOILED, AND PRESERVED IN FAT

As a general principle, the first requisite for preparing all preserves successfully is to use none but the best and freshest provisions.

Another important point is the careful soldering of the tins.

FILLET OF BEEF

Trim a fillet of beef weighing about 8 lbs.; lard it with strips of fat bacon, fry it in a stewpan with some butter for twenty minutes, and put it on a dish until cold;

Procure a tin large enough to hold the fillet without compressing it;

Line the inside of the tin with very thin slices of fat bacon (this bacon should be very fresh, as the smallest rancid part would spoil the whole contents of the tin; this remark will apply to all bacon used for preserving meat in tins);

Place the beef in the tin, and fill it up with equal quantities of clarified fat and *Mirepoix*, which latter is prepared in the following way:

Cut 1 lb. of fillet of veal, ¼ lb. of fat bacon, and 1 lb. of raw ham, half lean and half fat, in 1½-inch pieces, and put them in a stewpan with:

2 sliced carrots,
2 middle sized onions,
2 bay leaves,
1 small sprig of thyme,
2 shalots;

Fry till the meat is of a light brown colour, and pour in a bottle of Madeira and 2 quarts of General Stock; add $\frac{1}{4}$ oz. of *mignonette* pepper;

Boil; then simmer gently for two hours, and strain through a broth napkin: the *Mirepoix* is then ready for use.

Solder the cover on the tin.

Place a wicker mat at the bottom of a braizing stewpan or stockpot; put the tin on it, and pour in sufficient water to cover the tin to a depth of 3 inches;

Boil for three hours, and leave the tin in the water until cold; then take it out, and keep it in a cool place.

A 2-inch layer of straw may be substituted for the wicker mat at the bottom of the stewpan;

The water should boil gently, to prevent its reducing too rapidly; if any more water is required to keep up the quantity, it should be added boiling, so as not to stop the cooking.

A piece of ribs of beef boned, or of the rump, may be preserved in the same way.

NOIX, OR CUSHION OF VEAL

Trim a *noix* of veal weighing about 4 lbs.; lard it with strips of fat bacon, and proceed as above.

CALF'S HEAD EN TORTUE

Bone and blanch a calf's head, and prepare it in the same way as if it were about to be served.[1]

When thus prepared, put the calf's head in a tin; fill it up with Sauce à la Tortue;[2]

---

[1] *Vide* Calf's Head en Tortue, 'The Royal Cookery Book,' p. 401.

[2] Ibid. p. 325.

Solder on the cover, and boil the tin for two hours, as described above.

The garnish should be preserved in separate tins.

HIND-QUARTER OF LAMB

Trim a hind-quarter of lamb; put it to roast, and when two-thirds cooked, take it up, and let it get cold;

Procure a tin large enough to receive the joint;

Place the latter in the tin, solder on the cover, and boil the tin in water for two hours.

STUFFED SHOULDERS OF LAMB

Bone 2 shoulders of lamb;

Make some forcemeat with :

$\frac{1}{2}$ lb. of lean pork freed from skin and sinew,

$\frac{1}{4}$ lb. of fat bacon,

Season with spiced salt;

Stuff the shoulders with the forcemeat, tie them up to a round shape, and braize them in a stewpan;

When two-thirds cooked, take them out of the stewpan, and put them on a dish until they are cold;

Put the joints in tins; fill these up with equal quantities of broth and of the braize in which the lamb has been cooked;

Solder on the covers, and boil the tins in water for two hours and a half.

LAMB CUTLETS

Trim some necks of lamb into cutlets;

Fry them slightly in a *sauté*-pan with a little butter;

When cold, pack the cutlets tightly in tin cases;

Solder on the covers, and boil the tins in water for two hours.

LAMB SWEETBREADS

Choose some large lamb sweetbreads;

Steep them in cold water;

Blanch them in boiling water for five minutes; cool, drain, and trim them, and boil them in salted water until they are half cooked;

When cold, put the sweetbreads into tin cases, fill them up with water slightly salted, solder on the covers, and boil the tins in water for an hour.

VEAL CUTLETS

Trim a neck of veal into cutlets of an even size;

Butter a *sauté*-pan; place the cutlets in it, sprinkle them with salt, and fry them until they are two-thirds cooked;

When cold, pack them tightly in tin cases, and fill these up with broth or weak *consommé*;

Solder on the covers, and boil the tins in water for two hours.

ROAST LEGS OF MUTTON

Trim some legs of mutton, and put them to roast until they are three-quarter cooked;

When cold, put each joint in a tin, solder on the covers, and boil the tins in water, allowing half an hour's cooking for every pound of meat.

MUTTON CUTLETS

Trim some necks of mutton into cutlets;

Fry them in a *sauté*-pan with a little butter until half cooked;

When cold, pack the cutlets tightly in tin cases;

Solder on the covers, and boil the tins in water for an hour and a half.

CARBONADES OF MUTTON

Take 3 loins of mutton;

Bone them entirely, without separating the under-fillets, and tie them up to an oblong shape;

Put the rolled loins, or *carbonades*, in a stewpan with a little butter; sprinkle them with salt and pepper, and fry them for five minutes; then pour in sufficient broth or stock to cover them, and boil them until they are half cooked;

When cold, put the *carbonades* in tin cases; fill up with the broth in which the mutton has been cooked; solder on the covers, and boil the tins in water for two hours.

BRAIZED POULARD

Pick, draw, and singe a poulard; truss it as for boiling, and tie a thin slice of fat bacon over the breast;

Line a tin, large enough to hold the poulard without compressing it, with thin slices of fat bacon; place the poulard in it; add 3 gills of diluted chicken *consommé* and 1 pint of clarified poultry fat;

Solder on the cover, and boil the tin in water for three hours.

POULARD STUFFED WITH TRUFFLES

Prepare a poulard as above;

Fill the inside with 1½ lb. of peeled truffles;

Place the poulard in a tin, previously lined with thin slices of fat bacon; solder on the cover, and boil the tin in water for three hours and a half.

FRICASSEE OF CHICKEN

Pick, draw, and singe a fowl or large chicken;

Cut it up into joints, as for fricassee;[1]

Steep the pieces in cold water for twenty minutes; drain, and put them in a stewpan; cover them with General Stock, and add:

 a faggot,

 an onion,

 a pinch of salt;

Boil; skim, and strain the broth into a basin;

Make a *roux* in a stewpan with some butter and flour; add the broth, and stir over the fire for twenty minutes; skim the sauce, and thicken it with yolks of egg;

Wipe the pieces of chicken, place them in a tin, and pour in the sauce when cold;

Solder on the cover, and boil the tin in water for two hours.

CHICKEN À LA BONNE FEMME

Cut a fowl or large chicken as directed in the preceding recipe;

Butter a *sauté*-pan; sprinkle in a little salt, and place the

---

[1] The recipe for preparing Fricassee of Chicken will be found *in extenso*, p. 135 of 'The Royal Cookery Book.' Sampson Low, Son, and Marston, 1869.

pieces of chicken in it; sprinkle them with salt, and putting *sauté*-pan on the fire for twenty-five minutes, turning pieces at the end of fifteen; then dredge some flour the chicken, cover it with broth, perfectly free of fat, cook it for twenty minutes; at the end of that time put pieces of chicken on a dish to cool;

Put 2 oz. of butter in a stewpan, together with:

4 oz. of onions, peeled and cut in thin slices,

4 oz. of the red part of some carrots, cut in shreds;

Stir over the fire until the vegetables acquire a golden tinge; then strain in the liquor in which the chicken has been cooked; boil gently for twenty minutes, and add 4 oz. of sliced mushrooms and $\frac{1}{4}$ oz. of coarsely chopped parsley;

Boil for ten minutes more, and put the sauce by till cold;

Pack the pieces of chicken in a tin case, and pour in the sauce and vegetables;

Solder on the cover, and boil the tin in water for tw hours.

CHICKEN À LA MARENGO

Cut up a fowl or large chicken as directed for Fricassee of Chicken;

Put the pieces in a *sauté*-pan, with:

1 gill of salad oil,

2 bay leaves,

1 sprig of thyme,

1 clove of garlic, unpicked;

Season with salt and pepper;

Fry until the chicken acquires a bright golden tinge on both sides, and put the pieces on a dish to cool;

Add 1 oz. of flour to the oil in the *sauté*-pan, stir over the fire for four minutes, and add 1 pint of broth; stir for twenty minutes more, and strain the sauce through a gravy strainer;

ack the pieces of chicken in a tin; pour in sufficient of above sauce, when cold, to cover them entirely;

older on the cover, and boil the tin in water for two

's.

DUCK OR WILD DUCK FOR ENTRÉES

'ick, draw, and singe a duck; truss it as for boiling, and wrap it in thin slices of fat bacon tied on with string;

Put the duck in a tin, and pour in 3 gills of diluted chicken *consommé* and 3 gills of clarified poultry fat;

Solder on the cover, and boil the tin in water for two hours.

PIGEONS

Pick, draw, and singe 3 house-pigeons;

Cut off the heads and necks;

Put back the livers in the inside of the birds, and truss lem with the legs inward;

Tie the pigeons up in thin slices of fat bacon; put them in a tin, and finish as directed in the preceding recipe.

QUAILS

Take 8 quails;

Prepare them, and finish as above.

PHEASANT

Pick, draw, and singe a pheasant; truss the legs inward, as for boiling, and wrap it in thin slices of fat bacon;

Put the pheasant in a tin; pour in 3 gills of clarified poultry fat and 3 gills of essence of game.

This essence of game is made by boiling the bones and

any trimmings of game in some General Stock, seasoning with herbs and spices, and reducing it.

Solder the cover on the tin and boil it in water for two hours.

PARTRIDGES

Pick, draw, and singe 3 partridges; truss the legs inward, as for boiling, and tie the partridges up in thin slices of fat bacon;

Put the birds in a tin, and finish as described in the preceding recipe.

WOODCOCKS

Take 3 woodcocks, and prepare them as directed in the preceding recipe.

SNIPE

Take 6 snipe; prepare and finish as directed for Pheasant.

PLOVERS, ORTOLANS, WHEATEARS, AND LARKS

For a good sized tin take 6 plovers, and proceed as above.

12 ortolans, wheatears, or larks will be required for a tin of the same size.

LEG AND LOIN OF ROEBUCK

Take a haunch of roebuck, and separate the leg from the loin;

Trim both carefully, and tie the loin with string;

Procure two tins—one to hold the leg, and the other the loin;

Put each joint in its respective tin, and fill up the tins with a cold marinade, prepared as follows :—

Put in a stewpan :

4 oz. of butter,
7 oz. of sliced onions,
7 oz. of sliced carrots,
2 oz. of parsley,
2 unpicked cloves of garlic,
6 shalots,
$\frac{1}{4}$ oz. of bay salt,
30 grains of whole pepper ;

Fry over the fire for a quarter of an hour, until the vegetables acquire a light golden colour; then add 5 gills of vinegar and 2 quarts of water;

Boil gently for half an hour, and strain the marinade.

Solder the covers on the tins, and boil them in water for three hours.

CAPON GALANTINE

Pick, draw, singe, and bone a large capon ;
Make some forcemeat with :

1 lb. of fillet of veal, free from sinew,
1 lb. of fat bacon, freed from rind and gristle ;

Season with spiced salt ;

Cut in $\frac{3}{4}$-inch dice :

4 oz. of truffles,
4 oz. of cooked tongue,
4 oz. of partially boiled fat bacon ;

Mix the whole in the forcemeat ;

Spread out the capon, skin downwards; sprinkle it with spiced salt, and spread the forcemeat on it; fold over the capon, so as to enclose the forcemeat, and give it an oval shape ;

Line a plain mould with thin slices of fat bacon ; place the capon in the mould, pressing it well in ;

Put the *galantine* in the oven to cook for an hour, without colouring it, and, when cold, take it out of the mould ;

Line a tin with thin slices of fat bacon ; place the *galantine* in it, and pour in $\frac{1}{2}$ pint of *Mirepoix* (*vide* Fillet of Beef, page 56) and 3 gills of clarified poultry fat ;

Solder on the cover, and boil the tin in water for three hours.

PHEASANT GALANTINE

Prepare the pheasant in precisely the same way as directed in the foregoing recipe.

PARTRIDGE GALANTINES

Make some forcemeat as described for Capon *Galantine*, adding the truffles, tongue, and fat bacon cut in $\frac{1}{8}$-inch dice.

Bone 3 partridges ; spread them out, skin downwards, on a cloth, and put some forcemeat on each bird ; fold them over so as to enclose it, and tie each partridge tightly in a napkin ; put them thus tied in a stewpan, cover them with *Mirepoix* (*vide* page 56), and boil them for an hour ;

When nearly cold, drain and untie the *galantines*, place them in a tin, and strain in sufficient of the liquor in which they have been cooked to cover them entirely ;

Solder on the cover, and boil the tin in water for two hours.

QUAIL GALANTINES

Make some forcemeat as described in the preceding recipe ;

Bone 12 quails ; spread them out on a cloth, skin downwards ; put a layer of forcemeat on each, fold the bird over so as to enclose the forcemeat, roll each to a round shape, and tie them tightly in broth napkins ;

Boil and finish the *Galantines* as directed for Partridge *Galantines*.

LARK GALANTINES

Prepare 18 larks as described for Quail *Galantines*, and finish in precisely the same manner.

GOOSE PRESERVED IN FAT

Pick, draw, and singe a goose ;

Remove each fillet whole, with the pinion attached, and cut this off to the first joint ;

Cut off the legs; trim them, and remove the thigh bones ;

Season the fillets and legs with spiced salt, and put them in a *sauté*-pan with some clarified goose fat ;

Fry for twenty minutes, turning the pieces once ;

When cold, place the fillets and legs in an earthenware jar, pressing them well down ; place some bay leaves on the top, and fill up the jar with clarified goose fat, slightly warmed, so as to fill up all interstices ;

When quite cold, place a round of paper on the top, tie a bladder on the jar, and keep it in a cold place.

Ducks and wild ducks are preserved in the same way, substituting some lard for the goose fat.

FOIES-GRAS

Great care must be shown in the selection of *foies-gras* ; they should be fresh, white, and very firm.

Cook 2 *foies-gras* for half an hour in some diluted *Mirepoix* (*vide* page 56) ;

Let them get nearly cold in the liquor

Drain; and when quite cold, wrap each liver up in thin slices of fat bacon;

Put them in a tin; pour in ½ pint of the *mirepoix*, and fill up the tin with clarified poultry fat;

Solder on the cover, and boil the tin in water for three-quarters of an hour.

Allow the tin to get cold in the water; which remark applies to all preserves in tins.

PAIN DE FOIE-GRAS OR FOIE-GRAS FORCEMEAT CAKE

Cut in dice 1 lb. of calf's liver free of sinew, and 1 lb. of fat bacon without rind or gristle;

Put the bacon in a *sauté*-pan, with :

 2 bay leaves,

 1 sprig of thyme,

 2 shalots,

 1 unpicked clove of garlic,

 ½ oz. of spiced salt;

Melt the bacon over a slow fire; then add the liver, stir over a brisker fire for five minutes, and put the whole on a dish to cool;

When cold, pound it in a mortar, adding 14 oz. of panada, prepared as directed for Pig's Liver Cheese (*vide* page 26), and 2 eggs, one after the other;

When well pounded, pass the forcemeat through a wire sieve;

Blanch 2 *foies-gras* in boiling water; drain and put them by to cool, and cut each liver in four pieces;

Cut 7 oz. of well cleaned and peeled truffles into ¾-inch dice;

Butter a plain round mould; line the bottom with forcemeat, and fill up the mould with pieces of *foie-gras*, truffles, and forcemeat alternately, finishing with a layer of forcemeat;

Boil the forcemeat cake *au bain-marie* for an hour;

When cold, turn the cake out of the mould, and place it in a tin large enough to leave a ½-inch space all round; fill up this space and the tin with clarified poultry fat; solder on the cover, and boil the tin in water for three hours.

COCKS' COMBS

Choose some large and white cocks' combs;

Trim the part which has been cut off the head, to free it of all feathers;

Put them in a stewpan, and cover them entirely with water; stir over a brisk fire till the skin begins to rise; then pour in some cold water, to stop the cooking of the combs instantly;

Strip off the skin very carefully, for were this not removed, the blood would coagulate underneath, and it would be impossible to whiten the combs.

Soak the combs in salted water for six hours, after which steep them in plenty of cold water for two days, changing the water frequently;

Drain the combs, which should now be perfectly white; put them in a tin, and cover them with some cold water previously boiled and slightly salted:

Solder on the cover, and boil the tin in water for two hours.

COCKS' KERNELS.

Choose these white, firm, and unbroken; wash them carefully, put them in a tin with some slightly salted water, and finish as described for Cocks' Combs.

TRUFFLES

Choose these sound, as a single stale or strong truffle will taint a whole tin.

Brush and peel the truffles carefully ; put them in tins, and solder on the covers ;

Two hours and a half's boiling will be requisite for a tin 6 inches high and $3\frac{1}{2}$ inches in diameter.

The truffles are sometimes salted, or Madeira is poured in the tins, but I think it preferable to preserve them *alone*, so that none of the flavour of the truffle be impaired.

When required to be served whole, or to garnish silver skewers, very large and round truffles should be chosen, brushed carefully, put into tins, the covers soldered on, and finished as above.

Observation.—Wherever a steam cooking apparatus is at hand, the above preserves can be cooked by subjecting the tins to the same number of hours' steaming, instead of the boiling I have indicated in the recipes.

CHAPTER VI

FISH PRESERVED IN TINS

SALMON

Take a salmon weighing about 8 lbs ;

Boil it in salted water until three-parts cooked ;

When cold, drain the fish, and put it in a tin of such a shape as to preserve that of the salmon ;

Strain, through a silk sieve, the water in which the fish has been cooked, and fill up the tin with it ;

Solder on the cover, and boil the tin in water for three hours.

Pieces of salmon weighing from 2 to 6 lbs. may be preserved in the same way.

TURBOT

I recommend preserving only the fillets of this fish.

Remove the fillets of some turbot ; boil them for a minute in slightly salted water, to set them ;

When cold, drain ; and put the fillets in a tin, one above another, being careful to place the thick end of one fillet on the thin end of the other, so as to pack them as closely as possible ;

Strain in sufficient of the water in which the fish has been boiled to cover the fillets ;

Solder on the cover, and boil the tin in water for two hours.

Brill is prepared in precisely the same way.

STURGEON

Take a piece of sturgeon, cut from the middle of the fish, and weighing about 6 lbs;

Clean and scale it, and remove the skin;

Tie up the piece of sturgeon in thin slices of fat bacon, and place it in a tin; fill up the tin with cold salted water, previously boiled;

Solder on the cover, and boil the tin in water for three hours and a half.

FILLETS OF SOLES

Take the fillets of 4 soles, and trim them carefully.

Fold each fillet over in half, and flatten it slightly with the handle of a knife; sprinkle them with salt and pepper, and place the folded fillets in a buttered *sauté*-pan;

Cook them; and put them to cool on a dish, placing another dish on the top, so as to press them at the same time;

When cold, trim the fillets again;

Pack them closely in a tin, and fill it up with slightly salted water;

Solder on the cover, and boil the tin in water for two hours.

RED MULLET

Take 8 red mullet;

Cut off the fins, scale the fish, and remove the gills;

Put 4 of the fish at the bottom of a tin, reversing the remaining 4 on the top; sprinkle over a little salt, and cover the fish with salad oil and 4 bay leaves;

Solder on the cover, and boil the tin in water for an hour.

EEL MATELOTE

Prepare the *matelote* in the following way :

Skin and clean 2 eels, weighing about 1¼ lb. each ;

Steep the eels in boiling water for two or three minutes, to be able to rub off their second oily skin with a cloth ;

Pare off the fins and cut the eels into pieces 3 inches long ;

Fry 20 peeled and blanched button onions in a stewpan with 2 oz. of butter, until they are coloured; then dredge in 1½ oz. of flour, stir for ten minutes, and add :

1 quart of French red wine,

2 pinches of salt,

2 small pinches of pepper,

1 double faggot,

1 unpicked clove of garlic ;

Simmer for ten minutes; then put in the pieces of eel, boil gently for five minutes, and put the pieces of eel on a dish to cool ;

When cold, place them in a tin, and pour in the sauce and onions, previously taking out the faggot and garlic ;

Solder on the cover, and boil the tin in water for two hours.

LOBSTERS

Take some live lobsters ;

Boil them in water, adding some vinegar, salt, thyme, bay leaf, parsley, shalots, garlic, and whole pepper ;

Middle sized lobsters will require twenty minutes' boiling;

When cold, take the meat from the claws and tails, pack it in tins, and fill these up with cold salted water, previously boiled ;

Solder on the covers, and boil the tins in water for three hours.

PRAWNS

Choose 1 lb. of large prawns, and put them, unpicked, in a tin ; cover them with cold salted water, previously boiled ;

Solder on the cover, and boil the tin in water for two hours.

CRAYFISH

Choose 25 even-sized crayfish : those which are of a reddish tinge under the claws are considered the best ;

Reject those which have a black tinge on the underneath part.

Wash the crayfish, and put them in a stewpan, with some water, salt, whole pepper, vinegar, parsley and sliced onions ;

Boil for ten minutes, and let them cool in the liquor;

When cold, put the crayfish in a tin, and cover them with cold salted water, previously boiled ;

Solder on the cover, and boil the tin in water for two hours.

When required, take the crayfish out of the tin, and warm them in a stewpan with 1 gill of boiled and salted vinegar, keeping the stewpan closely covered.

CHAPTER VII

VEGETABLES PICKLED IN VINEGAR

RED CABBAGE

TRIM off the outside leaves of some red cabbages, and remove the middle stalks of the remaining leaves ;

Cut the cabbage into thin shreds and as evenly as possible ;

Put the cut cabbage in a basin, and cover it with pounded salt, allowing 4 oz. of salt to every pound of cabbage; stir the whole up, to mix the salt, and drain the cabbage after four days' salting.

Take some jars; fill them three parts full with the cabbage, completing with some good vinegar ; add 12 grains of whole pepper and 1 bay leaf to each pound of cabbage ;

Tie some bladder over the jars, and keep them in a cool place.

Each time the jars have been in use and require recovering, I would recommend first damping the bladder before tying it on again.

RED CABBAGE (ANOTHER WAY)

Cut and salt the cabbage as above ;

Add to the vinegar :

    20 button onions, peeled and blanched,

    10 cloves,

    $\frac{3}{4}$ oz. of Chili capsicums,

    $\frac{1}{2}$ oz. of whole ginger ;

Finish and put into jars as above.

BEETROOT

Take 2 lbs. of beetroots;

Peel, trim, and cut them in slices $\frac{3}{8}$ inch thick;

Should the beetroots be exceptionally large, cut them in two lengthwise, and trim each half to a round shape before cutting it in slices.

Take some glass or earthenware jars; fill them three-parts full with the beetroot, and add:

1 oz. of pounded sugar,

8 cloves,

$\frac{1}{2}$ oz. of coriander seeds;

Fill up the jars with boiled vinegar, partially cooled, so as not to break the jars;

Cork down tightly, and tie some bladder on the top of the jars.

BEETROOT FLAVOURED WITH CARRAWAY SEEDS

Take 2 lbs. of beetroots;

Peel and cut them as described above;

Put the cut beetroot into jars, and add:

1 oz. of pounded sugar,

1 oz. of carraway seeds;

Fill up the jars with boiled vinegar, partially cooled; cork them, and tie some bladder on the top.

CAULIFLOWER

Divide some white cauliflowers into small even-sized heads, and throw them into cold water, to prevent their turning black;

When all the cauliflowers are thus cut up, throw the small heads into a stewpan of slightly salted boiling water; boil for four minutes; drain the cauliflower, put it in a basin, and pour in sufficient boiling vinegar to cover it; put some paper over the basin; and let the cauliflower pickle for twenty-four hours; then drain it;

Boil up the vinegar, adding a little salt;

Put the cauliflower into jars, fill them up with the vinegar, and finish as above.

CUCUMBER

Take 2 cucumbers; cut them lengthwise into quarters, take out the seeds, and peel and cut the quarters into slices $\frac{1}{2}$ inch thick.

Put the cut cucumber in a basin, with a $\frac{1}{4}$ lb. of pounded salt, and let it pickle for eight hours, stirring it occasionally;

Drain, and put the cucumber into a jar, with 3 bay leaves and 25 grains of whole pepper; fill up with cold boiled vinegar, cork the jar, and tie a bladder on the top.

ONIONS

Choose 2 lbs. of small white button onions;

Put them in a stewpan with plenty of water; boil for five minutes, and cool them by pouring cold water over them;

Peel the onions, and put them in a basin; pour over some boiling salted vinegar, and cover the basin with a round of paper;

After twenty-four hours' pickling, drain the onions, and finish as directed for Cauliflower.

GHERKINS

Take 2lbs. of gherkins, about 2 inches long;

Put them on a cloth, and rub them well with bay salt, so as to cleanse them thoroughly; scrub them in water, and dry them with a cloth;

Put the gherkins in a basin, with 1 lb. of pounded salt, and let them remain therein for six hours, tossing them occasionally;

Drain and put the gherkins in a jar, with:

25 small button onions, previously blanched and peeled,
2 cloves of picked garlic,
6 shalots,
4 pepper corns,
1 oz. of sea-fennel,
1 oz. of tarragon;

Fill up the jar with cold boiled vinegar, cork it, and tie a bladder over the top.

MAIZE, OR INDIAN CORN

Take 2 lbs. of green maize ears about 2 inches long;

Trim off the stalks, and blanch the ears in water, with a little salt; boil for five minutes; drain and put them in a basin; pour over some boiling vinegar, and let them remain thus for twenty-four hours;

Drain, and put the ears into jars;

Boil up the vinegar, adding a little salt, and fill up the jars with it, when partially cold;

Cork down the jars, and tie some bladder over the top.

CARROTS

Take 50 small spring carrots, and remove the green part near the stalk;

Put the carrots in boiling water, so as to be able to rub off the skin;

Boil the carrots in slightly salted water until they are half cooked; drain, and put them in a basin;

Pour over some boiling vinegar, and let them pickle for

twenty-four hours; then drain the carrots, and put them in a jar, with :

3 bay leaves,

4 cloves ;

Boil up the vinegar, adding a little salt; fill up the jar with it, and cork it up when cold, tying a bladder over the top.

Carrots, Chili capsicums, and Beetroot will be found very useful for mixing with other pickles in *hors-d'œuvre* dishes, as they afford a pleasant relief by their bright colouring.

CELERY ROOTS

Trim 4 solid roots of celery ;

Cut them into 1½-inch square pieces ¼ inch thick ;

Boil these in salted water until they are half cooked ; drain, and put them in a basin, with :

½ oz. of fennel,

1 oz. of whole pepper ;

Pour over some boiling vinegar, and cover the basin with paper ;

After twenty-four hours' pickling, drain the celery, and put it into a jar ;

Mix some mustard in the vinegar, season with Cayenne pepper, and fill up the jar with it ;

Cork down the jar, and tie a bladder over the top.

This pickle should be highly seasoned with pepper and mustard.

CHILI CAPSICUMS

Choose 2 lbs. of small and even-sized Chili capsicums ;

Cut off the part next the stalk ;

Put the capsicums in a jar, fill it up with vinegar, cork it, and tie a bladder on the top.

NASTURTIUM SEEDS

Take 1 lb. of small nasturtium seeds;

Put them in a jar, fill it up with vinegar, and finish as above.

MIXED PICKLES. PICCALLILI

Take some square pickle bottles, and fill them up with a mixture of:

Cauliflower,

Gherkins,

Carrots,

Chili capsicums,

Onions,

Cucumber,

Maize;

Prepared as directed in the foregoing recipes;

Add:

20 grains of whole pepper,

20 juniper berries;

Mix some mustard in vinegar, season with Cayenne pepper, and fill up the bottles; cork them well, and tie some bladders over the top.

TARRAGON VINEGAR

Dry 1 lb. of tarragon in the hot-closet for twenty-four hours, and put it in an earthernware jar, together with:

1 oz. of long pepper,

12 picked shalots,

3 quarts of vinegar;

Cork up the jar, and tie some bladder on the top;

After one month's steeping, filter the vinegar through some filtering-paper, bottle it, and keep it in a cool cellar.

COMPOUND VINEGAR

Dry in the hot-closet for twenty-four hours:

    4 oz. of elder blossoms,

    6 unpicked cloves of garlic,

    10 picked shalots,

    1 lb. of tarragon ;

When dried, put all the above in an earthenware jar, together with :

    1 gallon of vinegar,

    4 oz. of mustard seeds,

    2 oz. of whole pepper,

    $\frac{1}{4}$ oz. of cloves ;

Cork up the jar; and after two months' steeping, filter the vinegar, put it into bottles, cork them carefully, and keep the vinegar in a cool place.

CHILI VINEGAR

Put some Chili capsicums in an earthenware jar; fill it up with vinegar, and cork it up ;

After one month's steeping, filter the vinegar, and bottle it for use.

REMARKS ON HORS-D'ŒUVRE

In the dressing of small *hors-d'œuvre* side dishes, I would recommend that pickles of different colours should be placed together in the same dish; tastefully arranged, they look very well on the table.

When these *hors-d'œuvre* dishes return from table, it will be best to put the pickles back into their respective jars.

Lastly, I would advise keeping all the foregoing pickles in small jars, as their quality is impaired by being left too long in opened jars.

M

PLAIN MUSTARD

Mix the mustard with cold water when required.

ANCHOVY MUSTARD

Take 8 anchovies;

Scale, scrape, wash, and wipe them with a cloth ;

Pound the anchovies, and rub them through a silk sieve ;

Mix $\frac{1}{4}$ lb. of mustard with some cold water; add the pounded anchovies; mix, and keep the mustard in small well-corked jars.

RAVIGOTE MUSTARD

Pick $\frac{1}{2}$ lb. of chervil, tarragon, burnet and garden cress;

Steep the herbs in boiling water for one minute ; drain and cool them in water; drain them again on a cloth, and press out all the water;

Pound the herbs in a mortar, rub them through a silk sieve, and add them to $\frac{1}{2}$ lb. of mustard mixed with water and $\frac{1}{2}$ gill of vinegar ;

Put the mustard into small jars, cork them up, and put the mustard by for use.

Garlic may be added to the herbs.

CHAPTER VIII

VEGETABLES PRESERVED IN SALT WATER

ENDIVE

TAKE 100 heads of endive ;

Remove all the green leaves, and wash the heads several times in cold water ;

Blanch the endives in plenty of boiling water for ten minutes; drain and cool them in cold water ;

When cold, drain the endives ; press each head in a cloth, without breaking it, and set them in layers in a small barrel; cover them with cold water, previously boiled and salted until it registers 18° on the saccharometer ;

After two days, pour off the water, and boil it again, adding some more salt until it registers 18°; when cold, pour the water into the barrel so as to come $2\frac{1}{2}$ inches above the endives, and close the barrel.

When required, steep the heads of endive in cold water for six hours, and boil them in water until they are done.

CABBAGE LETTUCES

Prepare the lettuces precisely as directed. in the preceding recipe.

ARTICHOKE BOTTOMS

Remove the outside leaves of the artichokes, and cut off the tips of the remainder ;

Boil the artichokes in water until the leaves and the choke can be easily removed;

Trim the bottoms to a round shape, and rub them over with lemon juice;

Place them in a barrel capable of holding the quantity prepared, and fill it up with cold water, previously boiled and salted until it registers 18° on the saccharometer;

The next day, drain off the water; boil it again, adding more salt to bring it back to 18°; when cold, pour it over the artichoke bottoms, and close the barrel.

When required, steep the artichoke bottoms for twenty-four hours in lukewarm water; drain, and warm the artichokes, without any salt, in a dressing made in the following way:—

Melt $\frac{1}{2}$ oz. of butter in a stewpan;

Stir in $\frac{3}{4}$ oz. of flour; when well mixed, add 1 quart of water and the juice of a lemon, and stir over the fire until it boils; then put in the artichoke bottoms, and place a round of paper on the top;

Simmer gently until the artichokes are warm, keeping the stewpan well covered.

FRENCH BEANS

Pick and wash 10 lbs. of young and tender French beans;

Boil them for five minutes; drain, cool, and drain them again, and put them in a small barrel;

Cover them with cold water previously boiled and salted until it registers 18° on the saccharometer;

After two days, drain off the water, boil it again, adding more salt to bring it back to 18°; when cold, pour it over the beans, covering them entirely, and close the barrel.

When required, steep the beans in cold water, and complete the cooking by boiling them in water.

CAULIFLOWERS

Wash some cauliflowers in plenty of cold water ;

Trim off the leaves, and cut each cauliflower into four or five even-sized heads ;

Blanch these in boiling water for five minutes; cool and drain them ;

Put the cauliflowers in a small barrel, and finish as directed in the preceding recipe.

GREEN PEAS

Choose 10 quarts of fresh-shelled and even-sized green peas ;

Blanch them in boiling water for ten minutes; cool, drain, and put them in a barrel, covering them with salted water, as described for French Beans, and finish in the same way.

CELERY

Choose some fresh and white heads of celery ;

Cut them into 5-inch lengths, and trim off the outside ;

Wash the celery, and boil it for fifteen minutes in plenty of water ;

Drain, and finish as directed for Endive (*vide* page 83).

SAUERKRAUT

Take 24 lbs. of white Savoy cabbages ;

Remove the stalks and all green leaves ;

Cut the cabbages into $\frac{1}{8}$-inch shreds ;

Take a barrel capable of holding the quantity prepared ;

Place a few cabbage leaves at the bottom of the barrel ; sprinkle them with pounded salt ; on this spread a 2-inch layer of the cut cabbage; strew this with salt, and continue alternating the layers of cabbage and salt until the barrel is full, scattering in at intervals 10 bay leaves and 4 oz. of juniper berries.

Cover the cabbage with a cloth; on this place a piece of board, fitting into the barrel, with a 10-lb. weight on the top;

As the salt melts and the water rises, remove the board and cloth, and wash the latter;

Take the scum off the water; replace the cloth, board, and weight, and repeat this process every third day for a fortnight; then allow the cabbage to ferment.

Should the pickle not be sufficient to cover the cabbage, add some salted water, previously boiled.

After five weeks' salting, the sauerkraut will be ready for use.

As portions of the sauerkraut are taken out of the barrel, it should be filled up with salted water; otherwise the sauerkraut would become discoloured.

Observation.—6 lbs. of finely pounded and dry salt will be requisite for 24 lbs. of cabbage.

Sauerkraut, when properly prepared, should be perfectly white.

When a large quantity of sauerkraut is prepared, I would recommend the use of a machine for cutting the cabbage into shreds, to ensure a more even appearance.

CHAPTER IX

CONSOMMÉS, SAUCES AND PURÉES

CONSOMMÉ

TRIM, bone, and tie with string:

> 4 lbs. of gravy beef,
>
> 2 lbs. of leg of beef,
>
> 2 lbs. of knuckle of veal;

Pick, draw, and singe two hens;

Put all the above in a stockpot, with $2\frac{1}{2}$ gallons of General Stock;[1] boil and skim the broth, adding $\frac{1}{2}$ pint of cold water, to accelerate the rising of the scum; repeating this operation three times will secure a clear and limped appearance to the *consommé*;

When the *consommé* is well skimmed, put in the following vegetables, previously peeled and thoroughly washed:

> 11 oz. of leeks,
>
> 7 oz. of carrots,
>
> 7 oz. of onions,
>
> 1 oz. of celery,
>
> 2 oz. of salt,
>
> 3 cloves;

Boil gently until the meat is cooked, and strain the *consommé* through a broth napkin;

When cold, carefully remove all the fat, and put the *consommé* into quart tins, solder on the covers, and boil the tins in water for two hours.

---

[1] 'General Stock.' 'The Royal Cookery Book,' p. 266.

It is a mistake to think that by over-cooking the meat, the *consommé* or sauces will be improved thereby; when thoroughly cooked, all nutriment is extracted from the meat.

ESPAGNOLE SAUCE

Butter a stewpan, and put in a layer of onions cut in $\frac{1}{2}$-inch slices; upon this place 6 lbs. of boned leg of veal and 4 lbs. of gravy beef; moisten with 1 pint of General Stock, and set it boiling over a brisk fire; when the stock is reduced one half, glaze the meat of a bright and even colour, by simmering gently and turning it frequently.

When the meat is well glazed, take the stewpan off the fire, cover it, and let it stand for five minutes before adding any more stock; then pour in 2 gallons of General Stock; boil, skim, and add:

4 oz. of carrots,
1 onion, with 3 cloves stuck in it,
1 oz. of parsley,
1 large bay leaf,
1 sprig of thyme;

Boil and simmer, keeping the stewpan only three-parts covered;

When the meat is done, take it out, and strain the stock through a broth napkin, previously rinsed in hot water.

Take a stewpan large enough to hold the stock;

Make a *roux* with 11 oz. of clarified butter and 11 oz. of flour, and cook it over a slow fire for an hour and a half;

Add the strained stock, pouring it in by degrees, and stirring all the time;

Put the stewpan on the fire, and continue stirring until the sauce boils; then simmer for an hour and a half; skim and free the sauce of fat, and strain it through a tammy cloth into a glazing stewpan;

Reduce the sauce one half by boiling and stirring it over the fire for twenty minutes;

When cold, pour the sauce into tins, solder on the covers, and boil the tins in water for an hour and a half.

VELOUTÉ SAUCE

Take 6 lbs. of leg of veal, and tie it with string;

Pick, draw, and singe two hens;

Never make use of old hens, as they will not improve any preparation they may be added to;

Butter a stewpan, and put in a layer of onions cut in $\frac{1}{2}$-inch slices; on this layer place the veal and hens; pour in one quart of General Stock, and simmer very gently, so as not to colour the meat, for an hour and a half; then add 2 gallons of General Stock; boil, skim, and add:

A faggot of thyme, bay leaf and parsley,

1 onion, with 3 cloves stuck in it,

7 oz. of carrots;

Boil, and simmer until the meat is cooked, and take it out;

Strain the stock through a broth napkin; skim, and free it of fat;

Make a *roux*, without browning, in a stewpan; finish and put the sauce into tins, as described in the preceding recipe.

TRUFFLE PURÉE

Scrub and peel 2 lbs. of truffles;

Pound them well in a mortar, adding 4 oz. of fresh butter whilst pounding; and rub them through a fine hair sieve;

Fill some pint tins with the *purée*, solder on the covers, and boil the tins in water for an hour and a half.

When about to use the *purée*, add half a pint of *Espa-*

gnole Sauce reduced with Madeira, and 2 oz. of butter ; and warm it without boiling.

I have not indicated the use of any salt in preparing the *purée*, as the sauce added to it will be sufficient to season it.

MUSHROOM PURÉE

Pick, wash, and turn 4 lbs. of mushrooms, throwing them, as soon as they are turned, into a stewpan with some lemon juice and a little salt ;

When all the mushrooms are turned, put the stewpan on the fire, and boil them for four minutes ; let them cool in the liquor, and drain them on a cloth ;

Pound the mushrooms in a mortar, adding 4 oz. of fresh butter, and rub the whole through a fine hair sieve ;

Put the *purée* in pint tins, solder on the covers, and boil the tins in water for an hour and a half.

When about to use the *purée*, add ½ pint of *Velouté* Sauce reduced with Essence of Mushrooms, and warm both together.

Observation.—Mushrooms should be washed and drained quickly ; otherwise, being of a spongy nature, they would absorb the water, which would make them waste away when cooking.

ARTICHOKE PURÉE

Remove all the leaves of 36 artichokes ;

Blanch the bottoms in boiling water for fifteen minutes, cool them in cold water, remove the choke, and trim and turn the bottoms ; rub them with lemon juice to keep them white, and boil them until done in a dressing prepared as directed for Artichoke Bottoms (*vide* page 83) ; let them cool in the liquor ; then drain, and wipe each artichoke ; pound them in a mortar, and rub them through a fine hair sieve ;

Fill some pint tins with the *purée*, solder on the covers, and boil the tins in water for an hour and a half.

When about to use the *purée*, warm it with some reduced *Velouté* or *Béchamel* Sauce.

CARDOON PURÉE

Take all the tender part of 4 cardoons ;

Trim, and blanch them in boiling water for ten minutes, and rub off the skin ;

Boil the cardoons in a white dressing prepared as described for Artichoke Bottoms (*vide* page 83) ;

When done, drain the cardoons, and rub them through a tammy cloth ;

Fill some pint tins with the *purée*, solder on the covers, and boil the tins in water for one hour and a quarter.

Mix some *Béchamel* Sauce with the *purée*, when about to use it, and warm both together.

CELERY PURÉE

Trim off all the outside of 12 heads of celery, using only the white and tender part ;

Blanch the celery in boiling water for five minutes, cool it in cold water, drain, and put it in a stewpan, pouring in sufficent water and clarified poultry fat to cover one inch above the celery, and boil until it is quite tender ;

Skim off the fat, drain the celery, and rub it through a tammy cloth ;

Fill some pint tins with the *purée*, solder on the covers, and boil the tins in water for an hour and a half.

Mix and warm the *purée* with some reduced *Velouté* or *Béchamel* Sauce, when about to use it.

CARROT PURÉE FOR SOUPS

Scrape and wash some carrots ; slice off all the red outside part, say about 4 lbs. ; put this in a stewpan with some diluted broth, and boil gently until the carrot is done ;

Drain, and rub it through a tammy cloth, and fill some pint tins with the *purée* ;

Solder on the covers, and boil the tins in water for an hour and a half.

GREEN PEA PURÉE

Boil 6 quarts of fresh-shelled peas in plenty of water, adding $\frac{1}{2}$ oz. of Vichy salt to every quart of water ; this salt will keep the peas of a good colour ;

When done, drain, and rub the peas through a tammy cloth, and fill some pint tins with the *purée* ;

Solder on the covers, and boil the tins in water for two hours.

REMARKS ON PRESERVED VEGETABLES

Experience has shown me that, to preserve vegetables successfully, one should adhere to the simplest mode of preparation, and use but little salt and butter and no aromatic herbs.

Formerly it was customary to prepare peas for preserving in exactly the same way as if they were intended for serving immediately, without however thickening them with flour, and then soldering them down in tins.

But it is now universally recognised by all the large Preserved Vegetable dealers, that it is preferable merely to boil the vegetables in water slightly salted.

MEAT JELLY

Take :

6 calf's feet, previously blanched, boned, and tied with
string,

6 lbs. of leg of beef, boned, and tied with string,

2 knuckles of veal,

2 hens,

2½ gallons of water ;

Put the whole in a stockpot ; boil and skim the stock,
and add :

10 oz. of onions, with 3 cloves stuck in one,

10 oz. of carrots,

10 oz. of leeks,

2 oz. of salt,

¼ oz. of whole pepper,

A faggot of parsley, thyme, and bay leaf ;

Simmer until the meat is cooked, taking out each piece
as the cooking is completed, for it would not improve the
jelly were it to remain in the stock afterwards ;

When the calf's feet—which will require the longer
boiling—are done, strain the stock through a broth napkin
into a stewpan ; free it of fat, boil, skim, and simmer gently,
so that the jelly may be perfectly clear ;

Try it on the ice or a cold plate ; if it is not firm enough,
reduce it on the fire till it is ;

Before clarifying the jelly, taste it for seasoning, which
should be full flavoured ;

To clarify the above quantity of jelly, use 10 whites of
egg, adding 1 gill of Madeira and half a tablespoonful of
lemon juice to every quart of jelly ;

Put 1 quart of cold jelly in a stewpan with the eggs,
wine, and lemon juice ; stir it quickly over the fire with a
wire whisk, and, when well mixed, add the remainder of the

jelly, and continue stirring with the whisk over a brisk fire until the jelly boils; take it off the fire, and let it stand for two minutes; then strain the jelly through a jelly-bag; pour it through again, and repeat the straining until the jelly is perfectly clear;

The jelly will strain through quicker if the bag is hung in a warm place;

Fill some quart tins with the jelly, solder on the covers, and boil the tins in water for two hours.

I cannot impress too strongly on the reader the great importance of having perfectly clean stewpans in which to prepare jellies; the jelly's clearness and transparency depends in a great measure on attention to this point.

In some large establishments this precaution is carried to the extent of having all the utensils retinned each time jelly is prepared.

MEAT GLAZE

Put in a large stockpot :
 10 lbs. of gravy beef,
 3 boned knuckles of veal,
 2 hens,
 2 oz. of salt,
 $2\frac{1}{2}$ gallons of General Stock ;
Boil, skim, and add :
 10 oz. of carrots,
 10 oz. of onions,
 10 oz. of leeks ;
Simmer until the meat is cooked ; take it out, and strain the stock through a broth napkin ;

Free the stock of fat, put it in a glazing stewpan, and reduce it over the fire until it becomes of the consistence of treacle ; stirring with a wooden spoon, to prevent the glaze burning ;

Take some large skins, previously salted and steeped in cold water, and tie one end with string ;

When the glaze is nearly cold, fill up the skins with it, tie the ends with string, and hang the glaze in a cold and dry place.

When required for use, cut off a slice of the glaze, remove the skin, dissolve the glaze in warm water, and put it on the fire till it boils.

With this glaze it is easy to prepare soups and sauces ; it is also a capital substitute for beef-tea.

CHAPTER X

VEGETABLES PRESERVED BY STEAM OR BY BOILING AU BAIN-MARIE

IN small establishments it will be found most convenient to prepare all preserved vegetables by the process known as boiling *au bain-marie*, viz. immerse the tins or bottles in water in a large stewpan or stockpot, and boil them the time indicated in the recipes ;

Steam cooking, on the other hand, is preferable for the preparation of Preserves on a large scale.

Great care should be exercised in the selection of vegetables ; they should be chosen full-grown and freshly gathered ; it will also always be best to prepare them as quickly as possible, and only to prepare small quantities at a time, even in cases where there may be large quantities to preserve.

MUSHROOMS

Choose these fresh gathered, white, full, and firm ;

Cut away the gritty part near the stalk, and throw the mushroooms into a basin of cold water ; wash them quickly, and drain them on a cloth ;

Put in a stewpan, the juice of a lemon, an equal quantity of water, and a pinch of salt.

The above quantities are calculated for 2 lbs. of mushrooms.

Turn each mushroom ; put them into the stewpan containing the lemon juice, and toss them to impregnate them with the liquid;

Cover the stewpan, put it over a brisk fire, and boil the mushrooms for four minutes, tossing them occasionally; and pour the whole into a basin;

When cold, put the mushrooms in quart tins, cover them entirely with the liquor in which they have been boiled, filling up the tins with cold water, previously boiled, if the liquor is insufficient;

Solder on the covers, and boil the tins in water for two hours.

MUSHROOM TRIMMINGS

Wash and chop the mushroom trimmings, put them in the corner of a cloth, and squeeze out the water;

Wash, drain, and chop some parsley, say about half the quantity of chopped mushrooms; add an equal quantity of chopped shalot, also well washed and drained, and put the whole in a stewpan, with some fresh butter and a little salt and pepper, and fry for five minutes, stirring with a wooden spoon;

When cold, put the chopped trimmings into small tins; solder on the covers, and boil the tins in water for an hour.

These mushroom trimmings are used for *Gratins*, and for Sharp and Italian Sauce.

ARTICHOKES PRESERVED WHOLE

Prepare three artichokes for each tin;

Remove the outside leaves, cut off the tips of the remainder, and turn the bottoms;

Blanch the artichokes in boiling water, so as to be able to remove the choke;

Rub the bottoms with lemon juice, and put the artichokes in cold water; drain, and put them in tins, filling them up with water seasoned with salt and lemon juice;

Solder on the covers, and boil the tins in water for two hours.

ARTICHOKE BOTTOMS

Take nine artichokes, trim off the outside leaves, blanch the artichokes in boiling water, and cool them in cold water;

Remove the choke and the remainder of the leaves, turn the bottoms of an even size, and rub them with lemon juice;

Put in a stewpan:

$\frac{1}{2}$ oz. of butter,

1 oz. of flour;

Mix the butter and flour together, and add:

2 quarts of water,

the juice of 2 lemons,

$\frac{1}{2}$ oz. of salt;

Boil for twenty minutes; then add the artichoke bottoms, and boil for fifteen minutes; let them cool in the liquor; rinse them in lukewarm water, and dry them with a cloth;

Pack the artichokes in a tin; fill it up with water seasoned with salt and lemon juice; solder on the cover, and boil the tin in water for two hours.

ARTICHOKES PRESERVED IN QUARTERS

Take four young and fresh-gathered artichokes, remove the outside leaves, and turn the bottoms;

Cut each artichoke into quarters, blanch them in boiling water; cool, drain, trim, and rub the bottoms with lemon juice; cook them in a white dressing, and finish as directed in the preceding recipe.

CUCUMBERS

Prepare 8 middle-sized cucumbers for a quart tin ;

Cut each cucumber into quarters, lengthwise; peel them, and remove the seeds; then cut each quarter diagonally into $\frac{3}{4}$-inch pieces ; trim these to an oval shape, and throw them into a basin of cold water, seasoned with lemon juice.

Drain and put the cucumber in a stewpan, with plenty of water, and boil it until it is half cooked; take the stewpan off the fire, and let the cucumber cool in the liquor.

When cold, drain the pieces on a cloth; pack them closely in a tin, and fill it up with water seasoned with salt and lemon juice ;

Solder on the cover, and boil the tin in water for an hour.

ENDIVE

Prepare 50 heads of endive, trimming off all the green and tough part ;

Wash them thoroughly, and blanch them in boiling water until they are soft to the touch ;

Drain and cool the endives in cold water; drain them again, and press out all the water with a cloth ;

Chop the endive very fine; put it in a stewpan with some butter, and stir it over the fire, to expel all moisture ;

When cold, fill some tins with the endive ; solder on the covers, and boil the tins in water for two hours.

GREEN PEAS

Choose these of an even size, freshly gathered, and shelled ; the success of the preparation depends in a great measure on the careful selection of the peas ;

Boil the peas in water, with a little salt, until they are

three-parts cooked; drain, and spread them on a cloth to cool;

When cold, put the peas into tins; fill these up with cold water, previously boiled with $\frac{1}{8}$ oz. of carbonate of soda, or Vichy salt, to every quart;

Solder on the covers, and boil the tins in water for two hours.

WHITE HARICOT BEANS

Select these fresh-gathered and shelled;

Wash the beans in cold water, and boil them in slightly salted water until they are half cooked;

When cold, put the beans into tins; fill them up with cold salted water, previously boiled;

Solder on the covers, and boil the tins in water for two hours.

CARROTS FOR GARNISH

Take some spring carrots of an even size, about two inches long, and turn them to a pear shape;

Blanch the carrots in slightly salted water, and finish as directed in the preceding recipe, merely boiling the tins for an hour and three-quarters, instead of two hours.

CARDOONS

Cut the tender part of some sound cardoons into $3\frac{1}{2}$-inch lengths, carefully removing the prickles from the sides;

Blanch the cardoons in boiling water, so as to be able to rub off the skin with a cloth; trim the pieces without altering their shape, and boil them in a white dressing, as directed for Artichoke Bottoms (*vide* page 98);

When about two-thirds cooked, take the stewpan off the fire; let the cardoons cool in the liquor; then drain, and rinse them in lukewarm water, wiping each piece carefully with a cloth;

Put the cardoons into tins, and finish as directed for Artichoke Bottoms (*vide* page 98).

CELERY

Trim ten heads of celery, and cut off the tops, leaving each head 4 inches long; scrub and wash them well, and blanch them in boiling water for ten minutes; cool them in water; drain, and boil them in a white dressing until half cooked;

Put the celery into tins, and finish as directed in the preceding recipe.

CABBAGE LETTUCES

Take 48 cabbage lettuces, remove the outside leaves, and trim off the stalks;

Wash and blanch the lettuces in boiling water for ten minutes; cool them in water; drain, and cook them in some broth;

When done, drain and cut each lettuce in half; lay them open on a cloth; cut the stalks out, and fold the leaves over, so as to give each piece an oval shape, about 3 inches by 2;

Set the lettuces in tins, or preferably in a large square one; solder on the cover, and boil the tin in water for two hours.

Cabbage lettuces can also be preserved chopped, and prepared as directed for Endive (*vide* page 99).

TURNIPS

Turn the turnips to a pear shape; blanch, and finish them as directed for Carrots (*vide* page 100).

ASPARAGUS

Select some higher tins than those used for other vegetables, and capable of holding about eighteen large heads of asparagus in each tin ;

Scrape the asparagus carefully, and blanch it for five minutes in salted water ; take it out, dip it into cold water, and drain it on a cloth ;

Place the asparagus regularly in the tins, all the points in one direction ; make a mark outside the tins, to know which is the top, in order that after they are closed they may not be reversed and placed so that the asparagus stand on their points ;

Fill up the tins with cold water, slightly salted ; solder on the covers, and boil the tins in water for an hour and a half.

SORREL PURÉE

Pick 8 lbs. of sorrel, wash and drain it, and boil it in one gallon of water, until it is melted, stirring it occasionally, to prevent its adhering to the stewpan ;

Drain the sorrel on a hair sieve ; and when the water has drained off, rub it through the sieve ;

Fill a tin with the *Purée* ; solder on the cover, and boil the tin in water for an hour and a half.

TOMATOES

Choose preferably the tomatoes grown in the south of France ;

Cut off the stalk of each tomato and the green part round it ;

Put the tomatoes in boiling water for half a minute, to facilitate taking off the thin skin ; drain them ; and when cold, make an opening $\frac{3}{4}$ inch in diameter where the stalk has been cut off, to allow of taking out the seeds with the handle of a teaspoon ;

Pack the tomatoes closely together in tins ; solder on the covers, and boil the tins in water for half an hour.

Tomatoes preserved whole as described above, are generally intended for stuffing.

TOMATO PURÉE

Cut off all the green part of 15 large tomatoes ; cut them in pieces, and put them in a stewpan, with :

    1 bay leaf,

    1 small sprig of thyme,

    1 onion with 2 cloves stuck in it ;

Stir over the fire till the tomatoes are melted, and drain them on a sieve ;

Rub the tomatoes through a tammy cloth;

Boil the water drained from the tomatoes so as to reduce it to half the quantity, and add it to the *Purée* ;

Fill some wide-necked bottles with the *Purée* ; cork them, tie the corks down with string, and boil the bottles in water for half an hour ;

The means employed to prevent the bottles breaking will be described in the following recipe.

Observation.—The water which drains from the tomatoes is often thrown away, which is a mistake, as it possesses nearly the same qualities as the pulp, and will improve the *Purée* when added to it.

ANOTHER WAY OF PRESERVING PEAS

Take some wide-necked bottles, fill them to within an inch of the cork with some freshly gathered and shelled peas ;

Choose some firm and sound corks ;

Cork the bottles very carefully, and tie the corks on with string ;

The success of the preparation depends on the perfect corking of the bottles, so that they may be entirely air-tight ;

Put a wicker mat at the bottom of a stockpot ; on this place the bottles, filling up the spaces between with hay, to prevent the breaking of the bottles ; pour in some water, so as to fill the stockpot three-parts, and put it over a brisk fire until it boils ; then take the exact time, and let the water boil very gently for three hours, renewing the water as it evaporates with boiling water, so as not to interrupt the cooking ;

When cold, take out and wipe the bottles, and keep them in a cool place.

Observation.—All vegetables can be preserved in this manner, merely selecting suitable bottles or jars for the different vegetables.

CHAPTER XI

FRUIT PRESERVED IN SYRUP AU BAIN-MARIE OR BY STEAM

ALL the following recipes should be executed with great care;

The fruit must be chosen perfectly sound and fresh-gathered;

It should be pared with as little handling as possible, and bottled without bruising it;

All the processes should be carried on quickly, so that the colour of the fruit may not be impaired by too long exposure to the air;

The syrup should be prepared, and be ready beforehand;

The bottles well rinsed, and the corks carefully selected;

It will be well to prepare only the quantity of fruit which may be required for the year.

These general directions should be kept in view: they apply to the whole of the ensuing recipes.

PINEAPPLE PRESERVED WHOLE

Cut the whole of the peel off a pineapple weighing about 2 lbs., and put it in a tin capable of holding it, and leaving a $\frac{1}{2}$-inch space all round it;

Fill up the tin with syrup registering 24° on the saccharometer; solder on the cover, and boil the tin in water for half an hour.

PINEAPPLE FOR COMPOTES

Cut off the peel, and trim some pineapples; these trimmings will be found useful in the preparation of ices or punch;

Cut off three slices $\frac{1}{3}$ inch thick, and cut the remainder of each pineapple in half, lengthwise; then cut each half into $\frac{1}{3}$-inch slices;

Put the slices in wide-necked bottles; fill them up with syrup registering 24° on the saccharometer, cork and tie the bottles with string, and boil them in water for ten minutes.

Observation.—When about to prepare the compote, boil $\frac{1}{4}$ lb. of sugar to a syrup registering 38°; drain the slices of pineapple, put them in the syrup, and let them steep for two hours;

Strain the juice left in the bottles through a fine hair sieve; add it to the syrup and slices, and steep them for one hour more;

Drain the pineapple; dress the half-slices in a circle in a compote glass, putting a whole slice in the centre;

Strain the syrup into a sugar-boiler, and boil it up to 34°.

Five minutes before serving the compote, pour the cold syrup over it.

PINEAPPLE TRIMMINGS

Put the trimmings left from the preceding recipe into a bottle, fill it up with syrup registering 20°; cork, and tie the bottle with string, and boil it in water for ten minutes;

These preserved trimmings will be useful for punch or ices.

Observation.—Should the sugar be boiled above the degrees indicated in the recipes, it would be likely to impair the flavour of the fruit.

APRICOTS

Choose some fine standard apricots, of a bright yellow colour, and of such ripeness that the stones may be easily removed;

Cut the apricots in halves, take out the stones, and, with a wooden spoon, place the apricots in wide-necked bottles, putting the cut part uppermost; press them down, and leave an interval of two inches between the apricots and the cork;

Fill up the bottles to within $\frac{1}{2}$ inch of the corks with syrup registering 28° on the saccharometer;

Cork the bottles, tie down the corks, and boil the bottles in water for two minutes.

GREEN APRICOTS

Take some green apricots before the stone is set;

Blanch them in boiling water, adding $\frac{1}{4}$ oz. of soda to every quart of water;

Steep the apricots in cold water for an hour, drain them on a sieve, and wipe them with a cloth;

Put the apricots into bottles, filling up with syrup registering 28°, adding $\frac{1}{8}$ oz. of Vichy salt to every quart of syrup;

Cork the bottles, tie them with string, and boil them in water for two minutes.

I should advise the use of small pint bottles for preserving these green apricots.

PEACHES

Take some small, ripe, and sound peaches;

Cut them in halves, and put them in boiling water for a

minute or two, to facilitate taking off the skin ; take out the stones, and put the peaches into bottles, as directed for Apricots (*vide* page 107), filling up with syrup registering 32° on the saccharometer ;

Cork and tie the bottles, and boil them in water for two minutes.

PEARS

Blanch some scarcely ripe early pears for one minute ; cool them in water ; drain, and peel them smoothly, leaving the stalk about $\frac{1}{2}$ inch long ;

Put the pears into bottles as you peel them, and fill them up with syrup registering 32° ;

Cork and tie the bottles, and boil them in water for eight minutes.

BON CHRÉTIEN PEARS

Cut some *Bon Chrétien* pears into halves ; blanch them in boiling water for two minutes ; cool, and drain them ;

Peel each half, lengthwise, with three cuts of the knife, putting them into bottles as you peel them ;

Fill the bottles up with syrup registering 38° ; cork, tie, and boil them in water for eight minutes.

BAKING PEARS

Cut some large and sound baking pears into quarters ; cut a few pears into halves only, and trim these to a round shape, to be used for the centres when dishing compotes ;

Peel the quarters, lengthwise, with three cuts of the knife, and throw them into cold water as you peel them ;

When all the pears are peeled, place them in a newly-tinned stewpan, pour in sufficient water to come a few inches above the pears, adding ½ lb. of sugar and a teaspoonful of prepared cochineal for three quarts of water and pears ;

When the pears are about three-parts done, take the stewpan off the fire, and, when they are cold, take them out, drain, and put them into bottles, being careful to put one of the round halves in each bottle ;

Add some sugar to the liquor in which the pears have been cooked, and boil it until it registers 30° on the saccharometer ;

When cold, fill up the bottles with the syrup ; cork, and tie them with string, and boil them in water for sixteen minutes.

DUCHESSE PEARS (FOR JELLIES)

Cut some ripe and sound *Duchesse* pears into quarters ;

Peel, and throw them at once into cold water with some lemon juice added ;

Drain, and put the pears in a preserving-pan, cover them with water, adding the juice of a lemon and ¼ lb. of sugar to every quart of water and pears ;

Cover the pan, and boil the pears gently until they are half done ; let them cool in the water ; drain, and put them into bottles, filling up only two-thirds, and completing the filling with the syrup in which the pears have been cooked ;

Cork and tie the bottles, and boil them in water for ten minutes.

COLVILLE APPLES

Choose some round and even-sized Colville apples ;

Cut them in halves, take out the core, and peel each half with three cuts of the knife, namely : by the first cut remove the peel from the centre, and by each of the others that from the sides; to do this properly the apple should turn on the blade, and not the blade round the apple;

As the pieces of apple are peeled, throw them into a basin of cold water with a little lemon juice added;

Drain, and blanch the apples in plenty of boiling water for four minutes; when cold, drain the pieces, and put them into bottles;

Fill them up with syrup registering 30°; cork, and tie them with string, and boil them in water for two minutes.

The season for preserving these apples is from the middle of November to the middle of December.

CHERRIES FOR COMPOTES

Choose some May-Duke or Kentish cherries, of a bright red colour and perfectly sound, and cut off all but $\frac{3}{4}$ inch of the stalks;

Put the cherries into bottles; fill up the bottles with syrup registering 24° on the saccharometer; cork and tie them with string, and boil them in water for two minutes.

STONED CHERRIES

Take some large and sound May-Duke or Morella cherries; pick and stone them without bruising them;

Put the cherries into bottles; cover them with syrup registering 24°; cork the bottles, tie them with string, and boil them in water for two minutes;

CORNELIAN CHERRIES

Choose some large, ripe and sound Cornelian cherries, and cut off all but $\frac{3}{4}$ inch of the stalks;

Fill some bottles with the cherries, cover them with syrup registering 28°, and finish as directed in the preceding recipe.

MIRABELLE PLUMS

Choose these of a light yellow colour, unspotted, not too ripe, and perfectly sound ;

Cut off the stalks to within $\frac{1}{4}$ inch of the fruit ;

Fill some bottles with the plums, pressing them in slightly, and cover them with syrup registering 25° ;

Cork down the bottles, tie them with string, and boil them in water for five minutes.

GREENGAGES

Choose the greengages sound, unspotted, and not too ripe ;

Prick them with a needle, to facilitate cooking ;

Put the greengages in a preserving-pan, with plenty of water, and put it to simmer for five minutes, keeping the fire low, so that the air bubbles do not rise to the surface quicker than the plums ;

Drain the plums on a sieve, and when cold put them into bottles ; fill these up with syrup registering 38° ; cork, and tie them with string, and boil them in water for four minutes.

LADIES' APPLES

Choose some ladies' apples as nearly of a size as possible ;

Peel them very smooth, and throw them into cold water, with a little lemon juice added ;

Blanch them in boiling water for a few minutes ; take them out and remove the core with a $\frac{1}{4}$-inch cutter ;

Put the apples back into boiling water, and simmer until

they are soft to the touch ; then cool them in water, drain them on a sieve, and put them into bottles ; fill them up with syrup registering 38° ; cork, and tie them with string, and boil them in water for two minutes.

BARBERRIES

Pick some fine barberries, and put them into bottles, filling up with syrup registering 38° on the saccharometer ;

Cork the bottles, tie them down with string, and boil them in water for two minutes.

RED CURRANTS

Choose these of a large size, and not too ripe ;

Pick the currants carefully, put them into bottles, and fill these up with syrup registering 30°.

Cork the bottles, tie them with string, and boil them in water for two minutes.

WHITE CURRANTS

Proceed exactly as directed in the preceding recipe.

MULBERRIES

Choose these not over ripe; pick them, and put them into bottles ;

In bottling the mulberries, keep the bottle slightly inclined, so that the mulberries, sliding gently down its side, may reach the bottom unbruised ;

Fill up the bottles with syrup registering 38°; cork, and tie them with string, and boil them in water for two minutes.

STRAWBERRIES

Take some small Alpine strawberries; choose them not over ripe, and perfectly sound ;

Pick the strawberries, put them into bottles, and finish as directed in the preceding recipe.

RASPBERRIES .

Choose some not over ripe, and perfectly sound, red or white raspberries ;

Pick them quickly, and put them into bottles; fill these up with syrup registering 38°; cork them down, tie them with string, and boil them in water for two minutes.

PINEAPPLE PURÉE

Take three sound and ripe pineapples ; pound them in a mortar, and rub them through a fine hair sieve; put the *Purée* in a basin, and mix with it an equal quantity of pounded sugar ;

Put the *Purée* into bottles; cork, and tie them with string, and boil them in water for fifty minutes.

APRICOT PURÉE

Choose some ripe standard apricots, and rub them through a fine hair sieve ;

Add 1 lb. of pounded sugar to every pound of the *Purée*; mix; and fill some bottles with the *Purée* ;

Cork down the bottles, tie them with string, and boil them in water for two minutes.

PEACH PURÉE

Choose some fine ripe peaches;
Make the *Purée*; bottle, and finish it as directed in the
preceding recipe.

NECTARINE PURÉE

Proceed in precisely the same way as directed for Apricot
Purée.

PLUM PURÉE

Greengage, Orleans, or *Mirabelle* plums may be used;
Prepare the *Purée*, and finish it in the way indicated for
Apricot *Purée*.

STRAWBERRY PURÉE

Pick some fresh-gathered Alpine strawberries;
Rub them through a fine hair sieve;
Add 1 lb. of pounded sugar to every pound of the straw-
berries; mix both together; and fill some bottles with the
Purée;
Cork the bottles, tie them with string, and boil them in
water for two minutes.

RASPBERRY PURÉE

Proceed as directed in the preceding recipe.

MULBERRY PURÉE

Prepare and finish the *Purée* as directed for Strawberry
Purée.

PEAR PURÉE

Peel some ripe and sound pears ;

Put them in a stewpan, with ½ pint of water to every pound of pears, and boil them gently until they are done ; then drain, and rub them through a fine hair sieve ;

Add 1 lb. of pounded sugar to every pound of the *Purée*; mix thoroughly, and fill some bottles with the *Purée* ;

Cork, and tie the bottles with string, and boil them in water for four minutes.

APPLE PURÉE

Peel some sound and ripe apples ;

Have a stewpanful of water boiling on the fire, and throw the apples into it as they are peeled ;

Boil the apples until they become soft enough to be rubbed through a fine hair sieve ; then drain, and rub them through a sieve ;

Add 1 lb. of pounded sugar to every pound of apple; mix both together ; and fill some bottles with the *Purée* ;

Cork, and tie the bottles with string, and boil them in water for four minutes.

The water in which the apples have been boiled may be used for making Apple Jelly.

QUINCE PURÉE

Proceed precisely as directed in the preceding recipe.

GOOSEBERRY PURÉE

Pick 4 lbs. of green gooseberries ; boil them in ½ pint of water until they become soft to the touch, and rub them through a fine hair sieve ;

Add 1 lb. of sugar to every pound of gooseberries ; mix both together; fill some bottles with the *Purée*; cork, and tie the bottles with string, and boil them in water for twenty minutes.

This *Purée* will be found useful for puddings, tartlets, creams, and ices.

Gooseberry Fool may be prepared by adding some whipped cream to the *Purée.*

GOOSEBERRY PURÉE WITHOUT SUGAR

Boil the gooseberries as directed in the preceding recipe ;

Rub them through a fine hair sieve, and put the *Purée* into bottles ; cork, and tie the bottles with string, and boil them in water for twenty minutes.

Observation.—This unsweetened *Purée* is much appreciated when served with boiled fish or roast meat.

CHAPTER XII

FRUIT PURÉES PRESERVED WITHOUT BOILING

REMARKS ON FRUIT PURÉES

FOR all Fruit *Purées* preserved without boiling, prepare, in a very cool cellar, a small pit, 6½ feet long, 2 feet wide, and 8 inches deep ;

BOTTLES IN THE PRESERVING-PIT

At the bottom of the pit make a layer of sand one inch thick ;

When the pit is prepared as directed above, place the bottles of Fruit *Purée* therein, and fill it up with sand.

Although this pit will not exactly be a substitute for an

ice-well, still it will, in many cases, be preferable to boiling the bottles *au bain-marie*.

STRAWBERRY PURÉE

Pick some small Alpine strawberries, and rub them through a fine hair sieve ;

Add 1 lb. of pounded sugar to every pound of *Purée*; mix; and put it into bottles; cork, and tie them with string, and put them in the Preserving-Pit.

Raspberry, Peach, Apricot, and Greengage *Purées* are prepared in the same way.

PEAR PURÉE

Boil some sound pears in syrup registering 10° on the saccharometer ; drain, and rub them through a fine hair sieve ;

Add 1 lb. of pounded sugar to every pound of *Purée*; mix; and put it into bottles ; cork, and tie these with string, and place them in the Preserving-Pit.

PINEAPPLE PURÉE

Pound some pineapples, without first peeling them ; rub them through a fine hair sieve, and finish as directed in the preceding recipe.

CHAPTER XIII

FRUIT JELLIES

REMARKS ON APPLE JELLY

APPLE jelly can be prepared with almost all kinds of apples; however, to obtain a white and clear jelly, use in preference such apples as Colville, Orange Pippin, or American apples;

Equal proportions of Colville and American apples will be found to give the best result.

Apple jelly is the constituent part of Lemon, Orange, and all Flower Jellies.

The best season for making apple jelly is from the middle of November to the middle of December.

APPLE JELLY

Pour 2 quarts of water into a preserving-pan, and put it to simmer over a slow fire ;

Peel 2½ lbs. of Colville apples and an equal quantity of American apples; cut them into slices, and throw them into the water in the preserving-pan; put it over a brisk fire, and boil until the apples are melted down ; then pour the whole into a jelly-bag, and pour it back again two or three times, until the liquid is perfectly clear.

Weigh the strained juice, and put it in a preserving-pan,

adding sugar in the following proportion, say, 10 oz. of sugar to every pound of juice;

Boil the whole until it registers 28° on the saccharometer; pour the jelly into pots; skim it, and let it get perfectly cold; then place a round of paper, previously steeped in brandy, close on the top of the jelly; tie some paper over the pots, and keep the jelly in a dry and cool place.

APPLE JELLY DE ROUEN

Prepare the jelly as directed in the preceding recipe, merely adding some candied lemon peel, cut in very fine shreds, two minutes before taking the jelly off the fire.

APPLE JELLY FLAVOURED WITH VIOLETS

Prepare 4 lbs. of apple jelly as directed above;

Five minutes before the jelly registers 28° on the saccharometer, add $\frac{1}{2}$ lb. of scented violet petals, and boil it again to 28°, adding a few drops of prepared cochineal, to improve the colour;

Place a hair sieve over a basin; strain the jelly through the sieve and put it into pots;

When the jelly is quite cold, cover it with a round of paper steeped in brandy, and tie some paper over the pots.

APPLE JELLY FLAVOURED WITH ROSES

Prepare the jelly as directed in the preceding recipe, substituting 5 oz. of cabbage-rose petals for the violets.

APPLE JELLY FLAVOURED WITH ORANGE FLOWERS

Prepare the jelly as directed for Apple Jelly Flavoured with Violets, merely substituting 2 oz. of picked orange blossom for the violets, and omitting the cochineal.

APPLE JELLY FLAVOURED WITH CLOVES

Prepare the jelly in the way indicated above, using 1 oz. of clove petals and a few drops of prepared cochineal, to give the jelly a bright red tint.

POMEGRANATE JELLY

Put in a preserving-pan 4 lbs. of picked pomegranate, and 2 quarts of water; boil for twenty minutes, and strain the liquid through a jelly-bag, pouring it back again until it is quite clear;

Add 10 oz. of loaf sugar to every pound of the juice, and boil it until it registers 28° on the saccharometer;

A few drops of prepared cochineal may be added, if the jelly be too pale in colour;

Pour the jelly into pots, and, when cold, cover it with a round of paper steeped in brandy;

Tie some paper on the pots, and keep the jelly in a cool, dry place.

RED CURRANT JELLY

Pick 4lbs. of ripe red currants;

Put them in a preserving-pan; with 1 quart of water, and boil them until the currants are melted down; then pour the whole through a jelly-bag;

Add 10 oz. of sugar to every pound of juice, and boil it until it registers 28°;

Put the jelly into pots, and cover it as directed for Apple Jelly (*vide* page 119).

BLACK CURRANT JELLY

Prepare this in precisely the same way as directed in the preceding recipe.

BARBERRY JELLY

Boil 4lbs. of picked barberries in 3 quarts of water until they are soft when pressed between the fingers;

Strain the juice through a jelly-bag;

Add 10 oz. of sugar to every pound of the juice, and boil it until it registers 28°;

Put the jelly into pots, and cover it as indicated above.

QUINCE JELLY

Peel and core sufficient quinces to obtain 4 lbs. of fruit;

Throw the quinces into water as they are peeled, to prevent their being discoloured;

Drain, and boil the quinces in 1 gallon of water until they are melted down, and pour the whole through a jelly-bag;

Add 10 oz. of sugar to every pound of juice, and boil it until it registers 28° on the saccharometer;

Just before taking the jelly off the fire, add some candied orange peel cut in fine shreds;

Put the jelly into pots; skim it, and, when cold, place a round of paper steeped in brandy on the top; tie some paper over the pots, and keep the jelly in a dry and cold place.

LEMON JELLY

Boil some apples, and strain them through a jelly-bag, as directed for Apple Jelly (*vide* page 119), putting in the bag the yellow peel of three lemons for 4 lbs. of apple juice;

Add the filtered juice of six lemons to the strained juice;

Boil 2½ lbs. of the best loaf sugar *to the ball*; pour in the strained juice, and boil the whole until it registers 28° on the saccharometer;

Put the jelly into pots, and cover it as directed in the preceding recipe.

Observation.—The expression 'to boil sugar *to the ball*' will often recur in the ensuing pages. The following is the process to which this refers :—

Boil, say, $2\frac{1}{2}$ lbs. of the best loaf sugar with 1 quart of water; skim off the scum, and clean the edges of the sugar-boiler with a wet sponge, without dropping any water into the sugar ;

When the syrup begins to thicken, try it by dipping the tip of the finger into it, and transferring the finger rapidly to a basin of cold water held in readiness ;

If the portion of sugar adhering to the finger is easily removed, and rolled into a ball, the syrup may be considered to have reached the degree of boiling known as *to the ball*.

ORANGE JELLY

Proceed precisely as directed in the preceding recipe, substituting the juice of six oranges for the lemon juice, and adding a few drops of prepared cochineal, to give the jelly a pink tinge.

RASPBERRY JELLY

Pick 4 lbs. of fine raspberries, and boil them in 3 pints of water for ten minutes ; strain the whole through a jelly-bag, and add 10 oz. of sugar to every pound of the juice ;

Boil until it registers 28° ; pour the jelly into pots, and, when cold, place on the top a round of paper steeped in brandy ;

Tie some paper over the pots, and keep the jelly in a dry and cool place.

CHERRY JELLY

Pick and stone 4 lbs. of May-Duke or Kentish cherries, and boil them in 3 pints of water until they are done ;

Strain the juice, and finish the jelly as directed in the preceding recipe.

MULBERRY JELLY

Pick 4 lbs. of perfectly ripe mulberries, and make the jelly as described for Raspberry Jelly.

WHITE CURRANT JELLY (GROSEILLES DE BAR)

Pick 2 lbs. of fine white currants, and remove the pips with a quill ;

Boil 2 lbs. of sugar *to the ball*, as described for Lemon Jelly (*vide* page 122);

Put the currants, and any juice that may have drained from them, into the syrup, and take it off the fire ; toss the currants, so as to mix them with the syrup ; cover the sugar-boiler, and let it stand for ten minutes ; then put it on the fire, and let the contents boil up ;

Pour the jelly into pots or small glass jars ; skim it carefully, and, when it is cold, cover it.

RED CURRANT JELLY (GROSEILLES DE BAR)

Proceed in precisely the same way as described in the preceding recipe.

RED OR WHITE RASPBERRY JELLY (THE RASPBERRIES PRESERVED WHOLE)

Pick 2 lbs. of large and scarcely ripe raspberries ;

Boil 2 lbs. of sugar *to the ball*;

Add the raspberries carefully, so as not to bruise them, and toss them in the syrup, so as to mix both together;

Take the sugar-boiler off the fire; cover it, and let it stand for fifteen minutes; then put it on the fire, boil up the syrup, and pour the jelly into pots;

When cold, cover the jelly, and tie some paper over the pots.

CHERRY JELLY (THE CHERRIES PRESERVED WHOLE)

Take a sufficient quantity of May-Duke or Kentish cherries to weigh 4 lbs. when picked;

Pick and stone them very carefully;

Break up into small pieces 2 lbs. of loaf sugar; put it into a sugar-boiler, with 1 pint of water, and boil it *to the ball*; then add the cherries; boil them for one minute, and pour the whole into a basin; cover it, and let the cherries remain thus for twenty-four hours; then drain them, put the syrup in a preserving-pan, add $\frac{1}{2}$ lb. of sugar, and boil it for four minutes; add the cherries, and boil for one minute more;

Pour the jelly into pots, and cover it when cold.

STRAWBERRY JELLY (THE STRAWBERRIES PRESERVED WHOLE)

Pick 2 lbs. of not too ripe British Queens;

Boil 2 lbs. of sugar *to the ball*;

Add the strawberries to the syrup, cover the sugar-boiler, and let it stand for an hour; then put it over a brisk fire, and boil for two minutes; skim the syrup, pour the jelly into pots, and cover it when cold.

PEAR JELLY (THE PEARS PRESERVED IN QUARTERS)

Take 4 lbs. of sound and scarcely ripe pears;

Peel, core, and cut them into quarters; blanch them in

boiling water for ten minutes ; drain, and put them in a basin ;

Cover the pears with boiling syrup registering 20° on the saccharometer ; cover the basin, and let the pears steep for four days ;

Drain the pears, add some sugar to the syrup, and boil it until it registers 22°; pour it boiling over the pears, and let them remain thus for four days more; then drain them again, add some more sugar to the syrup, and boil it until it registers 30°; pour it on the pears, and put the jelly into pots ;

Let the jelly cool for twenty-four hours before covering it.

CHAPTER XIV

SALADS

IN the following recipes will be found salads proper to the different seasons, and also some mixed salads, which are much appreciated, and can be prepared at a very moderate cost.

SUMMER SALAD

Take :

8 cabbage lettuces,	some garden cress,
1 oz. of capers,	6 hard-boiled eggs ;
6 anchovies,	

Steep the anchovies in cold water; scrape and open them; take out the bones, and cut the anchovies into small dice ;

Trim off all the outside leaves of the lettuces, and cut the hearts each in eight pieces ;

Chop the yolks and whites of the eggs separately ;

Put the lettuces in a salad-bowl; add the anchovies, chopped eggs, the chopped cress, and the capers ;

Just before serving, season the salad with salt, pepper, oil, and vinegar.

SUMMER SALAD

Prepared with :

artichoke bottoms,	green peas,
asparagus,	French beans,
turnips,	cucumbers ;
spring carrots,	

Cook some artichoke bottoms as directed for Artichoke *Bottoms* (*vide* Chapter VIII., page 84), and cut them in $\frac{1}{8}$-inch dice;

Blanch, cool, and drain all the other vegetables ;

Cut the turnips, carrots and cucumbers into $\frac{1}{8}$-inch dice;

Cut the asparagus into $\frac{1}{2}$-inch lengths, and the French beans into diamond-shaped pieces;

Put the whole in a salad-bowl, together with some coarsely-chopped tarragon and chervil; season with a thin *Mayonnaise* Sauce, and serve.

MAYONNAISE SAUCE FOR SALADS

Break a yolk of egg into a basin, carefully separating it from the white; season with salt and pepper, and mix it with a tablespoonful of salad oil, pouring it in drop by drop, and stirring all the time ;

Add 3 tablespoonfuls of vinegar, mixing one thoroughly before adding another; then stir in, by degrees, a sufficient quantity of oil to make about eight tablespoonfuls of *Mayonnaise*, which will be about the quantity required for a salad.

The *Mayonnaise* should be highly seasoned.

WINTER SALAD

Prepare equal quantities of :

Dutch herrings,	radishes,
celery,	potatoes,
white haricot beans,	lentils,
French beans,	Ribston pippin apples ;

Boil separately, cool, and drain the celery, haricot beans, French beans, radishes, potatoes and lentils ;

Cut the apples and potatoes into $\frac{1}{4}$ inch dice, and put them in a salad bowl, pouring in a tablespoonful of vinegar to prevent the apples becoming discoloured ;

Cut the celery into strips $\frac{3}{4}$ inch long by $\frac{1}{4}$ inch broad ;

Remove the skin and bones of the herrings, and cut them into $\frac{1}{4}$-inch dice ;

Put the whole in the salad bowl, season with salt, pepper, and vinegar, and let it marinade for two hours ; add some oil and some coarsely chopped chervil when about serving the salad ; mix thoroughly, and taste for seasoning.

WINTER SALAD

Prepare :

$\frac{1}{2}$ lb. of salsify,

$\frac{1}{2}$ lb. of Dutch herrings,

$\frac{1}{2}$ lb. of Brussels sprouts,

$\frac{1}{4}$ lb. of red pickled cabbage ;

Trim the salsify and Brussels sprouts, and boil them in salted water ; take them out of the water before they are quite done ;

Steep the herrings in cold water, drain them, and remove the skin and bones, and cut the fish into small dice ;

Chop the pickled cabbage, and put the whole together in a salad bowl, adding some chopped chervil ;

Season with pepper, oil, and vinegar, very little salt, and a little Cayenne pepper.

WINTER SALAD

Take some :

    white haricot beans,
    French beans,
    potatoes,
    beetroot,
    onions ;

Blanch all the vegetables separately ; cool, and drain them ;

Chop the onions, and put them in the corner of a cloth ; dip this in cold water, and press the water out of the onion ; repeating this process two or three times will tend to make the onion easier of digestion ;

Cut the potatoes and beetroot in $\frac{1}{8}$-inch dice ;

Put all the vegetables into a salad bowl, adding some chopped chervil ; season with salt, pepper, oil, and vinegar, and mix the whole thoroughly.

WINTER SALAD

This salad is prepared with equal quantities of :

    potatoes,
    celery,
    beetroot ;
    half a quantity of Dutch herrings,
    2 oz. of chopped gherkins,
    1 oz. of chopped chervil ;

Boil the potatoes and beetroot separately ; cool, drain, and cut them into small dice ;

Steep the herrings in water, remove the skin and bones, and cut the fish into small dice;

Parboil the celery in salted water; cool, drain, and cut it into dice;

Put the whole, excepting the beetroot, into a salad bowl; season with salt, pepper, oil, and vinegar;

Add the beetroot when about serving the salad.

SALAD À LA CHASSEUR

For this salad take some:

    cooked smoked and salted beef,
    smoked salmon,
    cooked pickled tongue,
    pickled maize ears,
    pickled Chili capsicums,
    lemons,
    hard-boiled eggs,
    onions,
    potatoes,
    celery;

Boil the potatoes and celery separately, and cut both into dice; cut the beef, salmon, tongue, and maize in the same way;

Peel and trim the onions, cut them into dice, and put them in the corner of a cloth; dip this in cold water, and press the water out of the onion; repeat this process two or three times to make the onion more digestible;

Chop the capsicums and the whites and yolks of the eggs separately;

Remove the skin and pips of the lemons, and cut the pulp into pieces;

Arrange all the above ingredients in a salad bowl, and season with salt, pepper, oil, vinegar, and some mixed mustard.

MACÉDOINE SALAD

The following incident first led me to prepare this salad: Whilst staying once at a friend's country house, the mistress of the house came to me in great distress, and confided to me that, her supplies having failed, she was quite at a loss how to entertain her numerous guests, and asked me to assist her.

When I investigated the state of the larder, I found there nothing but cold meat, cold poultry, and cold game; all these I took, and, after carefully paring and cutting them up, I made them into a huge salad, which I mixed with an abundant and highly seasoned *Mayonnaise* Sauce, adding lettuces, olives, anchovies, hard-boiled eggs, pickles, and some chopped tarragon, chervil, and shalots.

This salad, preceded by a good soup, and followed by sweets and fruit, was highly appreciated by the hungry guests.

LETTUCE AND TUNNY SALAD

Cut up 2 fine lettuces, after removing the outside leaves;

Cut 4 oz. of onions into $\frac{1}{8}$-inch dice; wash them in plenty of water several times, and press out the water in a cloth, in order to make the onion more digestible;

Cut 4 oz. of marinaded tunny into $\frac{1}{4}$-inch dice;

Put the lettuces, onions, and tunny in a salad bowl, together with some chopped tarragon, and season with salt, Cayenne pepper, oil, and vinegar.

ENDIVE SALAD

Pick some fine white endives; wash and drain them carefully, and put them in a salad bowl;

Chop some shalots, wash them in several waters, and press out the water in a cloth;

Add them to the endive, together with some chopped tarragon, chervil, and burnet;

Season with some thin *Mayonnaise* Sauce, adding 2 finely chopped Chili capsicums.

NORWEGIAN SALAD

Take:

  $\frac{3}{4}$ lb. of cold boiled potatoes,

  $\frac{3}{4}$ lb. of russet apples,

  $\frac{1}{2}$ lb. of pickled herring, freed from skin and bones,

  $\frac{1}{2}$ lb. of smoked salmon,

  $\frac{1}{4}$ lb. of anchovies, previously steeped in water and scraped;

Cut all the above ingredients in small dice;

Put them into a salad bowl, and add:

  $\frac{1}{2}$ lb. of gherkins, cut in pieces,

  $\frac{1}{4}$ lb. of slices of lemon, previously removing the peel,

  $\frac{3}{4}$ lb. of stoned olives,

  $\frac{1}{4}$ lb. of capers,

  $\frac{1}{4}$ lb. of chopped tarragon, chervil, and shalot,

  $\frac{1}{2}$ oz. of finely chopped Chili capsicums;

Mix the whole together, season with oil and vinegar, and, just before serving, place 24 fresh-opened oysters on the top of the salad.

GERMAN SALAD

Blanch 1 lb. of sauerkraut in boiling water for five minutes; cool, drain, and chop it;

Blanch, cool, drain, and chop 2 oz. of onions;

Trim and cut ¾ lb. of smoked salt beef into dice;

Pick ½ lb. of crayfish tails;

Grate 2 oz. of horseradish;

Chop 1 oz. of tarragon;

Put the whole together in a salad bowl;

Season with salt, pepper, oil, and vinegar; mix, and serve.

RUSSIAN SALAD

Cook ½ lb. of smoked salmon in a *sauté*-pan, with a little butter, and put it on a dish to cool;

Cook ¼ lb. of fillets of chicken and ¼ lb. of fillets of sole in the same way;

Cut the salmon, chicken and sole, together with ¼ lb. of boiled tongue, into small dice;

Take ¼ lb. of the red part of some carrots, and cut it in small dice;

Cut ¼ lb. of French beans into diamond-shaped pieces;

Divide ¼ lb. of cauliflower into small even-sized heads;

Boil ¼ lb. of green peas and all the above vegetables, separately, in water, with a little salt added;

When the vegetables are cold, put all the ingredients in a salad bowl, add ¼ lb. of chopped *Ravigote*, and season with some *Mayonnaise* Jelly, prepared as follows:

Melt ½ pint of *Aspic* Jelly in a *sauté*-pan; when the jelly is melted, take the *sauté*-pan off the fire, and when the jelly is cold, whip it on the ice;

Put the *sauté*-pan on the fire, and melt the jelly slightly;

season it with oil, vinegar, and Cayenne pepper, and whip it again on the ice ;

Add the *Mayonnaise* Jelly to the salad, mix the whole thoroughly, and taste for seasoning, which should be highly flavoured.

CHAPTER XV

SYRUPS

MODES OF FILTERING

THERE are several different ways of filtering liquids; the first described will, however, be found the most successful.

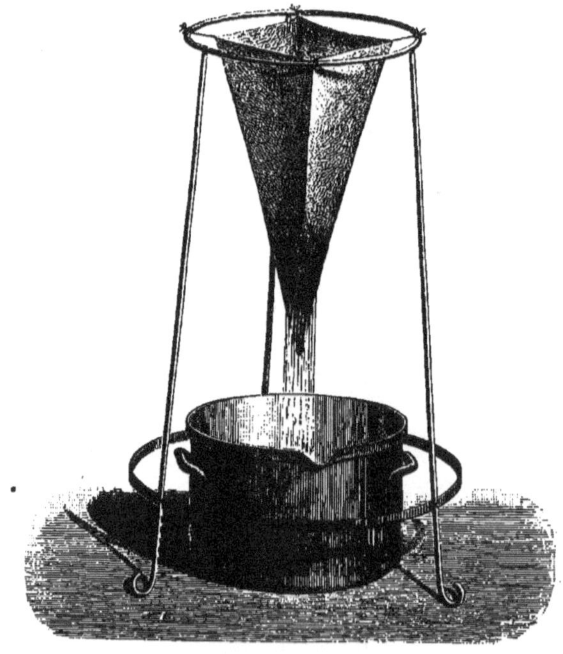

FILTERING PROCESS

Take three sheets of filtering-paper; put it in a sugar-boiler with plenty of water; put it on the fire, and whip the paper with a wire whisk, to reduce it to a pulp; drain the pulp on a sieve; then wash it several times in plenty of cold water; drain it again, and press out all the water;

Put the pulp in a basin, and mix with it the liquid to be filtered, and pour the whole into a felt filtering-bag; pour the liquid back again and again until it is perfectly clear.

FILTERING PROCESS

When a felt filtering-bag cannot be obtained, a hair sieve may be substituted; the juice and pulp should then be spread all over the surface of the sieve, to filter through it into a basin, and poured back again until quite clear.

Another mode of filtering is as follows:

Procure a large glass decanter and a glass funnel; fold a sheet of filtering-paper as directed at page 138;

Place the paper filter in the funnel and the latter in the

decanter; pour the liquid carefully in the paper filter, and continue pouring it back until it becomes quite clear.

When a certain quantity of the liquid has become clear, put it into another vessel, so that, if the paper should happen to break, the liquor which it contains may not fall through and spoil that which is already filtered.

DIRECTIONS FOR PREPARING A PAPER FILTER

Take a square of filtering-paper, and fold it in two diagonally from corner to corner;

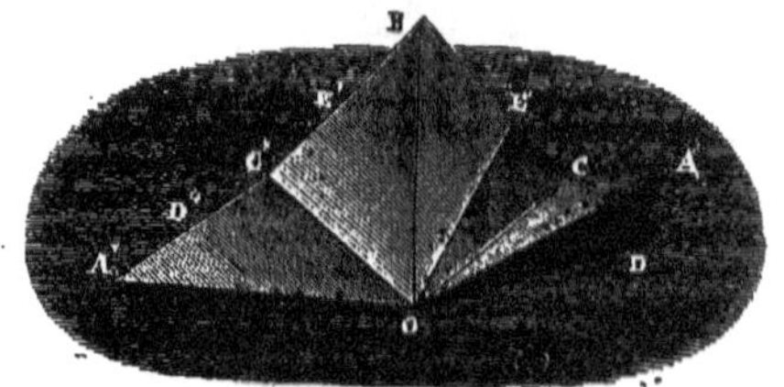

PAPER FILTER PARTLY FOLDED

Bringing the point A′ to A, the fold O B will be obtained.

O is the central point where all the folds meet; these are made by folding over each angle gradually into smaller ones, thus:

O A′ being brought to O B will give the fold O C′

O A	,,	O B	,,	O C
O A	,,	O C	,,	O D
O A	,,	O C′	,,	O E
O A′	,,	O C′	,,	O D′
O A′	,,	O C	,,	O E′

In this way seven folds will be obtained, all in one direction; it will then be necessary to separate them by eight folds in a contrary direction; namely, by bringing O A on O C, and then bringing it back to O D, in order to divide the angle A O D by a first reversed fold.

Leaving O A on O D, O D must be folded over to O E, and then brought back to O C, thus giving a second reversed fold in the middle of the angle D O C.

Similarly, leaving O A and O D on O C, O C must be brought to O B, and then folded back to O E; then again, still leaving O A, O D, and O C on O E, O E must be brought to O E', and then folded over to O B.

The same operation must be repeated in the portion A' O B.

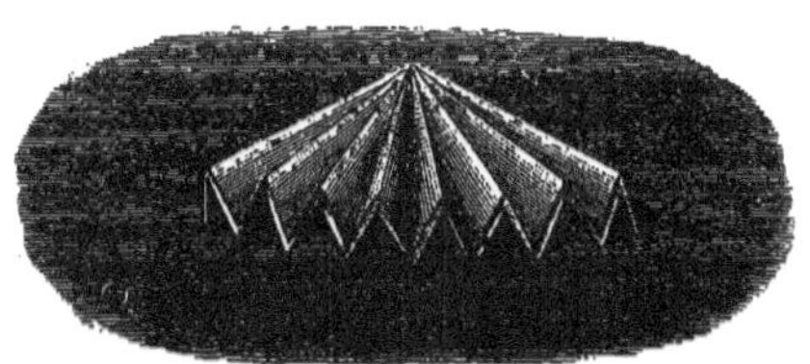

PAPER FILTER COMPLETED

After the edges have been cut even with scissors, the filter, as represented in the woodcut, will be obtained.

The folds of the filter will run alternately in contrary directions, with the exception of the two first right and left-hand folds, corresponding to the lines O A and O A'.

These two end-folds should be divided again by small reversed folds, and the filter will then be ready for use.

CHERRY SYRUP

Pick and stone 3 lbs. of Kentish cherries;

Cook them in a sugar-boiler with 1 quart of water, and pour the whole in a filtering-bag;

When the juice is quite clear, weigh it, and add 3 lbs. of sugar to every 2 lbs. of juice;

Boil till the syrup registers 32° on the saccharometer; then place the sugar-boiler in a basin of cold water, to accelerate the cooling of the syrup, and so avoid the crystallisation of the sugar in the bottles ;

Pour the syrup into bottles, cork them carefully, and keep them in a dry and cold place.

Observation.—No filtering-paper is required for fruit syrups, as the pulp of the fruit answers the same purpose.

CURRANT SYRUP

Boil 3 lbs. of picked red currants in 1 quart of water ;

When the juice is filtered, add 3 lbs. of sugar to every 2 lbs. of the juice, and finish the syrup as directed in the preceding recipe.

RASPBERRY SYRUP

Choose 3 lbs. of sound raspberries ; cook them in 1 quart of water, and make the syrup as described for Cherry Syrup.

ORANGE SYRUP

Remove the peel of 6 oranges, and steep it in cold water for two hours ;

Press out the juice of the oranges, together with 6 more, and filter the juice through paper ;

Boil 3 lbs. of sugar until it registers 34° on the saccharometer ; add the orange juice and the peel, and bring the syrup back to 32° ;

Strain the syrup through a hair sieve ;

When cold, pour it into bottles, and cork them carefully ;

When the orange syrup is made later than January, the juice of three lemons should be added, as the oranges will then have become too sweet.

LEMON SYRUP

Steep the peel of 6 lemons in cold water for two hours ;

Press out the juice of 12 lemons; filter it, and finish the syrup as directed in the preceding recipe.

STRAWBERRY SYRUP

Pick 2 lbs. of small Alpine strawberries ;

Boil 2 lbs. of sugar *to the ball* ;

Put the strawberries into the syrup; let it boil up, and pour the whole into a basin; cover it, and let the strawberries steep for two hours; then strain the whole through a filtering-bag, and pour the syrup into bottles; cork them carefully, and keep them in a cool place ;

Should the syrup register more than 32° when the strawberries have been added, a little boiling water may be poured in to bring it to the right degree.

BARBERRY SYRUP

Take 2 lbs. of barberries, and pick off all the green ;

Boil the barberries in 1 quart of water until they become soft to the touch ;

Strain the whole through a filtering-bag; weigh the juice, and add 3 lbs. of sugar to every 2 lbs. of it ;

Boil the syrup until it registers 32° on the saccharometer, and bottle it when cold ;

Cork down the bottles, and keep them in a cool and dry place.

POMEGRANATE SYRUP

Boil 3 lbs. of picked pomegranate in 1 quart of water ;
Filter, and make the syrup as described in the preceding
recipe.

MULBERRY SYRUP

Pick 3 lbs. of ripe mulberries ;
Cook the mulberries and finish the syrup as directed for
Strawberry Syrup (*vide* page 141).

ALMOND SYRUP

Blanch and peel 1 lb. of Jordan almonds and ¼ oz. of
bitter almonds, and steep them in cold water for four
hours ;
Pound the almonds to a smooth paste in a mortar, adding
¼ lb. of pounded sugar and moistening by degrees with
1 quart of water;
Press the almonds through a wet broth-napkin, straining
the almond milk into a basin ;
Boil 2 lbs. of sugar *to the ball*; take it off the fire, and when
it is nearly cold, add to it the almond milk and a tablespoonful of Orange Flower Water; shake the sugar-boiler, to
mix the whole together, cover it up, and put it by until the
sugar is quite melted ;
Pour the syrup into bottles, cork them carefully, and keep
them in a cool place.
As almonds can be obtained all the year round, it will be
better to prepare only small quantities of the syrup at a
time.

SIROP DE GOMME

Dissolve 1 lb. of the best gum Arabic in 1 quart of cold water, and strain it through a hair sieve ;

Boil 2 lbs. of sugar *to the ball* ; add the dissolved gum, and mix both together with the skimmer ; add a table-spoonful of Orange Flower Water, and boil the syrup until it registers 32° on the saccharometer ;

When cold, bottle the syrup, and keep it in a cool place.

ASPARAGUS SYRUP

Cut 3 lbs. of the green and tender part of some asparagus, and boil it in 2 quarts of water until the water is reduced to one quart ;

Pour the whole through a filtering-bag, and add 4 lbs. of loaf sugar, broken in pieces, to the asparagus water ;

Boil the syrup in a covered vessel *au bain-marie*—that is, by placing the vessel containing the syrup in a stewpan half filled with boiling water—until it registers 32° on the saccharometer ;

When cold, bottle the syrup, and keep it in a cool place.

NORWEGIAN FIR SYRUP

Take $\frac{1}{4}$ lb. of the budding shoots of some fir trees, and put them in a covered jar to steep for twelve hours in $\frac{1}{4}$ lb. of spirits of wine ;

Boil 1 quart of water, and add it, boiling, to the spirits of wine and fir shoots ; close the vessel carefully, and let the contents steep for six hours more ;

Strain through a broth-napkin, and, to every quart of the liquid, add 3 lbs. of sugar ;

Dissolve the sugar *au bain-marie*, keeping the jar covered ;

Skim the syrup, and bottle it when cold.

MULBERRY VINEGAR

Steep 2 lbs. of mulberries in 1 quart of vinegar for a few days, and filter the whole through a felt bag ;

Boil 3 lbs. of sugar *to the ball*, and finish as described for Strawberry Syrup (*vide* page 141).

MEDICINAL SNAIL SYRUP

Take 1 lb. of picked garden snails ; boil them very gently in 1 quart of water, and strain the liquor through a filtering-bag ;

Put the strained liquor in a sugar-boiler with $1\frac{1}{2}$ lb. of sugar, and boil it until the syrup registers 32° on the saccharometer ;

Hasten the cooling by placing the sugar-boiler in cold water ; bottle the syrup, and keep it in a cool place.

CITRIC ACID SYRUP

Put $\frac{1}{2}$ oz. of chopped lemon peel in 1 oz. of spirits of wine ; let it steep for eight days, and strain the liquid ;

Dissolve $\frac{1}{2}$ oz. of Citric Acid in 1 oz. of distilled water ;

Take $2\frac{1}{2}$ lbs. of plain syrup, registering 32° on the saccharometer ;

Mix the whole together, cold, and bottle the syrup.

A tablespoonful of this syrup, added to half a pint of water, will make an agreeable and refreshing drink.

Paris Pharmacopœia, 1866.

ORANGE FLOWER SYRUP

Put 2 lbs. of loaf sugar, broken in pieces, into 1 lb. of Orange Flower Water, and dissolve it without warming;

Filter the syrup, and keep it in well-corked bottles.

Observation.—Syrups are prepared in the same manner with aniseed, cinnamon, cherry-laurel leaf, and peppermint waters.   *Paris Pharmacopœia,* 1866.

POPPY SYRUP

Take 4 oz. of dried poppy petals, and put them in a jar with a cover to it;

Boil $2\frac{1}{2}$ lbs. of water; pour it, boiling, on to the poppies, and let them steep therein for six hours, keeping the jar closed;

Strain through a broth-napkin, and filter the liquid through a felt bag into a jar; add to it 3 lbs. 6 oz. of sugar; close the jar, and melt the sugar *au bain-marie;*

When cold, bottle the syrup, and keep it in a cool place;

Observation.—By using the quantities indicated in the above recipe, syrups may be successfully prepared with all the following:

Dried camomile flowers,

    honeysuckle „

    peony „

    scabious „

    hops,

    wormwood leaves,

    ivy „

    hyssop „

    saponaria „   *Paris Pharmacopœia,* 1866.

FLOWERING CLOVE SYRUP

Pick 1 lb. of fresh-gathered cloves, and put the petals in a jar closing hermetically ;

Boil 3 lbs. of distilled water, pour it boiling over the flowers, close the jar, and let them steep therein for six hours ;

Strain the whole through a broth-napkin, and filter the liquid ;

Put 3 lbs. of loaf sugar, broken in pieces, into a sugar-boiler ; add the filtered infusion, and boil until the syrup registers 30° on the saccharometer ;

When cold, bottle the syrup, and keep it in a cool place.

VIOLET SYRUP

Pick 1 lb. of fresh-gathered violet petals, and put them in a jar having a tight-fitting cover ;

Boil 3 lbs. of distilled water ; pour it boiling over the violets, and let them steep for twelve hours, keeping the jar closed ;

Strain the whole through a broth-napkin, previously rinsed in boiling water, and then dried ;

Let the infusion rest, and pour it off carefully into a sugar-boiler, so that the sediment may not be mixed ; add 5 lbs. of loaf sugar, broken in pieces, and boil until the syrup registers 30° on the saccharometer ;

When cold, bottle the syrup, and keep it in a cool place.

To obtain this syrup of a pleasing colour, none but silver or untinned copper stewpans should be used.

MARSHMALLOW SYRUP

Scrape 2 oz. of marshmallow roots, cut them in pieces, and put them in a jar ;

Boil ¾ lb. of distilled water, pour it boiling over the roots, close the jar, and let them steep for twelve hours; strain the infusion through a silk sieve, and add it to 3 lbs. of plain syrup registering 32° on the saccharometer;

Boil the whole until it registers 30°, and let it get cold;

Bottle the syrup, and keep it in a cool place.

Fifteen drops of Orange Flower Water may be added to the syrup. *Paris Pharmacopœia*, 1866.

TAR SYRUP

Break up 2 lbs. of loaf sugar, and put it in a jar with 1 lb. of Tar Water; close the jar, and boil the contents *au bain-marie* till the sugar is dissolved;

Filter the syrup, bottle it, and keep it in a cool place.
Paris Pharmacopœia, 1866.

SYRUP DES CINQ RACINES

Take :
    ¼ lb. of smallage roots,
    ¼ lb. of asparagus roots,
    ¼ lb. of fennel roots,
    ¼ lb. of parsley roots,
    ¼ lb. of small holly roots;

Cleanse the roots, and cut them into pieces; put them in a jar, and pour over them 3 lbs. of boiling water; close the jar, and let the roots steep for twelve hours, stirring them occasionally;

Strain through a broth-napkin, and filter the infusion in a cool place;

Put the roots back into the jar, pour over them 3 lbs. more boiling water, and let them steep therein for six hours, keeping the jar closely shut; and strain through a broth-napkin ;

With the second infusion thus obtained make a syrup by the addition of 4 lbs. of sugar, and by boiling and clarifying;

When the boiling syrup registers 30° on the saccharo-meter, let it boil on until it is reduced by a quantity equal to that of the first infusion ; then mix in this said infusion, and boil the syrup until it again registers 30°.

Strain, and bottle the syrup, and keep it in a cool place.

Paris Pharmacopœia, 1866.

Observation.—These medicinal syrups are often in request, and, as they are difficult to procure in the country, I have thought it of some use to describe their preparation.

A little practice is required to prepare them successfully, and particularly to get them clear.

As most of the recipes are according to the rules of the ' Pharmacopœia,' they can be followed in all confidence.

CHAPTER XVI

VARIOUS RECIPES FOR PARTIES

SMALL ROLLS WITH FOIE-GRAS

TAKE 24 small French rolls of an oval shape, 2½ inches by 1½ inch; rasp the rolls, and slit them open, lengthwise, without separating them entirely;

Spread some *Foie-gras* Forcemeat inside the rolls, close them up, and dress them on a napkin on a dish;

If the rolls are prepared beforehand, wrap them in a cloth to keep them moist.

SMALL ROLLS À LA FRANÇAISE

Take 24 rolls of an oval shape, 2½ inches by 1½ inch;

Rasp the rolls, cut out a 1¼-inch piece of the crust on the top, and remove the crumb from the inside;

Cut in small dice an equal quantity of cooked chicken fillets, tongue, and truffles; mix the whole, with some chopped *Ravigote*, in some *Mayonnaise* Jelly;

Fill the rolls with the mixture, replace the crust covers, and dish the rolls on a napkin.

The rolls may also be filled with some lobster cut in thin scallops, some cleansed and scraped anchovies cut in pieces, and some capers, the whole mixed in *Mayonnaise* Sauce.

SMALL ROLLS WITH CHAUDFROID OF WOODCOCKS

Procure some rolls, similar to those described in the preceding recipe, cut out a piece of the crust, and remove the crumb in the same way;

Fill the rolls with some cold fillets of woodcocks, cut in small dice and mixed in Game *Chaudfroid* Sauce, heaping up the meat $\frac{1}{4}$ inch above the top of the rolls.

The rolls can also be filled with fillets of chicken, red partridge, or other game, cut in the same way, and mixed in reduced *Velouté* Sauce.

SMALL ROLLS WITH TRUFFLES

Take some oval rolls, similar to those described above; rasp the rolls, cut them in two, lengthwise, and remove nearly all the crumb from the inside; fill each half with sliced truffles mixed in Madeira Sauce; replace the halves, and press them lightly together, and dish the rolls on a napkin.

HAM SANDWICHES

Cut off all the crust of a loaf baked in a tin;

Butter, and cut up the bread into slices $\frac{1}{16}$ of an inch thick;

Cover one slice of bread with thin slices of boiled ham, laid on the buttered side; spread a little mustard on the ham, and reverse another slice of bread and butter on the top;

Proceed in the same way until all the slices are used, press them lightly together, and cut them through into pieces $2\frac{1}{2}$ inches by $1\frac{1}{2}$ inch;

Dish the sandwiches on a napkin, and cover them with a cloth till wanted.

SMALL GALETTES, OR SALT BISCUITS

Sift 1 lb. of flour on to a pasteboard; make a hole in the centre of the flour, and put in:

2 oz. of butter,
$\frac{1}{4}$ oz. of salt,
2 gills of water;

Mix with the hands, and, when half mixed, sprinkle over the paste a little more water, to mix all the flour to a smooth paste;

Work the paste thoroughly, gather it into a lump, and let it rest for an hour;

Cut the paste into four parts; roll these out to $\frac{1}{4}$-inch thickness; let it rest a little, and roll it again to the same thickness should it have shrunk at all;

Cut up the paste with a $1\frac{1}{2}$-inch plain cutter; turn these little cakes on to a slightly buttered baking sheet, and prick the top of the paste with a fork;

Brush them over lightly with a little water; sprinkle them with some dry pounded salt, and bake them in a brisk oven;

When the cakes are done, put them to cool on a wire sieve.

These small *galettes* can also be served at dinners.

TIMBALES WITH CHAUDFROID OF CHICKEN

Make some *brioche* paste as follows:

Take 1 lb. of sifted flour; put a fourth part of it on a pasteboard to make the sponge;

Make a hollow in the centre of the flour, and put in $\frac{1}{2}$ oz. of German yeast dissolved in $\frac{1}{2}$ gill of warm water; mix the flour to a softish paste, and put it to rise in a warm place in a covered stewpan with a little warm water in it;

Put the remainder of the flour on the board, make a hollow in the centre, and put in:

$\frac{1}{4}$ oz. of salt,

$\frac{1}{4}$ oz. of sugar,

2 tablespoonfuls of water to melt the salt and sugar,

5 eggs,

$\frac{3}{4}$ lb. of butter;

Mix the paste, and add 3 more eggs, mixing in one egg thoroughly before adding another;

When the sponge has risen to twice its original size, mix it with the paste, and put the whole in a basin in a warm place, to rise for four hours;

Butter some small oval moulds $2\frac{1}{2}$ inches long, $1\frac{3}{4}$ inch broad, and $1\frac{3}{4}$ inch deep;

Work the paste with a wooden spoon, and put it into the moulds so as to half fill them;

When the paste has risen to nearly the top of the moulds, bake the *brioches* in a brisk oven;

When done, take the *brioches* out of the moulds, and, when cold, cut off the tops, so that the *timbales* may be able to stand upright, and remove all the inside, leaving only a $\frac{1}{4}$-inch crust all round.

Pick, draw, and singe a chicken; remove the fillets and minion fillets;

Put the remainder of the chicken in a stewpan, with a carrot, an onion, a little salt, and a faggot;

Boil, skim, and simmer gently until the chicken is done, and strain the broth through a broth-napkin;

Make a *roux* in a stewpan with 2 oz. of flour and $1\frac{1}{2}$ oz. of butter;

Moisten the *roux* with the strained broth, stirring over the fire until it boils; then simmer for twenty minutes; skim the sauce, and reduce it until it thickens and coats the spoon;

Strain the sauce through a fine hair sieve or tammy cloth, and stir it till it is cold, to prevent a skin forming on the top;

Trim the fillets and minion fillets of the chicken, and cook them without colouring them in a *sauté*-pan with a little butter;

Press them between two dishes, and, when cold, cut them into $\frac{1}{8}$-inch dice; mix them in the sauce, fill the *timbales* with the mixture, and dish them on a napkin.

TIMBALES WITH CHICKEN PURÉE

Make, cook, and prepare some *brioche timbales*, as directed in the preceding recipe;

Cook a chicken, without first removing the fillets, and make the sauce in the same way;

When the chicken is cold, remove the meat from the bones, and trim off all skin and fat;

Chop the meat, and pound it in a mortar, moistening whilst pounding with the sauce, which should be stiffly reduced;

Press the *purée* through a tammy cloth, and, when cold, fill the *timbales* with it.

TIMBALES WITH CHAUDFROID OF PARTRIDGES

Prepare some *brioche timbales* as directed for *Timbales* with *Chaudfroid* of Chicken;

Pick, draw, and singe two partridges;

Remove the fillets and minion fillets; trim, and flatten them slightly with a knife; fry them in a *sauté*-pan with a little butter, and put them on a plate to cool.

Put the remainder of the partridges in a stewpan, with :

 1 carrot,

 1 onion,

 a faggot of parsley, bay leaf, and thyme,

 a small quantity of salt,

 2 quarts of broth ;

Boil; skim; simmer till the partridges are done, and strain the broth through a napkin ;

Make a *roux* in a stewpan with 2 oz. of flour and $1\frac{1}{2}$ oz. of butter; moisten it with the broth, and stir over the fire till it boils ; simmer for twenty minutes; skim, and stir the sauce over a brisk fire until it coats the spoon ;

Strain the sauce through a tammy cloth, and stir it to prevent a skin forming on the top ;

Cut the fillets and minion fillets into $\frac{1}{8}$-inch dice ; add them to the cold sauce, and fill the *timbales* with the mixture.

Timbales of larks, woodcocks, snipe, and all small game, are prepared in the same way.

SNOW EGGS

Boil 1 quart of milk in a shallow stewpan, with 2 oz. of pounded sugar and a stick of vanilla ;

Break 6 eggs ; put the whites in a whipping bowl and the yolks in a basin ;

Whip the whites very firm, and mix in 2 oz. of pounded sugar and $\frac{1}{2}$ oz. of vanilla sugar ;

Take up a tablespoonful of the whipped whites, about the size of an egg, and drop it in the boiling milk ; repeat this process, bearing in mind that about six spoonfuls will be enough in the stewpan at a time ; when the eggs are set on one side, turn them over with the skimmer, and, when quite firm, put them on a sieve to drain; continue in the same way until all the whipped white of egg is used;

Put the yolks in a stewpan, with some of the milk in which the white has been poached, and stir over the fire until the egg begins to thicken; take the stewpan off the fire, continue stirring for a few minutes, and strain the custard through a sieve;

When cold, dish the snow eggs in a pyramid, pour over them some of the cold custard sauce, and serve the remainder in a boat.

SNOW EGGS FLAVOURED WITH CHOCOLATE

Boil 1 quart of milk in a shallow stewpan, with $1\frac{1}{2}$ oz. of pounded sugar and $\frac{1}{2}$ oz. of vanilla sugar;

Whip 6 whites of egg very firm, add 2 oz. of pounded sugar, $\frac{1}{2}$ oz. of vanilla sugar, and 2 oz. of grated chocolate; mix, and finish the snow eggs as directed in the preceding recipe;

For the sauce, put 6 yolks of egg in a stewpan, with a pint of the milk and 2 oz. of grated chocolate; stir over the fire, and finish the sauce as described in the preceding recipe.

SNOW EGGS FLAVOURED WITH COFFEE

Make 1 gill of very strong coffee;

Whip 6 whites of egg very firm, and add 2 tablespoonfuls of the coffee and $2\frac{1}{2}$ oz. of pounded sugar;

Boil 1 quart of milk with the remainder of the coffee and $1\frac{1}{2}$ oz. of pounded sugar;

Poach the eggs, and make the sauce with the coffee-milk in the way described for Snow Eggs (*vide* page 154).

The flavouring of Snow Eggs may be varied by substituting the grated peel of a lemon or orange, or a tablespoonful of Orange Flower Water, for the flavourings indicated above.

CURRANT BUNS

Take 1 lb. of sifted flour; put a fourth part of it in a basin to make the sponge;

Dissolve $\frac{3}{4}$ oz. of German yeast in 1 gill of warm milk; strain it through a hair sieve; add it to the flour in the basin, and mix it to a softish paste, adding some more hot milk if required, and put the sponge to rise in a warm place;

Put the remainder of the flour in another basin, with;

3 oz. of butter,
3 oz. of sugar,
$\frac{1}{4}$ oz. of salt,
1 egg,
1 gill of milk;

Mix the whole well together, and add two eggs, one after the other;

When the sponge has risen to twice its original size, add it to the paste in the basin, and work the whole well with the hand, mixing in 1 gill of milk and 2 oz. of well washed and dried currants;

Divide the paste into 1-oz. portions, roll them to a round shape, and put them on a buttered baking sheet.

When the buns have risen to twice their original size, bake them in a hot oven; take them out, brush them over with milk, and put them back in the oven for a minute to colour them; then take them out, and put them on a sieve to cool.

MUFFINS

Sift 1 lb. of flour into a basin;

Dissolve 1 oz. of German yeast in 3 gills of warm milk, and mix it with the flour; work the flour and yeast to a smooth paste with a wooden spoon, adding 1 gill of milk and $\frac{1}{2}$ oz. of salt;

Put the sponge to rise in a warm place till it has doubled its size; then put it on the pasteboard, and divide it into 2-oz. portions; roll these out to a $\frac{3}{4}$-inch thickness, and put them on some baking sheets, leaving plenty of space between each muffin; put the baking sheets in a warm place, and, when the muffins have risen to double their original thickness, bake them in a slow oven without colouring them;

When about to use the muffins, slit them all round with a knife, toast them slightly on each side, pull the halves apart, butter the inside, and replace them together; and serve the muffins on a hot plate.

PANCAKES

Sift $\frac{1}{2}$ lb. of flour into a basin; add:

   3 eggs,

   $\frac{1}{2}$ gill of brandy,

   a small pinch of salt;

Work it with a wooden spoon, and add a little milk if the paste becomes too stiff;

Melt 2 oz. of butter in 1 pint of milk, and add it, by degrees, to the flour and eggs in the basin;

Warm a pancake-pan, wipe it, and put in a small piece of butter; when the butter is melted, pour in two tablespoonfuls of the batter, and spread it so as to cover the pan entirely;

Fry the pancake till it is coloured on one side; then toss it over, and cook the other side, and turn the pancake out on to a dish;

Sprinkle the pancake with salt or sugar, according to taste, and keep it very hot till all the batter is cooked in the same way;

Serve the pancakes on a hot dish, with a cut lemon on a plate.

BEIGNETS SOUFFLÉS, OR PLAIN FRITTERS

Put in a stewpan:

$\frac{1}{2}$ pint of water,

$\frac{1}{4}$ lb. of butter,

$\frac{1}{2}$ oz. of sugar,

a pinch of salt;

Put the stewpan on the fire, boil the contents, and take it off the fire; mix in a $\frac{1}{4}$ lb. of flour, and stir over the fire for four minutes;

Take the stewpan off the fire, and mix in 4 eggs, thoroughly mixing one egg before adding another; the paste should then be stiff enough not to spread when dropped from a spoon;

Put the paste on to the cover of a stewpan, so as to have a $\frac{3}{4}$-inch thickness of paste;

Hold the stewpan cover in the left hand, and, with the hooked handle of a copper spoon, held in the right, detach portions of the paste about the size of a walnut, letting them fall into a kettle of hot clarified frying fat held in readiness on the stove corner;

When a sufficient quantity of fritters have been divided, place the frying-kettle on the fire; stir the fritters with the skimmer, so that they may be evenly coloured; drain them first on a sieve and then on a cloth, sprinkle them with sugar, dish them on a napkin, and serve.

A flavouring of orange or lemon peel, vanilla, or Orange Flower Water may be added to the paste.

ALMOND CUSTARD FRITTERS

Put 7 oz. of flour in a stewpan, with:

4 eggs,

2 oz. of pounded sugar,

1 oz. of blanched and pounded almonds,

½ oz. of bitter almonds, also blanched and pounded;

Mix, and pour in, by degrees, 1 pint of milk; add 1 oz. of butter, and stir over the fire for fifteen minutes, when the custard should be very smooth;

Spread the custard on a buttered baking sheet to a ¾-inch thickness, and, when cold, cut it into 1½-inch square pieces; dip these in egg, strew them with finely sifted bread-crumbs, and fry them in very hot fat until they assume a bright yellow tinge;

Drain the fritters on a sieve, sprinkle them with sugar, and serve very hot.

FLEMISH GAUFRES

Put 1 lb. of butter in a warmed basin, and work it with a wooden spoon;

Break ten eggs, and add the yolks, one at a time, to the butter in the basin; mix, and add, by degrees, 1 lb. of sifted flour and 1 pint of milk.

Much care is required to accomplish this mixing so as to obtain a smooth and not too stiff paste.

Dissolve ½ oz. of German yeast in 1 gill of warm milk; mix it in the paste, adding ½ oz. of sugar and a pinch of salt;

Whip 6 whites of egg, and mix them lightly with the paste, together with 1 pint of well whipped cream; and put the paste to rise for two hours in a warm place;

Heat a large square gaufre-iron, and turn it over to heat both sides equally;

Put a spoonful of the paste on one side of the gaufre-iron; close it, turn it over, and cook the gaufre on both sides, and take it out of the iron with a knife; trim the edges of the gaufre with some scissors, and keep it hot;

Continue in the same way until all the paste is used; sprinkle the gaufres with sugar, and serve them hot.

DUTCH WAFERS

Sift 10 oz. of flour on to a pasteboard; make a hollow in the centre, and put in:

6 oz. of pounded sugar,

5 oz. of butter,

the grated peel of a lemon,

a tablespoonful of rum,

a small pinch of salt,

two yolks of egg and one white;

Mix, and work the whole to a smooth paste;

Divide the paste into pieces the size of a walnut, and give them an oval shape;

Heat a wafer-iron, and place one of the pieces of paste on one side; close the iron carefully, so as to spread the paste and still preserve its oval shape, and cook it on both sides;

When the wafer is of a light golden colour, take it out of the iron, and put it to cool on a sieve;

Proceed in the same manner with the remainder of the paste, and put the wafers by for use.

ICE WAFERS

Put ½ lb. of flour in a basin, with:

½ lb. of pounded sugar,

3 eggs;

Mix the whole to a smooth paste;

Melt 2 oz. of butter in a stewpan with ½ pint of water, and add:

1 tablespoonful of brandy,

1 tablespoonful of Orange Flower Water,

a pinch of salt;

Add the above, in small quantities, to the paste in the basin, and work the whole to a smooth paste;

The paste should coat the spoon to $\frac{1}{12}$ inch thickness; add a little water if it is too stiff;

The proper cooking of these wafers is more easily accomplished than that of the Flemish Gaufres; the fire should not be so brisk, but of a moderate and even heat;

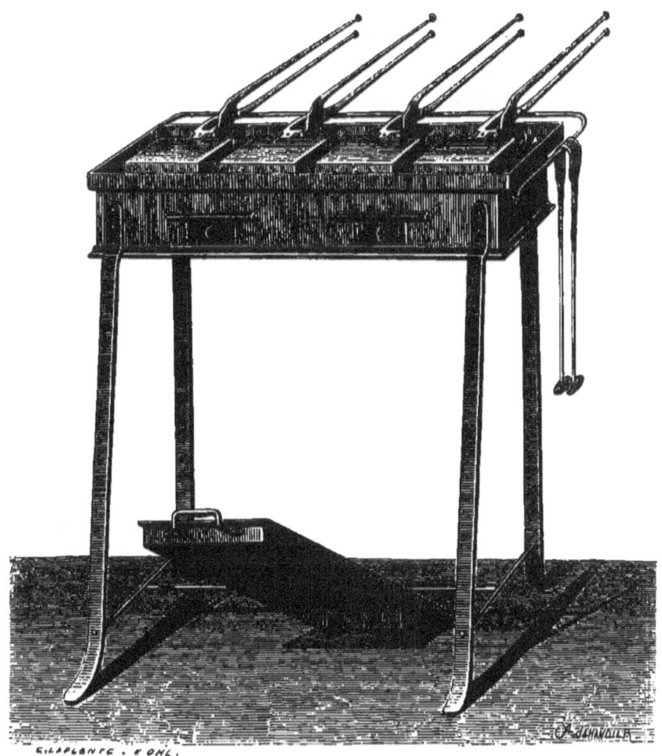

STOVE FOR COOKING GAUFRES

Heat a wafer-iron on both sides, butter it slightly, and wipe it with a cloth; heat it again, and hold it over the basin containing the paste; pour a spoonful of the paste on the iron, close it, cook the wafer on both sides, and take it out to be put aside, as this first wafer will merely have cleaned the iron;

Put another spoonful of paste on the heated iron; close it,

and cook the wafer on both sides; cut off the superfluous paste round the iron, open it, and place a stick on one end of the wafer, roll it quickly round the stick, and put the wafer on a sieve;

GAUFRE-IRON

Cook all the paste in a like manner, and keep the wafers in a tin box till wanted.

CALF'S FOOT JELLY

Put 4 boned calf's feet in a stewpan with 3 quarts of cold water, and put it on the fire;

When the water boils, skim it carefully, and simmer for eight hours, being careful to add some more boiling water as it evaporates; at the end of eight hours' boiling, there should be about 2 quarts of stock;

Strain the stock through a hair sieve into a basin, and put it in a cold place till the next day; then free the top of the jelly of all fat, wash it quickly with boiling water, and wipe it with a cloth ;

Put the jelly to clarify in a stewpan over the fire, with :

    1 lb. of loaf sugar,

    the juice of 5 lemons,

    ½ oz. of whole cinnamon,

    3 glasses of sherry or Madeira,

    4 cloves,

    A teaspoonful of coriander seeds ;

Put 3 whites of egg and 1 whole egg in a basin; whip them, adding a little water whilst whipping; then pour in part of the jelly and mix it with the whipped egg, stirring it with a wire whisk ;

Pour the whole into the stewpan containing the remainder of the jelly, and stir it till it boils; simmer for five minutes, close the stewpan, put some live coals on the cover, and simmer for ten minutes more ;

Put the yellow peel of two lemons in a jelly-bag, and pour the jelly through it ;

Pour it back again two or three times until it is perfectly clear, and put the jelly into basins on the ice ;

When the jelly is cold, chop it coarsely, and put it into jelly-glasses ;

The jelly can also be poured into small moulds, and set on the ice.

SMALL LOAVES À L'ALLEMANDE

Sift 1 lb. of flour; put a fourth part in a basin to make the sponge; dissolve 1 oz. of German yeast in 1 gill of warm milk, mix it with the flour, and put the sponge in a warm place to rise to double its size ;

Then put in the remainder of the flour, with :

    ¼ lb. of butter,

    ½ oz. of pounded sugar,

    ¼ oz. of salt ;

Mix the whole to a softish paste with ½ pint of warm milk, and put it to rise for three hours ;

Work the paste with a wooden spoon and let it rest for an hour ; then divide it into 2-oz. portions ; give each piece an oval shape, 3 inches long ; place them on a baking sheet, brush them over with egg, and put them to rise in a warm place ; then brush the loaves with egg again, strew them thickly with cummin seeds, bake them in a brisk oven, and put them to cool on a sieve.

SWISS CROQUETS

Rub ¼ lb. of almonds in a cloth, and cut them lengthwise in thin strips ;

Melt ¼ lb. of sugar in a basin with 1 gill of water, add :

    ½ oz. of ground ginger,

    a pinch of salt,

    ½ lb. of flour ;

Mix the whole to a softish paste, adding a few drops of water if required ; mix in the almonds, and divide the paste into 2-oz. portions ; roll each portion round into 2½-inch lengths ; place the croquets on some slightly buttered baking sheets, leaving a 2-inch space between each croquet ; bake them in a brisk oven until they are of a light golden colour, and put them on a sieve to cool.

GINGER-BREAD

Put in a stewpan :

    1 lb. of honey,

    2 oz. of treacle ;

Stir over the fire until both are melted; then add:

$\frac{1}{2}$ lb. of flour,

2 oz. of ground ginger,

$\frac{1}{2}$ oz. of carbonate of soda,

$\frac{1}{8}$ oz. of carbonate of ammonia;

Mix, and add another $\frac{1}{2}$ lb. of flour; mix the whole together, and work the paste for ten minutes by drawing it apart and folding it over;

Put the paste in a basin, and let it rest for eight days;

Before baking the paste, put it on the pasteboard, and work it again in the same way as before, namely: hold it with the left hand and draw it out with the right, fold it over, and continue thus for ten minutes; this working will make the paste light;

Mix in 7 oz. of candied citron cut in small dice; roll out the paste to $\frac{1}{4}$-inch thickness, and score it with a knife into rectangular sections 3 inches by $1\frac{3}{4}$ inch;

Brush over with egg, and bake the ginger-bread in a brisk oven until it attains a dark brown colour;

When cold, divide the pieces where they were scored, and keep the ginger-bread in a cool place.

ALMOND CROQUETS

Sift 1 lb. of flour on to a pasteboard; make a hollow in the centre, and put in:

$\frac{1}{2}$ lb. of sugar,

$\frac{1}{2}$ lb. of Jordan almonds previously rubbed in a cloth,

1 gill of water,

a pinch of salt,

the grated peel of 2 lemons;

Mix the whole to a stiff paste, and roll it out to a $\frac{3}{4}$ inch thickness;

Cut the paste into bands 3 inches wide; brush them over

with egg, and score them across, leaving a $\frac{1}{8}$-inch space between each cut ;

Put the paste in a brisk oven till it attains a light golden tinge ; take it out and cut it through where it has been scored ;

Replace the croquets on the baking sheet, and put them in the oven, so as to colour that part where they have been divided, and put them on a sieve to cool.

CRACKNELS, OR CRAQUELINS

Sift 1 lb. of flour on to a pasteboard ; make a hollow in the centre, and put in :

1 oz. of pounded sugar,

$\frac{1}{2}$ oz. of German yeast dissolved in $\frac{1}{2}$ pint of warm water,

$\frac{1}{2}$ oz. of salt ;

Work the paste with the hands, and put it to rise for two hours ;

Divide the paste into 2-oz. portions, give them a round shape, put them on a tinned copper baking sheet, brush them over with egg, strew them thickly with cummin seeds, egg them again to stick on the seeds, and bake them in a brisk oven.

KOUQUES, OR BUTTERED CAKES

Sift 1 lb. of flour into a basin ; make a hollow in the centre ; mix in $\frac{1}{2}$ oz. of German yeast dissolved in $\frac{1}{2}$ gill of warm milk, and put the sponge to rise in a warm place ;

When the sponge has risen to twice its original size, add :

$\frac{1}{2}$ oz. of pounded sugar,

$\frac{1}{4}$ oz. of salt,

6 oz. of butter,

3 gills of milk ;

Mix the ingredients and add 6 eggs, mixing one thoroughly before adding another ;

Work the whole to a smooth paste and put it, in a closed vessel, to rise for three hours in a warm place ;

Sprinkle the pasteboard with flour, place the paste on it and cut it into 2-oz. portions ; shape each piece something like a shuttle and put the cakes on a tinned copper baking sheet, leaving a 1½-inch space between each ; brush them over with egg and put them to rise for an hour ; then bake them in a hot oven ;

Take the cakes out of the oven, slit them open without separating them entirely, put some fresh butter in the opening, dish them on a napkin and serve very hot.

CINNAMON BISCUITS

Break 4 yolks of egg in a basin ; add ¼ lb. of pounded sugar and work both together with a wooden spoon ; add :

1 oz. of ground cinnamon,

2 oz. of butter, melted,

a pinch of salt ;

Work again for five minutes ; add 10 oz. of flour and work the whole to a smooth paste ;

Divide the paste into 2-oz. portions and roll each portion round to a stick shape, ⅝ inch in diameter ;

Wax some copper baking sheets ; place the biscuits on them, leaving an inch space between each biscuit ; brush them over with egg, bake them in a brisk oven until they attain a light golden tinge, and put them on a sieve to cool.

ANISEED BISCUITS

Sift ½ lb. of flour on to a pasteboard ; make a hollow in the centre and put in :

$\frac{1}{4}$ lb. of pounded sugar,

2 oz. of butter,

$\frac{1}{2}$ oz. of fresh aniseed, chopped,

1 whole egg and 4 yolks,

a pinch of salt ;

Work the whole to a smooth and softish paste, adding 1 or 2 yolks of egg if it is too stiff;

Divide the paste into 2 oz.-portions ; roll each round to a stick shape, $\frac{5}{8}$ inch in diameter; brush the biscuits over with some whipped white of egg, and turn over the side so wetted on to some small aniseed comfits ;

Put the biscuits on slightly buttered copper baking sheets, and bake them in a brisk oven.

SALT BISCUITS

Sift $\frac{1}{2}$ lb. of flour on to a pasteboard ; make a hollow in the centre and put in :

$\frac{1}{4}$ lb. of butter,

$\frac{1}{4}$ oz. of salt,

1 gill of water ;

Mix, and add, by degrees, one gill more water and work the whole to a very smooth paste ; let it rest for an hour, and divide it into 2-oz. portions ;

Roll out each piece to an oval shape, $\frac{1}{8}$ inch thick, put the biscuits on a copper baking sheet, brush them over with egg, prick the surface with a fork, sprinkle them with salt, and bake them in a hot oven ;

Dish the biscuits on a hot napkin, and serve.

ALMOND BISCUITS

Sift 1 lb. of flour on to a pasteboard ; make a hollow in the middle, and put in :

$\frac{1}{4}$ lb. of pounded sugar,

$\frac{1}{4}$ lb. of butter,

$\frac{1}{2}$ oz. of grated orange peel,

1 oz. of finely pounded bitter almonds,

1 egg,

1 pinch of salt,

1 gill of milk, added by degrees ;

Mix, and work the paste, adding more milk, by degrees, until a smooth and stiffish paste is obtained, and let it rest for an hour ;

Roll out the paste to $\frac{1}{4}$ inch thickness and cut it with a 2-inch fluted cutter ;

Brush lightly over the surface of the biscuits with some egg, and turn them over on to some coarsely sifted sugar ;

Put the biscuits on some slightly buttered baking sheets, bake them in a brisk oven, and put them on a sieve to cool.

SWISS LECRELETS

Melt 10 oz. of honey over the fire ; skim, and put it in a perfectly clean basin ; add :

$\frac{1}{4}$ lb. of unblanched Jordan almonds, cut in thin strips,

2 oz. of candied lemon peel, cut in small dice,

2 oz. of candied orange peel, cut in small dice,

$\frac{1}{2}$ oz. of ground cinnamon,

$\frac{1}{8}$ oz. of ground cloves,

$\frac{1}{8}$ oz. of grated nutmeg,

$\frac{1}{2}$ gill of Kirschenwasser,

the grated peel of a lemon ;

Mix all the ingredients with a wooden spoon ;

Dissolve $\frac{1}{4}$ oz. of soda in a little water ; add it to the ingredients in the basin, together with 1 lb. of flour ;

Mix, and put by the paste in the basin for four days ;

z

Work the paste for ten minutes by drawing it apart and folding it over ;

Sprinkle the pasteboard with flour, roll out the paste to $\frac{1}{2}$ inch thickness, and put it on a baking sheet sprinkled over with flour ;

Cook the paste in a brisk oven, take it off the baking sheet and put it on the pasteboard ; brush off the flour, and place the paste on a clean baking sheet ; put the baking sheet in the oven, to warm the paste, and cut it, without dividing it entirely, into pieces $3\frac{1}{2}$ inches by $1\frac{3}{4}$ inch ;

Boil some sugar *to the blow ;*

Dip a brush in the sugar, and pass it rapidly over the warm paste ; this should be done carefully, so as not to brush twice over the same place ;

When the sugar is dry, break off the *lecrelets* where they were previously cut, and place them on a sieve to cool.

ORANGE STICKS

Whip 6 eggs in a basin, together with :

    5 oz. of pounded sugar,

    the grated peel of an orange,

    a pinch of salt ;

Add a sufficient quantity of flour to form a stiffish paste ; and when the paste is quite smooth, let it rest for an hour ;

Roll the paste into stick-shaped pieces 3 inches long, $\frac{5}{8}$ inch in diameter ;

When the paste is all rolled in this manner, throw the sticks into a large copper sugar-boiler half full of boiling water ; shake the sugar-boiler, to prevent the sticks adhering to one another, and, as they rise to the surface of the water, take them off with a skimmer, and put them in a basin of cold water to steep for an hour ;

Drain, and put the sticks on a sieve to dry ; place them on buttered copper baking sheets, brush them over with egg, and bake them till they assume a light golden tinge.

SMALL SEED CAKES

Sift $\frac{1}{4}$ lb. of flour into a basin, and add :

$\frac{3}{4}$ lb. of pounded sugar,

$\frac{1}{2}$ oz. of chopped green aniseed,

10 yolks of egg,

a pinch of salt ;

Work the whole with a wooden spoon, and add 2 whipped whites of egg ;

Butter some oval tin moulds 3 inches long, 1 inch wide ; fill the moulds with the paste, strew some aniseed comfits on the top, and bake the cakes of a light golden colour.

SMALL PARISIAN LOAVES

Sift $\frac{3}{4}$ lb. of flour into a basin ; add :

$\frac{1}{4}$ lb. of butter,

$\frac{1}{4}$ oz. of pounded sugar,

$\frac{1}{4}$ oz. of salt,

6 yolks of egg ;

Mix the whole together, adding, by degrees, sufficient cream to form a softish paste ;

Work the whole with a wooden spoon, and, when the paste no longer adheres to it or to the basin, add $\frac{1}{2}$ oz. of German yeast dissolved in two tablespoonfuls of warm water, and let the paste rise for three hours ;

Put the paste on the pasteboard ; divide it into 2-oz. portions ; give these a long oval shape, and let them rise for an hour ; then brush the loaves over with egg, bake them in a brisk oven, and serve them hot for tea.

CANAPÉS FOR HORS-D'ŒUVRE

ANCHOVY CANAPÉS

Cut some crumb of bread into slices $\frac{1}{4}$ inch thick; cut these in pieces $2\frac{1}{2}$ inches long, $1\frac{1}{2}$ inch wide; and fry them in clarified butter till of a light golden colour;

When cold, spread the pieces with fresh, or Anchovy Butter;

Place 4 fillets of anchovies, previously steeped in cold water, lengthwise on each piece of bread; fill up the spaces between with chopped hard-boiled white of egg, chopped parsley, and chopped hard-boiled yolk of egg;

Cover each piece of bread in the same way, and serve the *canapés* at evening parties, or as a *hors-d'œuvre* for dinners.

CAVIAR CANAPÉS

Cut and fry some pieces of bread as directed in the preceding recipe;

Butter the pieces when cold, and spread a layer of fresh *caviar* on them.

When preserved *caviar* is used, moisten it, before spreading it, with a little oil and lemon juice.

HAM CANAPÉS

Cut, fry, and butter some pieces of bread as described in the preceding recipe;

Cover the surface with thin slices of boiled ham, and dress the *canapés* in a small dish.

TONGUE CANAPÉS

Prepare these as directed in the preceding recipe, substituting some slices of boiled tongue for the ham.

LOBSTER CANAPÉS

Cut some crumb of bread into slices $\frac{1}{4}$ inch thick ; cut these out with a plain 2-inch cutter, and fry the rounds in clarified butter until they are of a light golden colour ;

When cold, spread the rounds with Lobster Butter, and sprinkle over a little salt and Cayenne pepper ;

Put a lobster scallop on the centre of each round, and place a row of capers round the lobster.

SMOKED SALMON CANAPÉS

Cut and fry the bread as directed for Anchovy *Canapés* ;

Spread the pieces with fresh butter, and cover the butter with very thin slices of smoked salmon previously slightly broiled and allowed to cool.

TUNNY CANAPÉS

Prepare some pieces of bread as described for Anchovy *Canapés* (*vide* page 172).

Spread them with very fresh butter, cover the butter with very thin slices of preserved tunny, season with lemon juice, and strew the tunny with some chopped *Ravigote*.

BEEF CANAPÉS FOR SHOOTING-PARTIES

Cut and fry some rounds of bread as directed for Lobster *Canapés* ;

Spread the rounds with fresh butter, season with a little salt and pepper, cover the butter with very thin slices of cold roast beef, and pour a little meat glaze over the beef.

Observation.—In preparing all the above *Canapés* the bread may be slightly toasted on each side, instead of frying it in the clarified butter.

CHAPTER XVII

ICES AND SORBETS

REMARKS ON ICES

To prepare ices successfully, the freezing-pot should be well embedded in rough ice and bay salt; and the preparation to be iced should be in such quantity as only to half fill the freezing-pot;

ICE-PAIL, FREEZING-POT AND SPATULA

To set a freezing-pot:

Cut a piece of rough ice 3 inches thick to fit the bottom of the pail; place the closed freezing-pot thereon, and fill up the pail with pounded rough ice and bay salt mixed together;

Let the freezing-pot remain thus for five minutes; then take off the cover and wipe it;

Half fill the freezing-pot with the preparation to be iced;

To freeze it: with the left hand, twist the pot rapidly round in the ice-pail, and, as the ice sets on the sides, detach it with the spatula, and work the whole well together, so that the ice may freeze evenly;

Continue thus until the whole is firmly set and quite smooth; then take the ice out of the freezing-pot, and put it into an ice-mould; embed this in a pail filled with mixed pounded ice and bay salt;

Dip a cloth in salted water; fold, and place it on the top of the pail;

Leave the mould in the ice for two hours; then take it out, dip the mould in cold water, and turn the ice out on to a dish or plate covered with a folded napkin.

Observation.—I would recommend filling up the interstices of the cover of the ice-mould with butter before embedding it in the ice, in order that none of the salt may get in and spoil the ice.

VANILLA ICE

Boil 1 quart of double cream; take the stewpan off the fire, put a stick of Vanilla in the cream, and let it steep therein for an hour, keeping the stewpan covered;

Put 12 yolks of egg in a basin, with 14 oz. of pounded sugar; work both together with a spoon, add the boiled cream, and strain the whole through a silk sieve into a stewpan;

Stir over the fire, without boiling, till the cream thickens and coats the spoon; pour it into a basin, and continue stirring, to prevent a skin forming on the surface;

When the cream is cold, strain it into a freezing-pot set in ice; freeze, and work the cream with the spatula; and when the ice is frozen, mix in 3 gills of whipped double cream, continue working with the spatula until the whole is quite smooth, and close the pot ;

Draw off any water that might be in the ice-pail, and refill it with pounded ice and bay salt, covering the freezing-pot entirely ;

Put the Vanilla ice into ice-moulds, and embed them for two hours in pounded ice and bay salt ; and turn the ices out of the moulds on to a napkin on a dish.

Or, the ice may be merely taken out of the freezing-pot, and piled up in a china ice-pail, and served.

Observation.—In all cases, it will be advisable to postpone adding the flavouring until the cream has been boiled, otherwise both may be spoiled.

FILBERT ICE

Roast $\frac{1}{2}$ lb. of filberts in a copper pan, shaking the pan frequently, so as not to colour them ;

Boil 3 pints of double cream, and put the filberts to steep in it ;

When the cream is cold, drain the filberts, pound them in a mortar, adding the cream whilst pounding, and press the whole through a tammy cloth into a stewpan ; add :

12 yolks of egg,
14 oz. of pounded sugar ;

Stir over the fire till the cream coats the spoon, pour it into a basin, add a tablespoonful of Kirschenwasser, and continue stirring for a few minutes ;

When the cream is cold, strain it into a freezing-pot set in rough ice ; and freeze it as directed in the preceding recipe ;

Add 3 gills of whipped cream, and finish the ice in the same way.

CHOCOLATE ICE

Melt ½ lb. of chocolate in a stewpan ;

Boil 1 quart of double cream ; mix in the melted chocolate, and add a stick of vanilla ; cover the stewpan, and let the vanilla steep for an hour ;

Break 12 yolks of egg in a basin ; add ¾ lb. of pounded sugar ; work both together with a spoon, mix in the chocolate cream, and strain the whole through a silk sieve into a stewpan ;

Stir over the fire until the egg thickens, and finish precisely as described for Vanilla Ice.

COFFEE ICE

Boil 3 pints of double cream ; add ½ lb. of fresh-roasted unground coffee, and let it steep for an hour ;

Put 12 yolks of egg in a basin, with 14 oz. of pounded sugar ; work both together with a spoon ; add the boiled cream, and strain the whole through a silk sieve into a stewpan ;

Stir over the fire, without boiling, till the cream coats the spoon, and freeze it as directed for Vanilla Ice.

ICED FROTHS, OR MOUSSES GLACÉES

Before giving the several recipes for these Iced Froths, I will give a list of the utensils required for their preparation.

First. A frothing-stick : this is a boxwood mallet-shaped instrument about a foot long (*vide* woodcut) ; the head is hollowed out into ridges, to produce the froth quicker and in greater abundance ; the handle is cut to an octagonal shape, so that it may be twirled with greater ease between the hands.

This frothing-stick can be obtained at all respectable turners.

FROTHING-STICK

Secondly. 2 large basins.
Thirdly. Several hair draining-sieves.
Fourthly. A tinned copper skimmer.

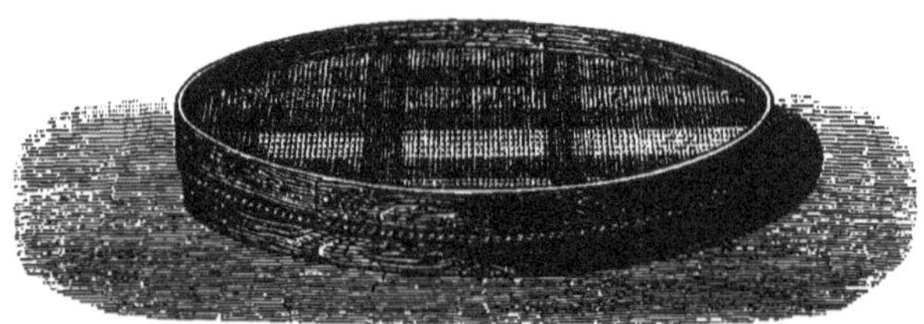

DRAINING-SIEVE

Fifthly. A large knife, to detach the froth from the skimmer.

Sixthly. A copper freezing-case.

Although this kind of ice is seldom served, I have thought it best to describe it; it is just possible that, in this transition period, we may see an attempt made to improve the indifferent quality of the refreshments now served at evening parties; and then such delicate preparations as these Iced Froths will be in request;

I consider these froths, on account of their lightness, superior to either Ices or *Sorbets*;

FREEZING-CASE

They are cool to eat, without freezing the palate, and do not increase thirst instead of slaking it, as so many sweetened drinks do.

Finally, they have the advantage of being perfectly wholesome and suited to the weakest digestion.

CHOCOLATE ICED FROTH

Put in a sugar-boiler :

    1½ lb. of chocolate, broken in pieces,

    ¾ lb. loaf sugar, also broken up,

    3 pints of water ;

Stir the chocolate over the fire until it is melted; boil for ten minutes, and strain the whole through a silk sieve into a large basin;

Allow the chocolate to cool for several hours and add 1 pint of double cream;

Place a draining-sieve on another basin;

Begin frothing the chocolate with the stick; whisk it at the edge of the basin rather than in the middle;

When the froth thickens, and its bubbles are small and close together, take it off with the skimmer, and put it on the sieve to drain;

Continue whisking until all the chocolate, even that which has dripped through the sieve, is converted into froth;

When thoroughly drained, heap the froth lightly into jelly-glasses;

Place the glasses in a freezing-case previously set in rough ice and bay salt; close the case, and let the glasses remain therein until wanted.

The preparation of the Iced Froth requires some practice;

The sieve containing the froth must not be shaken; the glasses must be filled properly without pressing the froth down, as its lightness is its principal attraction.

A stick of vanilla or a little vanilla sugar may be boiled with the chocolate.

COFFEE ICED FROTH

Mix in a basin:

    1 quart of double cream,

    $\frac{1}{2}$ pint of very strong coffee,

    $\frac{3}{4}$ lb. of pounded sugar;

Strain the whole through a silk sieve, and whisk and finish the froth as directed in the preceding recipe.

STRAWBERRY ICED FROTH

Mix in a basin :

 1 quart of double cream,

 3 gills of strawberry juice,

 $\frac{3}{4}$ lb. of pounded sugar,

 a few drops of prepared cochineal ;

Strain the whole through a silk sieve into a basin, and finish the froth as directed for Chocolate Iced Froth.

MARASCHINO ICED FROTH

Mix in a basin :

 1 quart of double cream,

 $\frac{1}{2}$ pint of Maraschino,

 $\frac{1}{2}$ lb. of pounded sugar ;

Strain and finish the froth as directed for Chocolate Iced Froth.

ALMOND MILK ICED FROTH

Blanch and peel $\frac{1}{4}$ lb. of Jordan almonds and 2 oz. of bitter almonds ;

Pound the almonds in a mortar, adding 3 gills of water whilst pounding ; press the almonds through a coarse broth napkin, previously washed in boiling water and rinsed in cold water ;

Put the almond milk in a basin, with :

 1 quart of double cream,

 $\frac{3}{4}$ lb. of pounded sugar ;

Mix, and strain the whole through a silk sieve into a basin, and whisk and finish the froth as described for Chocolate Iced Froth.

Observation.—Should the preparations not froth easily, add a little more cream.

STRAWBERRY ICE

Rub a sufficient quantity of small Alpine strawberries through a silk sieve to obtain $1\frac{1}{2}$ pint of juice; add 14 oz. of pounded sugar and 1 quart of double cream; mix, and strain the whole through a silk sieve, and add a few drops of prepared cochineal to give the ice a pale rose tint;

Pour the strawberry cream into a freezing-pot set in pounded ice and bay salt;

Freeze, and work the cream with the spatula until it is quite smooth;

Close the pot, draw off any water that might be in the ice-pail, and refill it with pounded ice and bay salt, covering the freezing-pot entirely.

Serve the ice in china ice-pails; or it may be moulded in different shaped ice-moulds and embedded in pounded ice and bay salt for an hour, and turned out of the moulds on to a napkin on a dish.

PINEAPPLE ICE

Peel and cut in pieces $\frac{3}{4}$ lb. of pineapple; put it in a basin, pour over it $1\frac{1}{2}$ pint of hot syrup registering 35° on the saccharometer, and let it steep for an hour;

Drain the pineapple, and pound it in a mortar, adding the syrup and $1\frac{1}{2}$ pint of double cream whilst pounding; strain through a hair sieve, add 2 tablespoonfuls of lemon juice, and strain the whole through a silk sieve;

Pour the cream into a freezing-pot set in ice; and work and finish the ice as directed in the preceding recipe.

RASPBERRY ICE

Rub sufficient raspberries through a silk sieve to obtain
1¼ pint of juice; add:

    1¼ pint of syrup, registering 35° on the saccharometer,

    1 pint of double cream,

    2 tablespoonfuls of lemon juice;

Mix and strain the whole through a silk sieve; pour it
into a freezing-pot set in ice, and finish the ice as directed
for Strawberry Ice.

RED CURRANT ICE

Rub some red currants through a silk sieve, so as to
obtain 1¼ pint of juice, and mix it with 1¼ pint of syrup
registering 35° on the saccharometer;

Strain the whole through a silk sieve; pour it into a
freezing-pot set in ice, and finish the ice as directed for
Strawberry Ice.

A flavouring of raspberries may be added by substituting
1 gill of raspberry juice for an equal quantity of currant
juice.

APRICOT ICE

Choose some not over ripe apricots;

Rub the apricots through a hair sieve so as to obtain 1¼
pint of juice; add:

    1¼ pint of syrup, registering 35° on the saccharometer,

    1 tablespoonful of Noyau,

    1 gill of water;

Strain the whole through a silk sieve; put it into a
freezing-pot set in ice, and work and finish the ice as
directed for Strawberry Ice (*vide* page 182).

Peach Ice is prepared in the same way.

CHAPTER XVIII

COOLING CUPS, PUNCHES, AND SABAYONS

CHÂBLIS CUP

PUT in a basin :

$\frac{1}{2}$ lb. of loaf sugar broken in pieces,

1 pint of water,

The peel of a lemon ;

Steep the lemon for an hour, and strain the whole through a silk sieve into a basin ;

Cut the peel off 2 lemons ; cut them across into slices, remove the pips, and add the slices to the syrup in the basin, together with 3 bottles of Châblis ; mix, and pour into glass jugs or into a punch bowl, and serve with some bottles of Seltzer water.

CHAMPAGNE CUP

Melt $\frac{1}{2}$ lb. of loaf sugar in a basin with $1\frac{1}{2}$ pint of water; add the juice of 4 oranges and the peel of one ;

Filter the whole through a paper filter placed in a glass funnel (*vide* Modes of Filtering, page 136);

Strain the syrup through a silk sieve into a basin ; add 3 bottles of Champagne, and pour the whole into a punch bowl or into glass jugs, and serve with some pieces of Wenham lake ice in a bowl.

SAUTERNE CUP

Put 1 lb. of picked Alpine strawberries in a basin, with 1 quart of syrup registering 30° on the saccharometer;

Let the strawberries steep for three hours; add 2 bottles of Sauterne; strain the whole through a filtering-bag, pour it into a punch bowl or into glass jugs, and serve with some bottles of Seltzer water.

RHINE WINE CUP

Put in a basin:

1 quart of syrup registering 30°,
$\frac{1}{2}$ oz. of cummin seeds,
$\frac{1}{2}$ oz. of coriander seeds;

Cover the basin, and steep the seeds for twenty-four hours; add 2 bottles of Rhine wine (Forster, Johannisberg or Sparkling Hock); filter the whole through a paper filter, and pour it into glass jugs or into a punch bowl.

PICARDAN CUP

Put in a basin:

1 quart of syrup registering 28°,
2 bottles of Picardan wine,
the juice of 2 lemons,
the peel of 2 Seville oranges;

Cover the basin, and let the orange peel steep thus for an hour;

Strain the whole through a filtering-bag, and pour it into a punch bowl or into glass jugs.

MARSALA CUP

Pick 1 lb. of May-Duke or Kentish cherries; slit them open, and put them in a basin with $\frac{1}{2}$ lb. of pounded sugar and 2 bottles of Marsala;

Cover the basin, and let the cherries steep for twelve hours; strain the whole through a filtering-bag, pour it into a punch bowl or into glass jugs, and serve with some bottles of Seltzer water and some pieces of Wenham lake ice in a bowl.

Observation.—When the glass jugs or bowls are filled with either of the foregoing Cups, they should be put on the ice for half an hour before they are served.

MULLED CLARET

Steep $\frac{1}{2}$ oz. of cinnamon and $\frac{1}{4}$ oz. of cloves in $\frac{1}{2}$ pint of hot syrup;

This infusion should be prepared in advance, and kept in a well-corked bottle for use;

Put $\frac{1}{2}$ lb. of loaf sugar in a copper sugar-boiler with one gill of water; melt it over the fire, and pour in:

2 bottles of claret,

4 tablespoonfuls of the spiced syrup;

Taste, and if the flavour is not strong enough, add a little more of the syrup;

Warm the wine, without boiling, and serve it in a silver stewpan or china bowl.

Slices of lemon are frequently added to mulled wine, but I do not recommend their addition, as the acid taste which results is a very questionable advantage; a little grated nutmeg or ground ginger may be substituted, and will, in my opinion, be much preferable to the lemon.

All red wines are mulled in the same way.

None but the best qualities should be used for mulled wine or for any of the preceding recipes.

HOT PUNCH

Put in a basin:

$\frac{3}{4}$ oz. of green tea,

the peel of 2 oranges,

the peel of 2 lemons;

Pour in 1 quart of boiling water, cover the basin, and infuse the contents for an hour;

Melt 10 oz. of sugar in a sugar-boiler with $\frac{1}{2}$ pint of water; pour in 1 bottle of Brandy and 1 bottle of Rum; set light to the spirit, and let it burn for eight minutes; then add the contents of the basin; mix, and strain the whole through a silk sieve into a *bain-marie* pan, and keep the punch hot;

Just before serving the punch, add the filtered juice of 6 oranges, and pour it into a bowl.

Should the punch be too strong, add a little boiling water.

AMERICAN PUNCH

Put in a basin:

$\frac{3}{4}$ oz. of green tea,

$\frac{1}{2}$ oz. of cinnamon,

$\frac{1}{4}$ oz. of whole ginger,

the peel of 2 Seville oranges,

a small pinch of Cayenne pepper;

Pour 1 quart of boiling water over the ingredients; cover the basin, and let them steep therein for an hour;

Put 10 oz. of loaf sugar in a sugar-boiler with $\frac{1}{2}$ pint of water; pour in 2 bottles of Rum, set light to it, and let it burn for five minutes;

Strain the contents of the basin through a silk sieve; add the infusion to the rum, together with the filtered juice of 3 lemons; make the punch very hot, and serve it in a bowl.

WHISKY PUNCH

Melt 14 oz. of loaf sugar in a sugar-boiler with 1 quart of water; let it boil, and strain it through a silk sieve into another sugar-boiler; pour in a bottle of Whisky, let it boil up, and serve the punch, very hot, in a bowl.

KIRSCHENWASSER PUNCH

Prepare this in the way described for Whisky Punch, substituting a bottle of Kirschenwasser for the whisky.

HOT PINEAPPLE PUNCH

Melt $\frac{1}{2}$ lb. of loaf sugar in a sugar-boiler, with 1 gill of water; pour in:

$\frac{1}{2}$ a bottle of Rum,

$\frac{1}{2}$ a bottle of Brandy;

Set light to the spirit, and let it burn for eight minutes; add 1 pint of reduced Pineapple Syrup and 1 bottle of dry Champagne;

Strain the whole through a silk sieve into a *bain-marie* pan, and keep the punch hot;

Add the filtered juice of 3 oranges to the punch; pour it into a bowl, and serve it hot.

PUNCH À LA ROMAINE

Set a freezing-pot in pounded ice and bay salt;

Mix in a basin:

1 bottle of Châblis,

the strained juice of 4 lemons,

3 gills of syrup, registering 24° on the saccharometer;

Strain the whole through a silk sieve into the freezing-pot; freeze the ice, and add 4 whites of egg of Italian *Meringue*, prepared in the following way:

Put 6 oz. of sugar in a sugar-boiler with a little water, and boil it until it registers 40° on the saccharometer;

Whip 4 whites of egg, and add the boiling sugar to them, whipping all the time; when the *Meringue* is cold, add it to the ice, as directed above;

Continue working with the spatula until the whole is well mixed; close the freezing-pot, and cover it with pounded ice and bay salt;

Five minutes before serving, add ½ gill of rum to the ice; mix, and serve the punch in glasses.

CHAMPAGNE PUNCH À LA ROMAINE

Set a freezing-pot in pounded ice and bay salt;

Pour in 1 pint of syrup registering 28°, and 2 bottles of Champagne;

Work the syrup with the spatula, and, when it is frozen, add 4 whites of egg of Italian *Meringue*, prepared with 4 oz. of sugar boiled *to the ball*;

Work the ice until the whole is well mixed, and cover the freezing-pot;

Serve the punch in glasses.

MARASCHINO PUNCH À LA ROMAINE

Set a freezing-pot in the ice;

Pour in 1 quart of syrup registering 24°, and ½ pint of Maraschino;

Work the ice until it is frozen, and add 4 whites of egg of Italian *Meringue*, prepared as described for Punch *à la Romaine*; and finish and serve the punch in the same way, without, however, adding the rum.

PINEAPPLE PUNCH À LA ROMAINE

Peel and pound 1 lb. of pineapple; put it in a basin, and pour over it 3 pints of hot syrup registering 28°; let it steep for an hour, and strain the whole through a silk sieve into a freezing-pot set in pounded ice;

Work the syrup until it is frozen, and add half a bottle of Champagne and 4 whites of egg of Italian *Meringue*;

Work the whole together; close the freezing-pot, and cover it with pounded ice and bay salt;

Serve the punch in glasses.

STRAWBERRY PUNCH À LA ROMAINE

Set a freezing-pot in the ice;

Rub sufficient Alpine strawberries through a hair sieve to obtain $1\frac{1}{2}$ pint of juice; add $1\frac{1}{2}$ pint of cold syrup registering 20°, and strain it through a silk sieve into the freezing-pot;

Work the syrup until it is frozen, and add:

 1 gill of Sauterne,

 2 tablespoonfuls of lemon juice,

 4 whites of egg of Italian *Meringue*,

 A few drops of prepared cochineal, to give the punch
  a bright rose colour;

Work the whole together with the spatula; close the freezing-pot, and cover it with pounded ice and bay salt;

Serve the punch in glasses.

MADEIRA SABAYON

The infusions for flavouring the *Sabayons* should be prepared in advance.

Put the spice or flavouring in a bottle; fill up the bottle

with hot syrup registering 28° on the saccharometer; cork the bottles, and keep the essences for use.

Put in a basin:

10 oz. of pounded sugar,

6 yolks of egg;

Work the sugar and egg together, and add, by degrees, 1½ pint of Madeira and 2 tablespoonfuls of Vanilla Essence;

Strain the whole through a silk sieve into a chocolate-pot; put the pot over the fire, and froth the contents with the frothing-stick, as you would chocolate.

Sabayons are served hot in china cups, and will be much appreciated towards the close of a ball.

MARSALA SABAYON

Prepare this precisely as directed in the preceding recipe, omitting the vanilla flavouring, and substituting an equal quantity of Marsala for the Madeira.

RUM SABAYON

Mix 6 yolks of egg in a basin with 1 pint of syrup registering 20°; add 1 gill of Rum and 2 tablespoonfuls of Cinnamon Essence;

Strain and froth the *sabayon*, and serve it hot, as directed for Madeira *Sabayon*.

KIRSCHENWASSER SABAYON

Put 6 yolks of egg in a basin, with:

1 gill of Kirschenwasser,

1 pint of syrup registering 20°;

Mix all together; strain, and finish the *sabayon* as directed for Madeira *Sabayon*.

VANILLA SABAYON

Put 6 yolks of egg in a basin with ½ lb. of pounded sugar; work both together with a spoon, and add:

1 pint of cream,
1 gill of Vanilla Essence;

Mix, and strain the whole through a silk sieve into a stewpan; stir it over the fire till the egg coats the spoon, and pour it into a chocolate-pot;

Froth and serve the *sabayon* as directed for Madeira *Sabayon* (*vide* page 190).

CHOCOLATE SABAYON

Melt 6 oz. of chocolate in 1½ pint of milk;

Put 6 yolks of egg and ½ lb. of pounded sugar in a basin; work both together with a spoon, and add the melted chocolate;

Mix the whole well together, and strain it through a silk sieve into a chocolate-pot; put the pot on the fire, and froth and serve the *sabayon* as directed above.

COFFEE SABAYON

Put 6 yolks of egg in a basin, with 10 oz. of pounded sugar; work both together with a spoon, and add 1 pint of strong coffee and ½ pint of boiled cream;

Strain the whole through a silk sieve into a chocolate-pot; froth it over the fire, and serve as directed for Madeira *Sabayon* (*vide* page 190).

FRUIT SALADS

PINEAPPLE SALAD

Peel a pineapple, and cut it in two lengthwise; trim off the tough part in the centre, and cut each half across into slices $\frac{1}{4}$ inch thick;

Put the slices in a deep compote dish, and strew some pounded sugar over them, say 2 oz. of pounded sugar to every pound of pineapple;

Let the pineapple remain thus for two hours; then add 1 gill of Maraschino; mix the salad carefully, so as not to bruise the fruit, and serve.

ORANGE SALAD

Cut the peel off 4 large oranges, and cut each orange into 10 pieces; put them into a deep compote dish, strew them with pounded sugar, and let them remain thus for two hours; then add 1 gill of brandy, mix, and serve the salad.

PEAR SALAD

Take 10 fine *Duchesse* or *Bon Chrétien* pears;

Cut each pear in 8 pieces; peel and core them carefully, and put the pieces into a basin with some lemon juice;

When all the pieces are peeled, drain, and put them in a deep compote dish, and strew 5 oz. of pounded sugar over them;

Add 1 gill of Kirschenwasser; mix, and serve the salad.

Pear Salad should not be prepared long in advance, as the pears would be liable to become discoloured.

PEACH SALAD

Cut 8 fine peaches each in 8 pieces ;

Peel each piece, and put them into a deep compote dish ;

Strew the peaches with pounded sugar ; add 1 gill of Sauterne, and mix and serve the salad.

This salad should also be served as soon as it is prepared, or the peaches will become discoloured.

Claret may be substituted for the Sauterne, if preferred.

FRUIT MACÉDOINE SALAD

Prepare equal quantities of :

    pineapples,

    oranges,

    pears,

    peaches ;

Put all the fruit in a deep compote dish, strew some sugar over, add 1 gill of Maraschino, mix the salad, place 20 fine strawberries on the top, and serve.

SUGARED ORANGES

Peel 4 oranges very carefully ;

Cut the oranges, across, in slices, $\frac{3}{8}$ inch thick ;

Strew a sheet of paper thickly over with finely pounded sugar ;

Beat up some whites of egg with a fork ;

Dip each round of orange into the egg; place it on the sugar, cover it thickly with sugar, and let it remain thus for five minutes; then place the rounds very carefully on a wire drainer till the sugar is quite dry;

Dress the slices, in diminishing circles, on a compote dish, and serve.

CHAPTER XIX

FRUIT COMPOTES

COMPOTE OF BON CHRÉTIEN PEARS

TAKE 5 even-sized *Bon Chrétien* pears ; cut them in halves ; core, peel, and trim them, giving one piece a round shape ;

Throw the pieces of pear, as they are peeled, into a basin of water with a little lemon juice ;

Drain the pears, and put them in a large sugar-boiler ; cover them entirely with syrup registering 16°, with some lemon juice added;

Boil the pears over a brisk fire, and put them in a basin, pouring over them all but 1 quart of the syrup ; and cover the pears with a round of paper ;

Add $\frac{1}{2}$ lb. of loaf sugar to the quart of syrup left in the sugar-boiler ; melt it, and strain the syrup through a hair sieve into another sugar-boiler;

Reduce the syrup to such a density, that, when taking some of it up on a skimmer and pouring it gently off, it flows in a stream or sheet an inch to an inch and a half in width ;

Skim, and put the syrup into a basin ;

When the pears are cold, drain them, and dress them in a circle in a compote glass, putting the round piece in the centre ; and pour the reduced syrup over the compote just before it is served.

All white fruit compotes can be garnished with either :
Preserved cherries,
currants,
angelica,
Or with layers of apple jelly, prepared as follows :
Make the Apple Jelly as directed at page 119 ;
Pour in a layer of it, $\frac{1}{8}$ inch thick, on a plate ; when it is set, and in order to get it off the plate, press a sheet of white paper on the top, warm the plate slightly for half a minute, and take up the jelly, which will then adhere to the paper ;
Cover the compote with the layer of jelly, and remove the paper by damping it with a brush, and detaching it with the point of a knife.

COMPOTE OF EARLY PEARS

Choose 12 scarcely ripe early pears ;
Remove the cores with a small cutter, and peel the pears whole, very smoothly, leaving the stalks $\frac{3}{4}$ inch long ;
Cook the pears and reduce the syrup as described in the preceding recipe ;
Stand the pears round a compote glass, and pour the reduced syrup over them.

COMPOTE OF RUSSET PEARS

Peel 12 russet pears very smooth, leaving the stalks $\frac{3}{4}$ inch long, and removing the cores with a small round cutter ;
Boil the pears gently in a tinned stewpan in syrup registering 16°, with a few drops of prepared cochineal to give them a bright rose tint ;
Drain the pears ; reduce the syrup to the density described for Compote of *Bon Chrétien* Pears ;

When cold, stand the pears round a compote glass, and cover them with the reduced syrup.

COMPOTE OF BAKING PEARS

Choose some even-sized baking pears;

Cut them into quarters; peel and core them; keep one half whole, and trim it to a round shape for the centre of the compote;

Boil the pears in syrup registering 16°, add a few drops of prepared cochineal, and, when done, drain the pears;

Dress the pears in a circle in a compote glass, putting the round piece in the centre;

Reduce the syrup, and pour it over the compote when cold.

This compote, being of a bright colour, will be found very effective on a dinner table amongst other fruit compotes; its agreeable aspect will be increased by placing a layer of Apple Jelly over the pears, as described for Compote of *Bon Chrétien* Pears (*vide* page 196).

COMPOTE OF APPLES

Cut 4 Colville apples into quarters;

Core and peel them carefully, and throw them, at once, into a basin of cold water with some lemon juice added;

Cook the apples in syrup, and simmer very gently, so as not to break them; drain, and put them to cool;

Add some sugar to the syrup, and reduce it as directed for Compote of *Bon Chrétien* Pears (*vide* page 196);

Dress the apples in a circle in a compote glass, pour the reduced syrup over, and place a layer of Apple Jelly over the whole.

STEWED APPLES À LA BONNE FEMME

Take 7 middle-sized orange pippin apples, remove the cores with a vegetable cutter, and prick the apples with a fork;

Put the apples in a shallow stewpan, with 2 oz. of pounded sugar and 1 gill of water;

Close the stewpan, and put some live coals on the cover, and simmer over a slow fire till the apples are done; or the stewpan may be put in the oven;

Dish the apples in a round dish, pour the juice over, and serve them hot.

Apples stewed in this way are well adapted for invalids.

COMPOTE OF ORANGES

Cut the peel off 3 large oranges, and cut them into quarters; keep one half whole, and trim it to a round shape;

Cut out the cores, and put the oranges in a basin with some syrup registering 32°, and let them remain therein for four hours;

Drain the oranges, and dress the pieces in a circle in a compote glass, putting the round piece in the centre;

Add $\frac{1}{4}$ lb. of sugar to the syrup, melt it *au bain-marie*, and strain the syrup through a silk sieve on to the compote.

COMPOTE OF PINEAPPLE

Peel a pineapple, and trim off all the tough part at both ends;

Cut 3 slices, $\frac{1}{4}$ inch thick, off the top of the pineapple; cut the remainder in half, lengthwise, and cut each half into slices $\frac{1}{4}$ inch thick;

Place a layer of pineapple in a basin, strew some sugar

over, make another layer of pineapple, strew some sugar over ; continue in the same way till all the pineapple is covered with sugar, and put the basin in a cool place for six hours ; then drain the slices, and dress them in a circle in a compote glass ;

Strain the juice through a silk sieve ; add $\frac{1}{2}$ gill of Maraschino, and pour it over the compote.

Pineapple Compote prepared thus, uncooked, retains the full flavour of the fruit.

COMPOTE OF CHESTNUTS

Choose 40 fine and even-sized chestnuts ; peel off the outer brown skin, and put the chestnuts into a stewpan, with plenty of water and 2 oz. of breadcrumbs ; and simmer until a thin wire enters easily into the chestnuts ;

Peel them carefully, and, as each chestnut is peeled, put it into a basin of cold water with a little lemon juice added;

Put in a large sugar-boiler, 1 quart of syrup registering 32°, a stick of vanilla, and the chestnuts ; boil, and take the sugar-boiler off the fire, and put it for four hours in the Hot-Closet, first covering the chestnuts with a round of paper ;

Drain, and dress the chestnuts in a compote glass ;

Strain the syrup through a fine hair sieve, reduce it as directed for Compote of *Bon Chrétien* Pears (*vide* page 196), and pour it over the chestnuts when cold.

COMPOTE OF VERMICELLI CHESTNUTS

Cook some chestnuts in syrup as directed in the preceding recipe ;

Fix a hair sieve on a stand, about 12 inches above a compote glass placed underneath ;

Drain, and warm the chestnuts, and pound them in a

mortar, adding the syrup whilst pounding; and rub the *purée* through the sieve into the compote glass, in such a way that it may fall through like vermicelli, and form a mound in the centre of the glass; to this end it is not necessary to shift the sieve about, the glass alone need be moved.

COMPOTE OF SUGARED CURRANTS

Choose 30 fine bunches of red currants and an equal quantity of white currants;

Beat up the white of an egg in a plate with a fork; add a tablespoonful of Maraschino, and mix both well together;

Strew a sheet of paper thickly with warm pounded sugar;

Dip each bunch of currants in the white of egg, and throw them in the sugar; strew some more sugar over them; take them out of the sugar, and put them on a sieve to dry;

Dress the currants, mingling the colours, in a compote glass, and serve.

COMPOTE OF CHERRIES

Take 1½ lb. of May-Duke or Kentish cherries, and cut off all but ¾ inch of the stalks;

Put the cherries in a copper sugar-boiler with 1 quart of syrup registering 35°; boil for five minutes, and pour the whole into a basin;

When the cherries are cold, drain, and dress them, stalks upwards, in a compote glass;

Strain the syrup into a sugar-boiler, and reduce it as described for Compote of *Bon Chrétien* Pears (*vide* page 196);

When the syrup is cold, pour it over the cherries.

COMPOTE OF APRICOTS

Choose 15 fine and sound standard apricots;

Cut the apricots in two, and remove the stones; break these, and blanch and peel the kernels;

Put the apricots in a sugar-boiler with 1 quart of syrup registering 35°; boil, and pour the whole into a basin, and let it remain thus for four hours;

Drain the apricots, and dress them in a compote glass;

Strain the syrup into a sugar-boiler, and reduce it as described for Compote of *Bon Chrétien* Pears (*vide* page 196); and pour it over the apricots when cold;

Place half a kernel on each piece of apricot, and serve.

COMPOTE OF GREENGAGES

Take 24 fine and not too ripe greengages, and blanch them in plenty of water with a little Vichy salt or soda added; cool the plums in cold water, and drain them;

When the water in which the greengages were blanched is cold, put them into it, and let them remain therein for an hour;

Boil some syrup registering 30°;

Drain the plums, put them in the syrup, and let it boil up; pour the whole into a basin, and put a round of paper on the top;

The greengages should be cooked the day before the compote is wanted;

Drain the plums on a draining-wire, and dish them in a compote glass;

Strain the syrup through a silk sieve into a copper sugar-boiler, and reduce it until it registers 32° on the saccharo-meter;

When the syrup is cold, pour it over the compote, and serve.

COMPOTE OF MIRABELLE PLUMS

Take 50 fine *Mirabelle* plums, not over ripe;

Blanch the plums in boiling water, cool them in cold water, and drain them;

Boil some syrup registering 32°; put the plums into it, boil it up, and pour the whole into a basin; and finish the compote as directed in the preceding recipe.

COMPOTE OF NECTARINES

Take 18 fine and ripe nectarines; remove the stones, without severing the fruit entirely;

Boil the nectarines for two minutes in syrup registering 32°, and pour the whole into a basin; put a round of paper on the top, and let the nectarines steep thus for two hours; then drain them on a draining-wire;

Strain the syrup through a silk sieve into a copper sugar-boiler; reduce it until it registers 32°, and let it get cold;

Dish the nectarines in a compote glass, and pour the syrup over them.

COMPOTE OF PEACHES

Cut 9 peaches in halves; remove the stones, break them, and blanch and peel the kernels;

Boil the peaches in syrup registering 20° until the skin peels off easily;

Drain the peaches; peel, and put them in a basin; pour the syrup over them, and cover the fruit with a round of paper;

Twenty minutes before serving the compote, drain the peaches on a draining-wire;

Strain the syrup through a silk sieve into a sugar-boiler, and reduce it till it registers 32° ;

Dress the peaches in a compote glass; pour the cold syrup over, and place half a kernel on each piece of peach.

COMPOTE OF RED AND WHITE CURRANTS

Pick 1 lb. of red and 1 lb. of white currants ;

Wash and drain them, and put them in a basin with 2 oz. of pounded sugar ; toss the currants, to melt and mix the sugar ; let them remain thus for an hour, and put the whole into a compote glass, adding $\frac{1}{2}$ gill of syrup registering 30° just before serving the compote.

COMPOTE OF POMEGRANATES

Pick sufficient pomegranates to obtain $1\frac{1}{2}$ lb. of fruit; put it in a basin with $\frac{1}{4}$ lb. of pounded sugar; toss it, to melt and mix the sugar, and let it remain therein for two hours ; then put the whole into a compote glass, and serve.

COMPOTE OF CUSTARDS FLAVOURED WITH MALAGA
A L'ESPAGNOLE

Break 8 yolks of new-laid eggs in a basin ;

Melt $\frac{1}{4}$ lb. of honey in a copper sugar-boiler, with $\frac{1}{2}$ gill of Malaga ; add it to the yolks of egg in the basin, with :

   $\frac{1}{2}$ gill of water,

   a pinch of salt,

   a pinch of ground cinnamon ;

Mix the whole together, and strain it through a silk sieve ;

Rub seven small *dariole*-moulds with sweet almond oil ; fill them with the mixture, and set the egg *au bain-marie*, without boiling ;

When the custards are set firm, take them off the fire, and let them get cold ;

Turn the custards out of the moulds on to a compote-glass, putting one in the centre ;

Melt some honey with a little Malaga ; let it get cold, and pour it over the custards.

When almond oil cannot be procured, rub the moulds lightly with a little salad oil.

COMPOTE OF CUSTARDS FLAVOURED WITH RUM

Melt ¼ lb. of honey with 1 gill of water, and add it to 8 yolks of egg broken in a basin with :

    a pinch of ground cloves,

    a small pinch of salt,

    ½ gill of rum ;

Mix, and strain through a silk sieve; put the custard into moulds; set, and dish them as directed in the preceding recipe ;

Melt ¼ lb. of honey with some rum and 1 gill of water, and pour it over the custards when cold.

COMPOTE OF CUSTARDS FLAVOURED WITH CARAMEL AND VANILLA

Boil ½ gill of syrup registering 30° to a *caramel*, being careful not to let it burn, and pour in ½ gill of water to dissolve the *caramel* ;

Break 8 yolks of egg in a basin, and add :

    half the dissolved *caramel*,

    a pinch of salt,

    1 gill of syrup registering 30°,

    ½ oz. of vanilla sugar ;

Mix, and strain the whole through a silk sieve ;

Rub 7 *dariole*-moulds with a little sweet almond oil ;

Fill the moulds with the egg mixture, and poach the contents *au bain-marie*, without boiling ;

When the custards are set firm, let them get cold, and turn them out of the moulds ;

Cut each custard across in four pieces, and dress them in a circle in a compote glass ;

Boil the remainder of the dissolved *caramel* with $1\frac{1}{2}$ gill of syrup registering 30° ; take it off the fire, and pour it, when cold, over the compote.

Compotes of Custards flavoured with Port, Madeira, or Alicant, are prepared in the same way.

These compotes are seldom in request ; however, as they may by chance be asked for, the above recipes may at times be useful.

CHAPTER XX

FRUIT GLACÉ AU CARAMEL

ORANGES GLACÉES AU CARAMEL

Choose some fine oranges, peel them very carefully, and divide them into their quarters;

Procure some very thin wooden skewers about 8 inches long; put a skewer in the point of each piece of orange, without going right through ; place the skewers on a sieve, in such a way that the pieces of orange hang all round the outside of the sieve, and let them dry thus for two hours;

Put 1 lb. of loaf sugar in a copper sugar-boiler, with 3 gills of water and a good pinch of cream of tartar;

When the sugar is melted, put it over a brisk fire; boil, and skim it;

Clean the edges of the sugar-boiler with a wet sponge, without dropping any water in the sugar;

When the syrup produces small air-bubbles, try it, by skimming off, with the tip of the finger, a small particle of the boiling syrup, and transferring the finger rapidly to a basin of cold water held in readiness;

If the sugar comes off the finger easily, and is brittle when tried with the teeth it has arrived at the degree of boiling known as *to the crack*.

Have a basin of pounded or brown sugar near at hand, to stick the skewers in for the orange to drain;

Dip each piece of orange into the boiled sugar, and stick

the end of the skewer into the sugar in the basin, so that the pieces of orange may drain outside the basin until they are dry ;

Take the pieces of orange off the skewers, and put them on a sieve.

DATES GLACÉES AU CARAMEL

Choose some fine fresh dates ; slit them open, without severing them entirely, and remove the stones ;

Pound $\frac{1}{4}$ lb. of blanched and peeled Jordan almonds with $\frac{1}{4}$ lb. of pounded sugar, moistening whilst pounding with sufficient Kirschenwasser to produce a stiffish paste ; colour the paste with a little green vegetable colouring, to give it a light green tint, and rub the whole through a fine hair sieve ;

Place some of this paste inside each date, and fold the halves together in such a way as to show a $\frac{1}{8}$-inch strip of the green paste down the slit ;

Stick a thin wooden skewer in each date ; dip them in sugar boiled *to the crack*, and stick the end of the skewers in a basin of sugar, as described in the preceding recipe ;

When the dates are dry and cold, take them off the skewers, and put them singly into oval paper bonbon cases.

GREENGAGES GLACÉES AU CARAMEL

Choose some large preserved greengages ;

Cut them in two, and remove the stones ;

Spread some white Vanilla *Fondant* Paste (*vide Fondant* Paste for Bonbons, page 257) on each half ;

Stick a thin wooden skewer in each piece of plum, dip them in sugar boiled *to the crack*, and, when dry, put each piece in a round paper bonbon case.

GREEN ALMONDS GLACÉES AU CARAMEL

Take some large green almonds which have been preserved in syrup ;

Slit them in two, and put a large Jordan almond,
previously blanched and peeled, in each half ;

Let the almonds dry, and then stick a thin wooden skewer
in each piece ; dip them in sugar boiled *to the crack*, and,
when cold and dry, put each piece into an oval paper bonbon case.

APRICOTS GLACÉS AU CARAMEL

Take some small even-sized preserved apricots ;

Stick a thin wooden skewer into each apricot, and, when
they are dry, dip them in sugar boiled *to the crack* ; and
when they are cold, place them in round paper bonbon
cases.

FRESH CHERRIES GLACÉES AU CARAMEL

Choose some fine not over ripe Kentish or May-Duke
cherries, and cut off all but $\frac{1}{4}$ inch of the stalks ;

Boil some sugar *to the crack*, and give it a pale rose tinge
by adding a few drops of prepared cochineal ;

Hold the cherries by the stalk, and dip each one singly
in the boiled sugar ; let the superfluous sugar drain off, and
put the cherry on a slightly oiled marble slab to cool ;

When all the cherries are glazed and cold, place each one
in a round paper bonbon case.

BRANDY CHERRIES GLACÉES AU CARAMEL

Take some cherries preserved in brandy ; drain, and dip
them in syrup registering 30° on the saccharometer ; drain
the cherries again, and put them to dry in the Hot-Closet ;

Boil some sugar *to the crack*, and add a few drops of prepared cochineal ;

Stick a thin wooden skewer into each cherry; dip them in the sugar, and let them dry ; and when cold, put them into small round bonbon cases.

FILBERTS GLACÉES AU CARAMEL

Take some even-sized filberts; crack them, and peel the nuts ;

Dip the nuts in sugar boiled *to the crack*, and put them to cool on a slightly oiled marble slab, placing three nuts together in a line, so that they may stick together when dry ;

When cold, put the filberts, three together, into some small oval bonbon cases.

MIRABELLE PLUMS GLACÉES AU CARAMEL

Choose some even-sized *Mirabelle* plums ; remove the stones, and fill up the plums with some pink *fondant* bonbon paste (*vide Fondant* Paste for Bonbons, page 257) ;

Stick a thin wooden skewer in each plum, and dip them in some sugar boiled *to the crack* ;

Let the plums drain till they are cold, and put them into small round bonbon cases.

CURRANTS GLACÉES AU CARAMEL

Take some fine bunches of red and white currants; choose them perfectly dry and not over ripe ;

Hold the end of the stalk, and dip each bunch into some sugar boiled *to the crack* ; let it drain a little, and put it on a slightly oiled marble slab to cool ;

When all the currants are cold, put the bunches into small oval bonbon cases.

GRAPES GLACÉS AU CARAMEL

Divide some bunches of grapes into small clusters of three or four grapes each ; dip them in some sugar boiled *to the crack* ; drain, and put the grapes to cool on a slightly oiled marble slab, and place each small bunch in a paper bonbon case.

CHESTNUTS GLACÉS AU CARAMEL

Choose some fine sound chestnuts ; slit the skin with a knife, and roast them in a frying-pan over a moderate fire, so that they may not be coloured ;

Peel the chestnuts carefully, and, when they are cold, stick a thin wooden skewer into each one ;

Dip the chestnuts in sugar boiled *to the crack*, and finish in the way described for Oranges *Glacées au Caramel* (*vide* page 207).

STRAWBERRIES GLACÉES AU CARAMEL

Choose some not over ripe and perfectly dry British Queen strawberries ;

Hold the stalk, and dip each strawberry singly into some sugar boiled *to the crack*, and put them to cool on a slightly oiled marble slab ;

When cold, put each strawberry into a paper bonbon case.

The sugar should be allowed to cool a little before dipping in the strawberries.

CHAPTER XXI

PETITS FOURS

PORTUGUESE BISCUITS

BREAK 6 eggs; put the whites in a whipping bowl and the yolks in a basin, with :

$\frac{1}{4}$ lb. of apricot jam, previously rubbed through a hair sieve,

$\frac{1}{2}$ lb. of finely sifted sugar,

20 blanched, peeled, and well pounded bitter almonds ;
Work the whole well together ;

Whip the whites very firm, and add them to the ingredients in the basin, mixing in at the same time 5 oz. of the best potato flour ;

Take some small oblong-shaped moulds, about 3 inches long, $1\frac{1}{2}$ inch wide, and $\frac{1}{2}$ inch deep ;

Butter the moulds and sprinkle them with fine sugar, and fill them with the biscuit paste ; dredge some fine sugar over, and cook the biscuits in a slow oven ; turn them out of the moulds and put them on a sieve.

ITALIAN BISCUITS

Put $\frac{1}{2}$ lb. of loaf sugar in a copper sugar-boiler with $\frac{1}{2}$ gill of water ; boil the sugar *to the ball*, and let it cool ;

Break 6 eggs ; put the yolks in a basin and the whites in a whipping bowl ;

Whip the whites very firm, add the yolks, the boiled sugar, and ½ oz. of vanilla sugar ;

Continue whipping with the whisk, and mix in 6 oz. of flour ;

Butter some moulds similar to those described in the preceding recipe ; dredge in some sifted sugar, fill them with the paste, dredge some sugar on the top, and bake the biscuits in a slack oven ;

When done, take the biscuits out of the moulds and put them on a sieve.

FINGER BISCUITS

Break 6 eggs ; put the whites in a whipping bowl and the yolks in a basin ;

WHISK AND WHIPPING BOWL

Add ½ lb. of pounded sugar and 2 tablespoonfuls of Orange Flower Water to the latter, and work them with a spoon for five minutes ;

Whip the whites very firm, and mix them lightly with the yolks, and add 5 oz. of sifted flour ;

Take a sheet of strong sized paper, and roll it to a conical shape ; fill it with the biscuit paste, and close the top ; cut off the point of the cone, so as to form a circular opening $\frac{1}{2}$ inch in diameter ;

Press out the biscuit paste upon some sheets of stiff paper, so as to form biscuits 3 inches long, leaving an inch-space between each biscuit ;

Dredge some sifted sugar over the biscuits ; bake them in a moderate oven, and let them cool before taking them off the paper.

DUTCH BISCUITS

Pound $\frac{1}{2}$ lb. of sugar in a mortar with 1 oz. of vanilla, and sift it through a hair sieve ;

Put 6 whites of egg in a whipping bowl ; whip them very firm, and add :

    the sifted sugar,
    $\frac{1}{4}$ lb. of flour ;

Mix the whole with a spoon, and put the paste into a paper cone, as described in the preceding recipe ;

Cut the point of the cone so as to form a circular opening $\frac{1}{4}$ inch in diameter, and press out the paste on to some sheets of paper, so as to form biscuits $2\frac{1}{2}$ inches long ;

Dredge some sifted sugar over the biscuits, and bake them in a brisk oven.

GINGER BISCUITS

Break 5 eggs into a tinned whipping bowl ;

Add $\frac{1}{2}$ lb. of pounded sugar, and whip both together over the fire until the paste is of a consistence similar to that prepared for Finger Biscuits ; add :

    1 oz. of ground ginger,
    $\frac{1}{8}$ oz. of ground cinnamon,
    $\frac{1}{4}$ lb. of flour,
    a small pinch of salt ;

Mix the whole well together;

Take some moulds similar to those described for Portuguese Biscuits (*vide* page 212); butter and flour them, and fill them with the paste;

Dredge some fine sugar over the biscuits, and bake them in a brisk oven.

BUTTER BISCUITS

Put $\frac{1}{4}$ lb. of butter in a basin, and warm it so as to soften the butter; add :

$\frac{1}{2}$ lb. of pounded sugar,

4 yolks and 1 whole egg;

Work the ingredients with a spoon for five minutes, and mix in $\frac{1}{4}$ lb. of flour and one egg ;

When this is well mixed, add another $\frac{1}{4}$ lb. of flour;

Whip the 4 remaining whites of egg and mix them with the paste;

Butter some moulds similar to those described for Portuguese Biscuits (*vide* page 212); dredge in some sifted sugar and fill them with the biscuit paste ; dredge some sugar over, and bake the biscuits in a moderate oven.

BOUCHÉES DE DAMES

Make some biscuit paste as directed for Finger Biscuits (*vide* page 213);

Put the paste in a paper cone, and squeeze it out, in rounds $1\frac{1}{2}$ inch in diameter, on to some sheets of paper ; dredge some sifted sugar over them, and bake them in a moderate oven ;

When done, trim the rounds with a 1½ inch plain round cutter ;

Spread the flat surface of a round with apricot jam, and place another round on it, to make the *bouchée* ;

Proceed in the same way for the remainder of the rounds, and glaze the *bouchées* with Chocolate Icing, prepared as follows :

Melt ¼ lb. of the best chocolate in a sugar-boiler with 1 gill of syrup ; add a tablespoonful of vanilla sugar, a table-spoonfnl of water, and sufficient pounded sugar, sifted through a silk sieve, to form a stiff paste ;

Stir the icing over the fire until it is warm ;

Stick a *bouchée* on the point of a thin skewer, dip it entirely into the chocolate, and put it on a draining-wire ; when all the *bouchées* are glazed, put them in the oven, on the wire, to dry for a minute, and put them on a sieve when cold.

Lemon, Orange, Strawberry or Raspberry Juice may be mixed to a stiff paste with finely sifted sugar, warmed, and used for glazing the *bouchées* in the manner described above.

For Coffee Icing, mix the sugar to a stiff paste with strong coffee.

I recommend the above manner of preparing the sugar for glazing the *bouchées* in preference to *Fondant* Icing, as being much easier, and therefore more likely to be accomplished successfully.

SOFT MACAROONS

Blanch and peel ½ lb. of Jordan almonds ;

Pound them in a mortar, adding the white of an egg in small portions, to prevent the almonds turning oily ;

When the almonds are half pounded, add ½ lb. of loaf

sugar, broken in pieces, and $\frac{1}{2}$ oz. of vanilla sugar, and continue pounding and moistening with some white of egg, added by degrees, until 4 whites of egg have been used;

The paste should then be softish, without spreading; if it is too stiff, add a little white of egg;

With a teaspoon, form the paste into balls $\frac{3}{4}$ inch in diameter; place them on sheets of paper, and leave a 2-inch space between each ball;

Beat up some white of egg, dip a brush in it and brush over the macaroons; dredge some fine sugar over, and bake them in a hot oven until they assume a light golden tinge;

Take the macaroons out of the oven, and let them cool; then turn the sheets of paper over, so that the macaroons may rest on the table; moisten the paper with a brush dipped in water, to facilitate taking off the macaroons, and put them on a sieve.

These macaroons should be soft when baked.

CRISP MACAROONS

Blanch, peel, and wash $\frac{1}{2}$ lb. of Jordan almonds, and chop them very fine;

Whip 4 whites of egg very firm, and add:

$\frac{1}{2}$ lb. of pounded sugar,

the chopped almonds,

the grated peel of an orange;

Work the whole together with a spoon; and, with a teaspoon, shape the macaroons, and put them on sheets of paper as directed in the preceding recipe;

Bake the macaroons in a moderate oven, and take them off the paper as described above.

These macaroons should be crisp and hard.

BITTER ALMOND MACAROONS

Make the macaroons precisely as directed for Soft Macaroons, merely using equal quantities of bitter and Jordan almonds.

CHOCOLATE MACAROONS

Make some paste as directed for Soft Macaroons, adding :
  $\frac{1}{4}$ lb. of grated chocolate,
  half a white of egg
  $\frac{1}{2}$ oz. of vanilla sugar ;
Shape and bake the macaroons in the same way.

MACAROONS SOUFFLÉS

Blanch and peel $\frac{1}{2}$ lb. of Jordan almonds, and cut them lengthwise into thin shreds ;
  Put in a basin :
  $\frac{3}{4}$ lb of pounded sugar sifted through a silk sieve,
  2 whites of egg,
  the grated peel of a lemon ;
Work the whole with a spoon to a stiffish paste, add the cut almonds, and half a white of egg if the paste is too stiff ;
  Put portions of the paste, the size of a small walnut, on some sheets of paper, leaving a 2-inch space between each macaroon, and bake them in a slow oven without colouring them ;
  Take the macaroons off the paper and put them on a sieve, as described for Soft Macaroons.

MACAROONS SOUFFLÉS WITH ORANGE FLOWERS

Prepare the paste as directed in the preceding recipe, using ¼ lb. of almonds cut in thin shreds and ¼ lb. of candied Orange Flowers; and finish the macaroons in the same way.

MACAROONS SOUFFLÉS WITH PISTACHIOS

Make the macaroons as directed for Macaroons Soufflés, preparing the paste with ¼ lb. of Jordan almonds and ¼ lb. of blanched and peeled pistachios, both cut in thin shreds, and adding a tablespoonful of Kirschenwasser.

BISCOTTES WITH ALMONDS PRALINÉES

Blanch and peel 4 oz. of Jordan almonds and ½ oz. of bitter almonds;

Pound the bitter almonds in a mortar, together with 2 oz. of the peeled Jordan almonds, and put them in a basin, with :

    ½ lb. of pounded sugar,

    ¼ oz. of grated lemon peel,

    a small pinch of salt,

    1 gill of rum,

    4 eggs ;

Whip the whole with a wire whisk for five minutes, and add ½ lb. of flour and 2 yolks of egg ; and continue whipping until the paste is quite smooth ;

Whip 2 whites of egg very firm, add them to the paste, with ¼ lb. of butter, melted, and work the whole together with a spoon ;

Take a copper baking sheet having a raised edge ; butter and flour it ;

Spread the paste on the baking sheet to a $\frac{3}{4}$-inch thickness, and bake it in the oven ;

Chop the remaining 2 oz. of almonds, and mix them thoroughly with 2 oz. of pounded sugar and half a white of egg ;

When the paste is done, take it out of the oven, brush it over with egg, and spread the chopped almonds thickly over the top ; dredge some fine sugar over, and put the paste back in the oven for ten minutes ;

When the paste is cold, cut it into *biscottes* $2\frac{1}{2}$ inches long, 1 inch wide.

CHOCOLATE BISCOTTES

Break 4 eggs ; put the whites in a whipping bowl and the yolks in a basin ; add $\frac{1}{2}$ lb. of pounded sugar to the latter, and work them with a spoon for five minutes ; then add :

$\frac{1}{2}$ lb. of grated chocolate,

$\frac{1}{2}$ lb. of flour,

2 eggs,

a small pinch of salt ;

Mix the whole thoroughly ;

Whip the whites of egg and add them to the paste ;

Take a copper baking sheet having a raised edge, and line it with paper ; spread the paste on it to a $\frac{3}{4}$-inch thickness, and bake it in a moderate oven ;

When the paste is done, take it out of the oven and put it on a sieve to cool ;

Cut the paste in pieces $2\frac{1}{2}$ inches long, 1 inch wide ;

Prepare some Vanilla Icing in the following way :

Steep a stick of vanilla, cut in pieces, in one gill of hot

syrup registering 30°, and, when it is cold, strain it through a silk sieve into a basin ; add sufficient finely sifted sugar to form a stiffish paste, and spread the icing on the *biscottes* ; put them in the oven for two minutes to dry the icing, and put them on a sieve to cool.

STRAWBERRY BISCOTTES

Make some paste, without the chocolate, as directed in the preceding recipe; and bake and cut it in the same manner ;

Make some Strawberry Icing as follows :

Rub ¼ lb. of Alpine strawberries through a silk sieve into a basin, and add sufficient finely sifted sugar to form a stiffish paste ;

Spread the icing on the *biscottes*, and finish as directed in the preceding recipe.

LEMON BISCOTTES

Make some paste as directed for Chocolate *Biscottes*, substituting a little grated lemon peel for the chocolate ;

Bake and cut the paste in the same way ;

Make some Lemon Icing as follows :

Steep the peel of a lemon in ½ gill of hot syrup, and, when it is cold, strain it through a silk sieve into a basin ; add the juice of a lemon and sufficient finely sifted sugar to form a stiff paste ;

Spread the icing on the *biscottes*, put them to dry in the oven for two minutes, and put them on a sieve to cool.

ALMOND PASTE LOAVES

Blanch and peel ½ lb. of Jordan almonds and ½ oz. of bitter almonds ;

Pound the almonds in a mortar, moistening with some white of egg; add ½ lb. of pounded sugar, and mix the whole to a stiffish paste;

Divide the paste into portions about the size of a walnut, and roll them to an oval shape;

Put some sheets of paper on some copper baking sheets, sprinkle them with fine sugar, and place the loaves on them, leaving an inch-space between each loaf;

Make an incision, ¼ inch deep, along the top of the loaves; brush them over with some yolk of egg beaten up with a little water, and bake the loaves in the oven for five minutes.

MASSEPAINS

Prepare some paste as directed in the preceding recipe;

Force the paste on to some sheets of paper, sprinkled with fine sugar, through a syringe with a ½-inch star at the end; cut the paste into 3-inch lengths, and turn each piece round into a ring;

Bake the *massepains* in a very brisk oven for three minutes, and put them on a sieve to cool.

ALMOND PASTE STICKS

Blanch and peel ½ lb. of Jordan almonds; pound them in a mortar, moistening with some white of egg; add ¾ lb. of pounded sugar and ½ oz. of vanilla sugar, and mix the whole to a stiffish paste;

Sprinkle a pasteboard with fine sugar;

Roll the paste out on it to ⅛ inch thickness, and cut it into strips 2½ inches wide;

Mix some finely sifted sugar to a softish paste with some white of egg, and spread it on the almond paste; cut the strips across into pieces ⅜ inch wide;

Butter and flour a baking sheet, and put the sticks on it, leaving a $\frac{3}{4}$-inch space between each :

Bake the sticks in a moderate oven, and put them on a sieve to cool.

Should the sticks adhere to the baking sheet, put it over the fire for a minute.

ALMOND AND PISTACHIO STICKS

Make some paste as directed in the preceding recipe, using $\frac{1}{4}$ lb. of Jordan almonds and $\frac{1}{4}$ lb. of pistachios ;

Roll out the paste, cut it into sticks, and bake it in precisely the same way ;

Mix some chopped pistachios, fine sugar, and Kirschenwasser to a stiff paste ;

Take the sticks out of the oven, spread them over with the pistachio paste, and strew the tops with some chopped pistachios ;

Put the sticks back in the oven, or in the Hot-Closet for a few minutes, and put them on a sieve to cool.

ALMOND PASTE STICKS À L'ANISETTE

Break 6 yolks of egg in a basin, add :
   $\frac{1}{2}$ lb. of pounded sugar,
   $\frac{1}{2}$ lb. of pounded almonds, previously blanched and
     peeled,
   $\frac{1}{4}$ oz. of chopped green aniseed,
   a pinch of salt ;

Beat up the whole with a wire whisk for five minutes, and mix in $\frac{1}{2}$ lb. of flour, working it with the hand ;

Roll out the paste to $\frac{1}{6}$ inch thickness and cut it into strips $2\frac{1}{2}$ inches wide ; cut the strips across into pieces $\frac{3}{8}$ inch wide; place the sticks on a buttered baking sheet, and cook them in the oven;

Make the icing in the following manner:

Put $\frac{1}{2}$ gill of syrup and 1 gill of *Anisette* into a basin, and mix in sufficient finely sifted sugar to form a stiff paste;

Spread the icing on the sticks, put them in a slack oven or in the Hot-Closet to dry the icing, and put them on a sieve to cool.

Observation.—All *liqueur* icings are prepared in the way described above.

ALMOND PASTE CRESCENTS

Make some paste as directed for Almond Paste Sticks;

Sprinkle a pasteboard with sugar; roll out the paste to $\frac{1}{8}$ inch thickness, and cut it out, with a 2-inch round cutter, into crescent-shaped pieces $\frac{3}{4}$ inch wide; and place the crescents on a buttered and floured baking sheet;

Put in a basin:

 $\frac{1}{2}$ lb. of finely chopped almonds,

 $\frac{1}{2}$ lb. of pounded sugar,

 1 tablespoonful of rum,

 half an egg;

Mix the whole with a spoon, and spread it on the crescents to $\frac{1}{8}$ inch thickness; sprinkle over some sifted sugar, and bake the crescents in a moderate oven till they are of a light golden colour, and put them on a sieve to cool.

CATS' TONGUES

Break 4 eggs in a basin, whip them with a wire whisk, and add:

¾ lb. of pounded sugar,

¾ lb. of flour,

1 oz. of vanilla sugar ;

Mix the whole to a soft paste, which should spread when dropped from a spoon ; if it is too stiff, add a little more egg ;

Rub some copper baking sheets with white wax ;

Put the paste into a paper cone, and squeeze it out on to the baking sheets, in portions 3 inches long, ⅜ inch wide, leaving a 3-inch space between each, as the paste is liable to spread ;

Bake in a brisk oven, and put the *cats' tongues* on a sieve to cool.

LADIES' PALATES

Whip 5 whites of egg in a basin, with ¾ lb. of pounded sugar, and add ½ lb. of flour by degrees ; when this is mixed, add 1 oz. of pounded candied Orange Flowers ;

Rub some baking sheets with white wax ;

Put the paste into a paper funnel, and squeeze it out on to the baking sheets in rounds 1½ inch in diameter ; let the top of the paste dry ; then brush it over lightly with some white of egg beaten up with a fork, and bake in a moderate oven.

ALMOND BISCUIT DAINTIES

Make some paste as directed for Finger Biscuits (*vide* page 213).

Mix some chopped almonds to a paste with pounded sugar and a little Maraschino ;

Put the biscuit paste in a paper funnel, and press it out on to some sheets of paper sprinkled with sugar, pressing out two round dots touching one another, so as to form figures of eight, 2½ inches long by ¾ inch broad ; strew them over with the chopped almonds and bake in a brisk oven ;

When cold, take the *dainties* off the paper, spread the flat side with apricot jam, and glaze the jam with some Maraschino Icing, prepared in the way described for Almond Paste Sticks *à l'Anisette* (*vide* page 223).

PATIENCES

Whip 4 whites of egg in a basin; mix in $\frac{1}{2}$ lb. of pounded sugar and 1 oz. of pounded and sifted vanilla, and add, by degrees, 6 oz. of flour, so as to make a smooth paste;

Roll a sheet of strong sized paper into a conical shape; secure it with sticking paste; and, when it is dry, fill it with the biscuit paste and close the top; cut the point of the cone so as to form a circular opening $\frac{1}{8}$ inch in diameter;

Rub some warmed copper baking sheets lightly over with white wax;

Squeeze out the paste, by pressing on the top of the cone, so as to form small biscuits 2 inches long, $\frac{1}{4}$ inch wide;

Put the biscuits in the hot-closet to dry for a few minutes, and bake them in a brisk oven for four minutes; then take them out of the oven, brush them over with some white of egg, beaten up with a fork, and put them in the oven for four minutes more;

Take the *patiences* off the baking sheet, and put them on a sieve to cool.

SMALL ITALIAN MERINGUES WITH APRICOT JAM

Whip 5 whites of egg in a whipping bowl;

Boil 1 lb. of sugar *to the ball*; when it has cooled for five minutes, let an assistant pour it gently into the whipped egg, holding the sugar-boiler some distance above the bowl, whilst you continue whipping the egg with a wire whisk; add a little vanilla sugar, and put the *meringue* paste in a paper cone;

Press out the paste on to some sheets of paper, in portions about the size of a pigeon's egg; sprinkle them with fine sugar, and cook the *meringues* in the oven on some boards;

When the *meringues* are slightly coloured, take them off the paper, and, with a teaspoon, remove some of the inside, put in a nut-sized portion of apricot jam, cover the jam with a reversed *meringue*, and, when all the *meringues* are prepared in the same way, put them on a sieve to dry in the hot-closet.

SMALL ITALIAN MERINGUES WITH PISTACHIOS

Prepare and shape the *meringues* as directed in the preceding recipe;

Blanch and peel some pistachios, chop them very fine, and mix them with some pounded sugar, some Kirschenwasser, and a little spinach greening, rubbed through a silk sieve;

Rub the pistachios between your hands, so as to dry them and prevent their clogging together;

Strew some of the prepared pistachios over the *meringues* and bake them on some boards in the oven;

Remove some of the inside of the *meringues* with a teaspoon, put in a well-drained preserved cherry, and cover it with a reversed *meringue*;

When all the *meringues* are filled, put them to dry in the hot-closet.

SMALL ITALIAN MERINGUES WITH APPLE JELLY

Prepare some sugar, to strew over the *meringues*, in the following manner:

Sift some pounded sugar, first through a fine hair sieve and then through a silk sieve ;

Put the sugar remaining *on* the silk sieve on to a sheet of paper, sprinkle some prepared cochineal and a few drops of water over the sugar, and rub it between the hands ;

Put the sugar in the hot-closet, stir it until it is dry, and sift it through a hair sieve ;

Prepare and shape the *meringues* as directed for Small Italian *Meringues* with Apricot Jam ; strew them with the prepared sugar ; bake and finish them as directed in the preceding recipe, substituting some apple jelly for the preserved cherry.

SMALL CHOCOLATE ITALIAN MERINGUES

Mix some whipped whites of egg and boiled sugar in the way described for Small Italian *Meringues* with Apricot Jam (*vide* page 226), adding some grated chocolate ;

Press the *meringue* paste, out of a paper cone, on to some sheets of paper in portions the size of a pigeon's egg ; put them on some boards, and bake them in the oven, without first sprinkling them with sugar ;

When the *meringues* are done, stick two pieces together, so as to form egg-shaped *meringues*, and put them to dry in the hot-closet.

PINEAPPLE TARTLETS

Sift $\frac{1}{2}$ lb. of flour on to a pasteboard, make a hollow in the centre, and put in :

$\frac{1}{4}$ lb. of blanched, peeled, and pounded almonds,

$\frac{1}{4}$ lb. of pounded sugar,

2 oz. of butter,

1 egg,

a pinch of salt ;

Mix the whole to a smooth paste, work it with the hands, and let it rest for an hour ;

Roll out the paste to $\frac{3}{8}$ inch thickness, and cut it out with a $1\frac{3}{4}$-inch fluted cutter ;

Line some $1\frac{3}{4}$-inch tartlet-moulds with the rounds of paste, and press it in slightly, so as to bring the paste a little beyond the edge of the mould ;

Put some Pineapple Jam (*vide* page 239) on the paste, and bake the tartlets in the oven ;

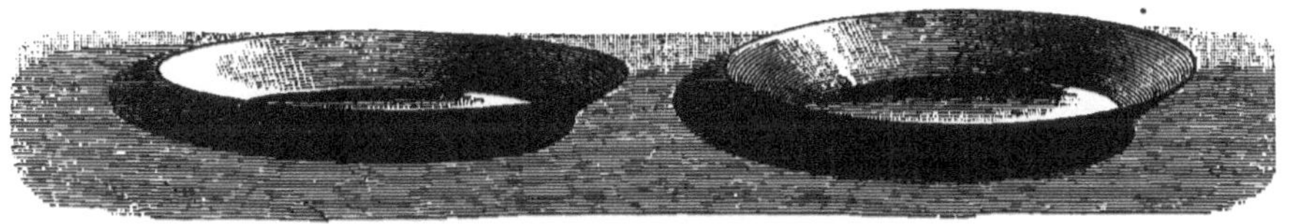

TARTLET MOULDS

When the tartlets are done, take them out of the oven, and let them cool ;

Make some Pineapple Icing in the following way :

Mix some pineapple juice with a sufficient quantity of finely sifted sugar to form a stiff paste ;

Spread some of the icing over the tartlets, keeping the paste edge clear ; place a large and well drained preserved cherry in the centre of each tartlet, and put them in the hot-closet for a few minutes to dry the icing.

APRICOT TARTLETS

Make the paste and line the moulds as directed in the preceding recipe ;

Fill the tartlets with reduced Apricot Jam (*vide* page 235), and bake them in the oven ;

When the tartlets are cold, glaze them with some Kirschenwasser Icing, prepared as described in the preceding recipe, substituting some Kirschenwasser for the pineapple juice ;

Put the tartlets in the hot-closet to dry the icing.

PEAR TARTLETS

Prepare the moulds with the paste as directed for Pine apple Tartlets ;

Put some Pear Jam (*vide* page 238), previously rubbed through a coarse hair sieve, on the paste, and bake the tartlets in the oven ;

When cold, glaze the tartlets with some Vanilla Icing, prepared with Vanilla Syrup, mixed with sufficient fine sugar to form a stiff paste ;

Put a preserved cherry in the centre of each tartlet, and put them in the hot-closet for a few minutes.

PAIN D'ÉPICES

Melt $\frac{1}{2}$ lb. of honey and $\frac{1}{2}$ lb. of treacle in a copper sugar-boiler ;

Sift 1 lb. of rye flour on to a pasteboard, make a hollow in the centre, and put in :

    the melted honey and treacle,

    $\frac{1}{4}$ oz. of ground cloves,

    1 oz. of ground cinnamon ;

Mix, and add :

    $\frac{1}{2}$ oz. of carbonate of soda dissolved in a little water,

    a few grains of carbonate of ammonia also dissolved in water ;

Work the paste thoroughly by pulling it apart and folding it over and over ; and put it in a basin to rest for eight days ;

Oil some brick-shaped wooden frames ; place them on

some floured baking sheets ; put the paste into them, and bake the *pain d'épices* in a moderate oven.

2 oz. of well washed and dried currants may be added to every pound of the paste, or the same quantity of stoned raisins may be added, if preferred.

DUCHESS PAIN D'ÉPICES NUTS

Make some paste as directed in the preceding recipe, mixing in 3 oz. of chopped candied citron to every pound of the paste ;

Divide the paste into portions, about the size of a small nut, and roll them round to a ball ;

Oil some small tartlet-moulds, and place a ball of the paste in each, flatten the paste slightly, and brush over the top with a little white of egg ; strew over some aniseed comfits, and bake the nuts in a moderate oven.

PAIN D'ÉPICES NUTS WITH ANGELICA

Make some paste as directed above, mixing in 2 oz. of preserved angelica, cut in small dice, to every pound of the paste ;

Divide the paste into 2 oz. portions, roll these round to a ball, and put them on to some floured baking sheets ;

Flatten the balls slightly, brush them over with a brush dipped in water, and bake them in a hot oven.

Some chopped candied orange peel may be substituted for the angelica.

PAIN D'ÉPICES STICKS

Roast ½ lb. of filberts in a copper pan, to remove the skins ; when the filberts are cold, chop them very fine, mix them with some white of egg and pounded sugar ; spread the whole on a sheet of paper, and put it in the hot-closet to dry for a few minutes ;

Make some paste as directed for *Pain d'Épices* ;

Divide the paste and roll it into stick-shaped pieces $2\frac{1}{2}$ inches long, $\frac{3}{4}$ inch in diameter ; brush the sticks over with water, and roll them in the chopped filberts ;

Put the sticks on some floured baking sheets, cover them with some sheets of paper, and bake them in a moderate oven.

PAIN D'ÉPICES RINGS

Add 3 oz. of chopped candied orange peel to every pound of some paste prepared as described for *Pain d'Épices* (*vide* page 230) ;

Shape the paste into rolls $\frac{3}{8}$ inch in diameter ; cut these into 5-inch lengths, and turn them round to form a ring ;

Brush over the rings with a little water ; strew them with some finely chopped candied orange peel ; place them on floured baking sheets, and bake them in a hot oven.

CROQUIGNOLES

Sift 1 lb. of flour on to a pasteboard, make a hollow in the centre, and put in :

6 oz. of pounded sugar,

2 eggs,

the grated peel of an orange ;

Mix the whole to a softish paste, and let it rest for an hour ;

Divide the paste into portions the size of a large nut, roll them round into balls, and put them on some slightly buttered baking sheets ;

Flatten the balls on the top, brush them over with egg, and bake them in a brisk oven.

ROLLED WAFERS À L'ITALIENNE

Put in a basin :

7 oz. of pounded sugar,
1 oz. of vanilla sugar,
½ lb. of blanched, peeled, and pounded almonds,
3 whites of egg ;

Mix the whole to a smooth soft paste, adding some more white of egg if necessary ;

Warm some copper baking sheets, and rub them with white wax ;

With a teaspoon, put portions of the paste on to the baking sheets, so as to form flat rounds 2 inches in diameter ; put them in the oven, and, when the rounds are half done, trim them with a 2-inch plain cutter, and put them back in the oven ;

When the wafers are done, take them off the baking sheet with a knife, and roll them quickly to a conical shape ;

Should the wafers cool before they are all rolled, put the baking sheet back in the oven to warm them ;

Stick the point of the cones in a basin of pounded sugar, and fill them with some Italian *Meringue* Paste (*vide* page 226) pressed out of a paper funnel ;

Place a preserved cherry on the top of each cone, and put them in the hot-closet to dry the *meringue*.

ALMOND WAFERS

Blanch, peel, and pound ½ lb. of Jordan almonds, add ½ lb. of pounded sugar and the grated peel of a lemon, and moisten the paste with 3 whites of egg ;

Warm some copper baking sheets, and rub them with white wax ;

When the baking sheets are cold, place on them small

portions of the almond paste, about the size of a small walnut; flatten each portion to a round 2 inches in diameter, and strew the top with well washed and dried currants, and with some coarsely sifted sugar;

Bake the wafers in the oven, and, when they are done, press them on a rolling-pin so as to curve them, and put them on a sieve to cool.

Some chopped pistachios may be substituted for the currants.

CHAPTER XXII

JAMS

APRICOT JAM

CHOOSE some sound and ripe apricots; peel them, and remove the stones;

Put 8 lbs. of apricots in a basin with 5 lbs. of coarsely pounded sugar, stir with a wooden spoon till the sugar is melted, and let the apricots remain thus for four hours;

PRESERVING-PAN

Put the contents of the basin into a preserving-pan, and boil for ten minutes, stirring with a wooden spoon;

To ascertain when the jam is done: dip a copper skimmer into the jam, and take it out; when the jam on the skimmer is cool, try it with the finger, and if it feels greasy, the jam is done; another way of ascertaining this is by taking up some of the jam on the skimmer, and pouring it off gently ; if it flows in a sheet an inch to an inch and a half in width, it is done ;

Break a few of the stones, blanch and peel the kernels, and mix them in the jam ;

Skim off any scum that may be on the jam, put it into pots, and, when cold, place a round of paper dipped in brandy close on the jam ; tie some paper on the pots, and keep the jam in a cool and dry place.

ORANGE JAM (THE ORANGES PRESERVED IN PIECES)

Blanch 12 not over ripe Seville oranges in plenty of water ; boil the oranges till they are tender when tried with a fork;

Drain the oranges, and put them in a basin of cold water, and let them remain thus for two days, changing the water twice a day ;

Drain and cut each orange into 8 pieces, take out the pips, and put the pieces in a basin ; pour in sufficient boiling syrup registering 28° to cover them entirely, and let them remain therein for two days ;

Drain the pieces of orange on a wire drainer ; strain the syrup through a hair sieve into a preserving-pan ; add some more sugar, and boil the syrup until it registers 30° on the saccharometer ;

Add the pieces of orange, let the syrup boil up again, and take the pan off the fire ;

Put the jam into pots, and, when perfectly cold, place a round of paper dipped in brandy close on the jam ; tie some paper over the pots, and keep them in a dry and cool place.

ORANGE JAM

Boil 12 Seville oranges in plenty of water until they are done ; drain, and cut them in quarters, and put them in cold water for thirty-six hours ;

Drain the oranges on a cloth, and rub them through a hair sieve;

Put some loaf sugar in a preserving-pan, using 14 oz. of sugar for every pound of fruit;

Boil the sugar *to the ball*, and add the orange pulp; stir over the fire, and try the jam as directed for Apricot Jam, and finish it in the same way.

ORANGE MARMALADE

Boil, and steep the oranges in cold water, as described in the preceding recipe;

Drain, and cut the oranges into thin shreds;

Boil the sugar as described in the preceding recipe, add the cut orange, and finish the jam in the same way.

PEACH JAM

Cut some peaches, each in 8 pieces; peel them and remove the stones; break a few of these, and blanch and peel the kernels;

Put the peaches in a basin with some sugar, using the same quantities of fruit and sugar as indicated for Apricot Jam, and cook and finish the jam in the same way.

MIRABELLE PLUM JAM

Cut some *Mirabelle* plums in half, remove the stones, and put the fruit in a basin with some coarsely pounded sugar, using the quantities indicated for Apricot Jam;

Let the plums remain in the sugar, and boil and finish the jam in precisely the same way.

GREENGAGE, ORLEANS, OR BRIGNOLLE PLUM JAM

Peel and stone some sound and not over ripe plums ;

Put the fruit into a basin with some pounded sugar as described for Apricot Jam, and finish the jam in the same way.

NECTARINE JAM

Cut the nectarines into quarters ; peel them, and remove the stones ;

Put the fruit in a basin with some coarsely pounded sugar, using the quantities indicated for Apricot Jam, and cook and finish the jam in precisely the same manner.

PEAR JAM

Choose some ripe early pears : cut them in quarters, core, peel, and throw them into a basin of cold water with some lemon juice added ;

For 8 lbs. of pears, boil 1 quart of water and 4 lbs. of sugar *to the ball* ;

Drain the pears, put them in the boiling sugar, and boil them for ten minutes, stirring with the skimmer ; and pour the whole into a basin till the next day ;

It is well to repeat the boiling to ensure the perfect preservation of the jam ;

Pour the contents of the basin into a preserving-pan, and boil, stirring all the time, until the jam flows off the skimmer in a stream from an inch to an inch and a half in width ;

Put the jam into pots, cover it, when cold, with a round of paper dipped in brandy, placed close on the jam ; tie some paper over the pots, and keep the jam in a cool and dry place.

BON CHRÉTIEN PEAR JAM

Prepare this as directed in the preceding recipe, using the same quantities of fruit and sugar as there indicated.

BERGAMOT PEAR JAM

Cut some Bergamot pears in quarters; core and peel them;

Put in a preserving-pan:

8 lbs. of pears,
1 quart of water,
1 lb. of sugar,
the juice of a lemon;

Simmer until the pears are half done; add 3 lbs. of sugar, and stir over the fire till the jam is cooked, which can be ascertained as directed for Pear Jam;

Put the jam into pots, and cover it in the same manner.

PINEAPPLE JAM

Peel some pineapples, and cut them in pieces;

Put the fruit in a preserving-pan, with 1 quart of water and a little sugar;

Simmer until the pineapple is cooked; drain it, pound it in a mortar, and rub it through a hair sieve;

Put some sugar in a preserving-pan in the proportion of $\frac{1}{2}$ lb. of sugar to every pound of the pineapple; boil it *to the ball* with the water in which the pineapple was cooked;

Add the pineapple *purée*, and stir the whole over the fire until the jam is cooked; try it as directed for Apricot Jam, and finish the jam in the same way.

STRAWBERRY JAM

Rub sufficient small Alpine strawberries through a coarse hair sieve to obtain 4 lbs. of *purée* ;

Boil 4 lbs. of sugar *to the crack* ; take the preserving-pan off the fire, and add the *purée* to the sugar ; let it stand for five minutes ; then stir the whole over the fire, and let the jam boil up ;

Put the jam into pots, cover it, when cold, with a round of paper dipped in brandy, and tie some paper over the pots.

RASPBERRY JAM

Make the jam as directed in the preceding recipe, using the same quantities of fruit and sugar as indicated therein.

GRAPE JAM, OR RAISINÉ

Take a sufficient quantity of baking pears to obtain 8 lbs. of fruit when peeled and cored ;

Throw the pears into a basin of water as they are peeled ;

Rub sufficient black grapes through a hair sieve to obtain 1 gallon of juice ; put it into a newly tinned stewpan, with the pears and 2 lbs. of sugar ;

Close the stewpan and simmer for twelve hours ; at the end of that time, should the jam be too thin, reduce it by stirring it over the fire ;

Pour the jam into pots, and put them in a slack oven or in the hot-closet for ten hours ;

When the jam is cold, place a round of brandied paper close on the top, and tie some paper on the pots.

APPLE JAM

Apple jam is prepared with the pulp of the apples used in making Apple Jelly (vide page 119);

Rub the pulp through a hair sieve ;

Boil some loaf sugar *to the crack*, using ½ lb. of sugar for every pound of the fruit ;

Mix the apple *purée* in the boiled sugar, and stir over the fire until the jam is cooked, which can be ascertained as described for Apricot Jam ; and finish it in the same way.

Apple jam is sometimes flavoured with Vanilla, or Lemon or Orange peel.

QUINCE JAM

Make the jam as directed in the preceding recipe, using the same quantities of fruit and sugar as indicated therein.

REMARKS ON JAMS

I think it will not be out of place to mention here, that although the foregoing recipes for the preparation of jams are intended to apply to fresh-gathered and picked fruit of a good quality, still owners of large gardens and orchards, who at times have much fruit which has fallen from over ripeness, or from high winds, may use it for making a somewhat inferior kind of jam, which will be very acceptable in poor households.

The gift of such jam will be an inexpensive and wholesome means of benefiting our poorer neighbours, and will be of special value where there are large families of children.

JAM FOR THE POOR

When there is much fallen fruit, such as apples, pears, all kinds of plums, apricots, peaches, &c. in an orchard or garden, gather it all up and rinse it in cold water; drain, peel, and stone the fruit, and cut it in pieces, trimming off any unsound part;

Put the fruit in a basin; add 1½ lb. of pounded sugar to every 2 lbs. of the fruit, mix the whole with a spoon, and let it remain thus for six hours; then pour it into a preserving-pan, stir over the fire, and cook the jam as described for Apricot Jam;

Put the jam into pots, cover it, when cold, with a round of brandied paper, and tie some paper over the pots.

CHAPTER XXIII

PRESERVED FRUIT

REMARKS ON PRESERVED FRUIT

FOR the preparation of preserved fruit, perfectly clean utensils, which have never been put to other uses, are required ;

Much attention should also be paid to the selecting of the fruit, as the proper degrees of ripeness vary in the different cases ;

My recommendations being the result of long experience, I would invite the reader to adhere to them exactly in what follows ;

The successful preservation of fruit depends on the blanching process ; this should be continued till the fruit is nearly cooked ; by shortening this boiling the fruit would become tough, and shrivel up in the syrup ;

Fruit of a proper ripeness should be preserved without altering in shape ;

Should the fruit be too ripe, preserve it in syrup registering only 28°, without boiling it.

PRESERVED CITRONS

Take some middle-sized fresh citrons ; select them well grown and not much coloured ;

Grate the citrons to make them smooth, not, however, taking off all the green ;

With a ¼-inch plain cutter, make an opening at the stalk end;

Boil the citrons in a newly tinned stewpan, with plenty of water, and keep filling up the stewpan with boiling water as it evaporates;

When the citrons are done, which will be when a thin wooden skewer enters into them easily, take them out of the stewpan and put them into cold water;

With a teaspoon, remove the inside of the citrons through the opening at the stalk; put them in a basin of cold water, and let them remain therein for forty-eight hours, changing the water four times a day;

Drain the citrons, and put them in a preserving-pan with sufficient cold syrup registering 24° to cover them entirely; put the pan on the fire, and let the contents boil up; then pour the whole into a basin, and let it get cold;

Drain the citrons, put them in a preserving-pan, and boil them up in some fresh syrup;

Continue this boiling and cooling twice a day for four days, making eight boilings in all; use some syrup registering 32° for the last boiling, and take the whole off the fire as soon as it boils;

Let the citrons cool a little, and pour the whole into pots or into glass jars, and, when cold, tie some paper over the top, and keep the preserve in a cool place.

CITRONS PRESERVED IN QUARTERS

Choose some citrons as directed in the preceding recipe; grate them smooth, and cut them in quarters;

Blanch and preserve the citrons as described in the preceding recipe, and put them into glass jars in the same way.

Citrons preserved whole and in quarters thus are used for compotes;

Place a whole citron in the centre of a compote glass, dress the pieces all round it, strain the syrup through a silk sieve, and pour it over the compote.

PRESERVED CITRON PEEL

Grate some citrons, cut them in quarters, remove the inside, and blanch and preserve the peel as directed for Preserved Citrons.

ORANGES PRESERVED WHOLE

Choose some scarcely ripe Seville oranges ;

With a $\frac{1}{4}$-inch cutter, make an opening at the top of the oranges where they have been picked off the stalks ;

Blanch the oranges in boiling water till they are done, and preserve them as directed for Preserved Citrons.

St. Michael or Valencia oranges are preserved in the same way.

Oranges preserved in quarters and preserved orange peel are both prepared precisely as indicated for Citrons.

PRESERVED LEMONS

Lemons are preserved whole, in quarters, or only the peel, in the way described for Citrons.

PRESERVED GREENGAGES

Choose some scarcely ripe greengages of an even size ; prick them with a needle, and put them in a preserving-pan with some water, adding $\frac{1}{8}$ oz. of Vichy salt to every quart of water ;

Boil the plums gently until they rise to the surface of the

water; take them off with the skimmer, and put them into cold water; then put them back into the water in the preserving-pan, and warm, without boiling them; the plums should then be green;

Drain, and put the plums in a basin, rejecting any plum that might be too soft, and pour over them some boiling syrup registering 30°; cover them with a round of paper, and let them remain thus till the next day; then drain the plums, and put them into a basin;

Boil up the syrup and pour it, boiling, over the plums; cover the basin, and let them remain thus for six hours;

Repeat this process six times, making eight times in all;

The eighth time, boil the syrup until it registers 32°; throw the plums into it, let it boil up again, and pour the whole into jars;

Cover them, when cold, and keep them in a cool place.

PRESERVED MIRABELLE PLUMS

Choose these sound and scarcely ripe;

Blanch the plums in water, and, when they rise to the surface, take them off with the skimmer, and put them into a basin of cold water;

Drain, and put the plums in a basin; pour some boiling syrup over them, and finish them as directed in the preceding recipe.

PRESERVED APRICOTS

Choose some scarcely ripe and even-sized apricots;

Cut them open without severing them entirely, blanch them in boiling water, drain them, and remove the stones;

Put the apricots in a basin, pour some boiling syrup over, and finish preserving them as directed for Preserved Green-gages.

PRESERVED PEARS

Choose some scarcely ripe and even-sized early pears ;

Peel them, and cut off all but $\frac{1}{4}$-inch of the stalk; remove the cores with a $\frac{1}{4}$-inch cutter, without cutting through to the stalks ;

Boil the pears in water till they are done ; cool them in cold water, drain, and put them in a basin ;

Pour some boiling syrup over the pears, and finish as described for Preserved Greengages.

PRESERVED WALNUTS

Choose some perfectly sound green walnuts ; peel them very smoothly, and throw them into a basin of cold water with some lemon juice added ;

Boil the walnuts in water till they are quite tender ; cool them in water ; drain, and put them in a basin ; pour some boiling syrup over, and finish the preserving in the way described for Preserved Greengages.

PRESERVED GREEN ALMONDS

Choose some fine green almonds of such ripeness that a needle may enter easily ;

Blanch the almonds in water, adding a little Vichy salt ; cool them in water, and, when the water in which they have been blanched is cold, put the almonds back into it and warm them without boiling them, so as to bring back their green colour ;

Cool the almonds in water ; drain, and put them in a basin ; pour over some boiling syrup, and finish in the way indicated for Preserved Greengages.

If the almonds are boiled until they are quite done, their taste and appearance will be improved thereby.

PRESERVED GREEN APRICOTS

Take some even-sized green apricots ;

Blanch and prepare them as directed in the preceding recipe, and preserve them in the way described for Preserved Greengages.

PINEAPPLE PRESERVED IN SLICES

Peel a ripe pineapple, and cut it into slices $\frac{1}{2}$ inch thick ;

Put the slices in a preserving-pan with sufficient syrup registering 15° to cover them entirely ;

Simmer gently until the pineapple is done, and pour the whole into a basin ;

When cold, drain the pineapple, and put it in another basin ;

Add some loaf sugar to the syrup, boil it until it registers 20°, and pour it on to the pineapple ;

Continue this cooling and boiling up, eight times in all, adding some sugar to the syrup every time of boiling it up, and increasing the density by 2° each time ;

The eighth time boil the syrup until it registers 32°, put the slices into it, let it boil up, and, when it is a little cool, pour the whole into jars :

When quite cold, tie some paper over the preserve, and keep it in a cool place.

PRESERVED CHERRIES

Choose 4lbs. of ripe Kentish cherries ;

Pick off the stalks, stone the cherries carefully, and put them in a preserving-pan with 1 pint of water and 1 lb. of loaf sugar ;

Simmer till the cherries are cooked, and pour the whole

into a basin, to remain therein till the next day; then drain the cherries;

Pour the syrup into a preserving-pan, with $\frac{1}{2}$ lb. of loaf sugar, and boil it up; add the cherries, let the syrup boil up again, and pour the whole into a basin, to remain thus till the next day;

Drain the cherries; pour the syrup into a preserving-pan, add $\frac{1}{2}$ lb. more sugar, and boil the syrup;

Try its density by dipping the skimmer into it, and when it flows off the skimmer in a sheet or stream an inch to an inch and a half in width, add the cherries to it, and let the whole boil up; take the pan off the fire, and, when the cherries are cold, put them on a draining-wire;

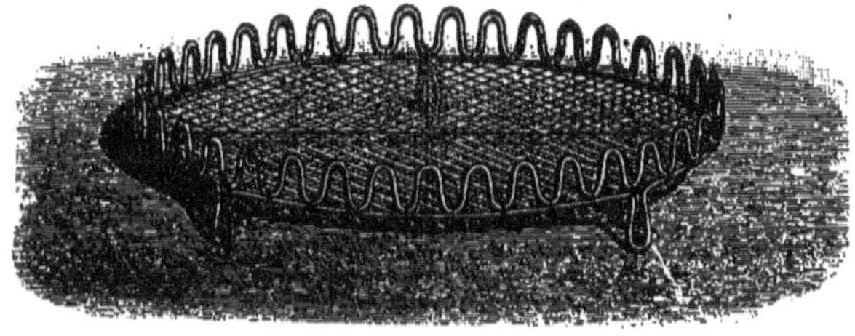

DRAINING-WIRE

Place the wire in the hot-closet to dry the cherries, and put them into tins when cold.

PRESERVED ANGELICA

Trim some fresh angelica and remove all the hard and stringy part;

Cut the angelica into 5-inch lengths, blanch them in boiling water to facilitate taking off the skin; trim the pieces again, and put them into a basin of cold water;

Drain the angelica, and cook it in some water with a little sugar added; let it cool in the water, drain, and put it into a basin;

K K

Pour some boiling syrup over, and finish the preserving as directed for Preserved Greengages.

PRESERVED CHESTNUTS

Italian chestnuts are the best for preserving, and the best season is from the middle of October to the middle of December;

Choose some fine even-sized chestnuts and remove the first brown skin ;

Mix some flour and water in a stewpan, and put the chestnuts in it ;

Put the stewpan over a brisk fire, boil, and then simmer gently until the chestnuts are done, which can be ascertained by pressing one between the fingers, when it should be soft ;

Drain the chestnuts and peel them very carefully, so as not to break them, and put them into a basin of cold water ; drain them on a sieve, and place them carefully in another basin ; pour over them some hot syrup registering 20°, and let them remain therein for two days ;

Drain the chestnuts, boil up the syrup to 24°, adding some more sugar ; pour it over the chestnuts placed in a basin, and let them remain thus for two days more ;

Continue boiling up the syrup, adding more sugar each time, and pouring it over the chestnuts four times in all, letting them steep for two days between each operation ;

The last time, boil the syrup until it registers 32°, put the chestnuts into it, let it boil up, and take the pan off the fire ;

When partly cold, pour the whole into jars and tie some bladder on the top.

When required for dessert, drain the chestnuts, and glaze them with some Icing made as follows :

Boil some sugar until it registers 36°, and work it with a spatula until it is quite smooth and white ;

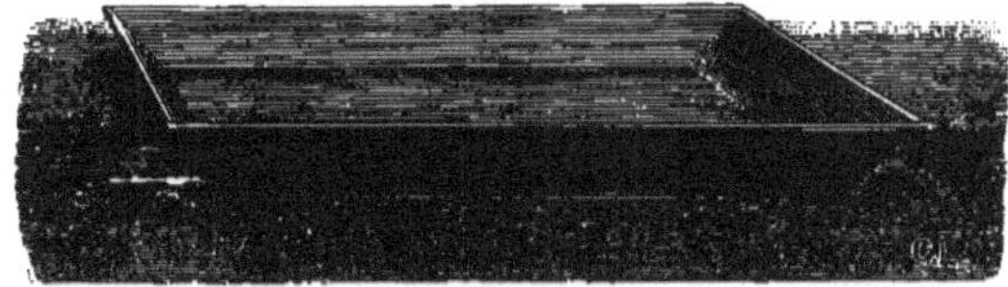

DRAINING-TIN.

Dip the chestnuts singly into the icing, and put them on a draining-wire in the hot-closet for a quarter of an hour ;

Put the glazed chestnuts in crimped paper bonbon cases, and dish them on stands or plates of mixed bonbons.

CHAPTER XXIV

BONBONS

REMARKS ON THE MOULDING OF BONBONS

To describe all the different kinds of bonbons, and the various shapes in which they can be moulded, would be tedious and unnecessary ;

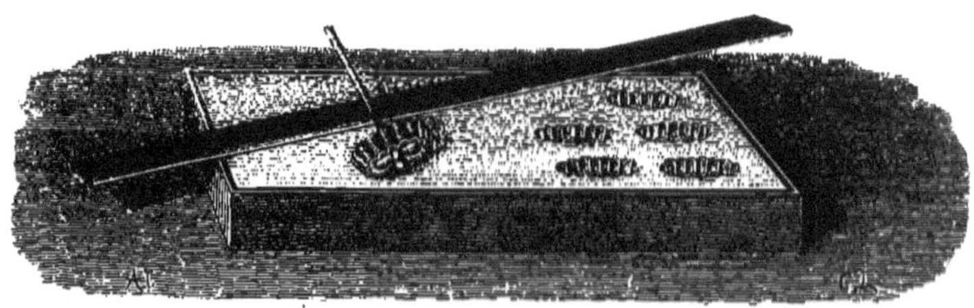

WOODEN TRAY FOR STARCH

I will merely touch upon a few of the most important, and state in a general way, that all bonbons are moulded either in starch powder or in plaster of Paris moulds.*

To prepare the starch moulds :

Sift some starch powder through a silk sieve, and warm it over the fire, stirring with a wire whisk ;

When the starch has become perfectly dry and light by this process, put it into a small flat wooden tray about 2 inches deep, and with a rule smooth the starch even with the top of the tray, without, however, pressing it too much down ;

* A great variety of these moulds can be obtained at Linder's, Hôtel Jabbach, Rue St. Méry, Paris.

Attach one of the raised imprinting-moulds, with some sealing wax, to the end of a stick, and press it carefully into

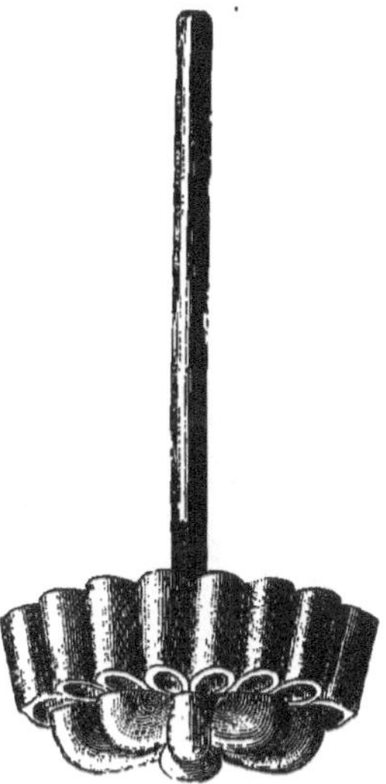

IMPRINTING-MOULD

the starch, so as to print therein a clear impression of the design ; be careful that, on withdrawing the mould, none of the starch should fall in and spoil the impression.

PLASTER MOULD FOR BONBONS

Moulding the bonbons in plaster of Paris moulds is a rather different process : the plaster moulds should be first dipped in cold water, and left to drain for three minutes before using;

SUGAR-BOILER FOR CASTING BONBONS

After the sugar has been run into them, it should be left to cool for twenty minutes; the bonbons should then be taken out and put upon a sieve, and should be left thus for three hours to set, before being candied.

REMARKS ON THE CANDYING OF BONBONS

For candying the bonbons, tin cases must be procured, about 3 inches high and spreading out towards the top (*vide* woodcut);

There should be a hole in one of the corners of the tin with a short pipe fixed in;

When using the tin, stop up this pipe with a cork, and lay the bonbons in the tin, resting them one on the other, and laying the pattern side downwards;

Pour over them some cold syrup registering 35° on the saccharometer; the syrup should be poured in gently at one of the corners of the tin, so as not to disturb the bonbons, which should be quite covered by the syrup ;

Cover the tin with a sheet of paper ;

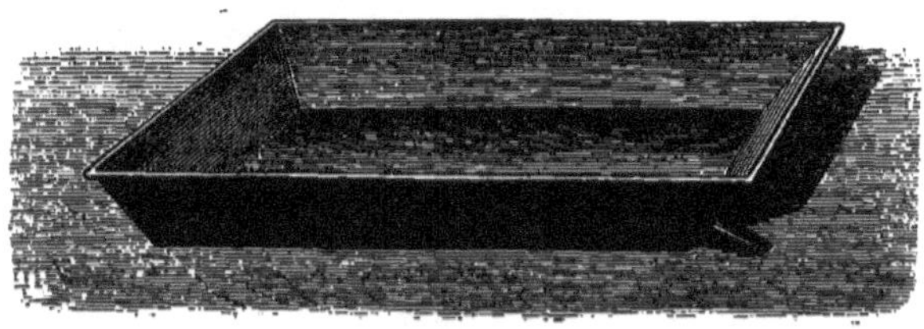

CANDY TIN

At the end of eight hours, take out one of the bonbons, and if it is thinly coated with crystallised sugar, the candying is completed ;

The stopper should then be withdrawn, and the syrup allowed to flow out into a basin ;

When the syrup has all drained off, place the bonbons on a draining-wire, and put it in the hot-closet for twenty minutes ;

Take out the bonbons and keep them in a dry place.

CLARIFIED SYRUP

Break 6 lbs. of loaf sugar, and put it into a preserving-pan with 1 quart of water ;

Whip 2 whites of egg in a basin with 1 gill of water ;

Pour the whipped egg into the sugar, put the pan on the fire, and stir with a wire whisk till the sugar boils up ; then pour in $\frac{1}{2}$ gill of cold water, let it boil up again, and let the syrup simmer ;

Remove the scum, pour in another half gill of cold water, and skim off the scum as it rises to the surface ;

Boil the syrup until it registers 30° ;

Place a large basin in a vessel of cold water, and strain

the syrup into it, either through a silk sieve or a broth napkin previously washed in boiling water and rinsed in cold water ;

Keep renewing the cold water in which the basin stands, so as to cool the syrup quickly, and so prevent its candying ;

Put the syrup into bottles, and put it by for use.

When the clarified syrup is used for making *Liqueurs*, it must be brought to the degree indicated in the various recipes by the addition of water ; and, when used for Compotes, Bonbons, or Ices, it must be boiled until it registers 32° on the saccharometer.

FLAVOURINGS FOR BONBONS

VANILLA FLAVOURING

Vanilla flavouring is prepared by steeping some sticks of vanilla in Spirit of Wine, or in syrup ;

Slit the sticks of vanilla lengthwise into four pieces, put them into a bottle, and fill it up with Spirit of Wine or syrup ;

Cork down the bottle and lay it in a warm place ;

To procure a strong essence, use 2 sticks of vanilla for every gill of spirits or syrup.

ORANGE AND LEMON FLAVOURING

Cut off all the yellow peel of some oranges, and put it into a bottle, fill it up with syrup registering 32°, cork the bottle, and put it by for use ;

Use $\frac{1}{2}$ oz. of peel for every gill of syrup.

Lemon Flavouring is prepared in precisely the same manner, substituting some lemon peel for the orange.

COFFEE FLAVOURING

Put 2 oz. of fresh-ground coffee in a percolator, press it well down, and pour over it 1 pint of boiling water; pour the water back again over the coffee, and, when it has strained through, bottle it for use.

STRAWBERRY, RASPBERRY, AND CURRANT FLAVOURING

Rub either of the above fruits through a silk sieve, and flavour the bonbons with the juice, adding a few drops of lemon juice if required.

When the fruit is not in season, use some preserved juice in the same way.

CHOCOLATE FLAVOURING

For Bonbons Flavoured with Chocolate : dissolve some chocolate over the fire with a little water and no sugar, and add it to the sugar before the bonbons are moulded.

FONDANT PASTE FOR BONBONS

Boil some sugar *to the ball*, and bring it back *to the blow* by adding some fruit juice or any of the flavourings described in the preceding recipes ;

When the sugar is cold, work it with a wooden spatula until it forms a smooth thick paste, and put it by in a basin.

When about to mould the bonbons, melt part of the paste in a small casting sugar-boiler (*vide* woodcut, page 254); rub some whiting under the spout, and pour the sugar into some plaster of Paris moulds, or into designs imprinted in starch (*vide* Remarks on the Moulding of Bonbons, page 252.)

When the bonbons are moulded, they should be set in the candy tin, some syrup should be poured over, and they should be left to candy for some hours (*vide* Remarks on the Candying of Bonbons, page 254).

When the bonbons are moulded into the shape of different fruits, they can, after they are taken out of the moulds, be coloured by hand, a soft camel hair brush being used for the purpose, and a very fine one to paint the smaller details.

Instead of moulding the bonbons, the paste can also be poured into fancy paper cases, $\frac{3}{4}$ inch in diameter, $\frac{3}{8}$ inch deep.

RED CURRANT BONBONS

Make some *Fondant* Paste by boiling the sugar and adding some Red Currant Juice, as described above;

Work the paste, melt it, and pour it into moulds or paper cases in precisely the same manner.

ORANGE BONBONS

Prepare some *Fondant* Paste by boiling the sugar and adding some Orange Juice and some of the Orange Flavouring, and finish the bonbons as directed above.

VANILLA BONBONS

Make some paste by boiling some sugar *to the small ball* and bringing it back *to the blow* by adding some of the Vanilla Flavouring;

Should the sugar be sufficiently flavoured, and yet not brought back to the right degree, complete it by adding a little water;

Work the paste, and finish the bonbons as described above.

VARIEGATED BONBONS

Prepare four different coloured *Fondant* Pastes (*vide Fondant* Paste for Bonbons, page 257).

Flavouring:

> a white paste with *Anisette*;
>
> a pink with Maraschino, adding a few drops of prepared cochineal;
>
> a green paste with Kirschenwasser, adding a little spinach greening;
>
> a fourth paste with chocolate;

When cold, roll out the pastes to a $\frac{1}{4}$-inch thickness, and, with a little white of egg, stick the pastes together, putting: the green paste on the chocolate, the white on the green, and the pink on the white;

Let the paste rest for ten minutes; then cut through the pastes to make bonbons $1\frac{1}{2}$ inch by $\frac{1}{4}$ inch;

Set the bonbons in a candy tin, and candy them as directed at page 254.

CHOCOLATE BALLS WITH CHOPPED FILBERTS

Put 1 oz. of pounded sugar in a sugar-boiler, and melt it over the fire until it acquires a brown tinge; add $1\frac{1}{2}$ oz. of chopped filberts, stir over the fire for a few minutes more, and spread the filberts and sugar on a baking sheet;

When cold, chop the filberts again, and mix them in an equal quantity of *Fondant* Paste, prepared as directed at page 257, and flavoured with Kirschenwasser;

Roll the mixture into balls $\frac{1}{4}$ inch in diameter, and put them in a sieve;

Melt some chocolate in a sugar-boiler, and add some cocoa butter or very fresh butter—about a fifth of the quantity of chocolate;

Keep the chocolate warm *au bain-marie* ;

Put each ball of chopped filberts into the chocolate, take it out with a two-pronged fork, and put the chocolate balls on a baking sheet till they are cold ; then take them off, and put them on a sieve to dry.

CHOCOLATE BALLS AU NOUGÂT

Blanch and chop some almonds ;

Melt 1 oz. of pounded sugar in a sugar-boiler, add the chopped almonds, and stir over the fire until they acquire a brown tinge ;

Spread the *Nougât* on a baking sheet, and chop it very fine when cold ; then mix it with an equal quantity of *Fondant* Paste flavoured with Kirschenwasser, and finish the balls as directed in the preceding recipe.

CHOCOLATE CREAMS

Make some Cream *Fondant* Paste by boiling the sugar *to the ball* and bringing it back *to the blow* by adding some double cream, and working the sugar, when cold, with a wooden spatula, until it forms a thick and smooth paste ;

Roll the paste into balls, dip them in some chocolate in the way described for Chocolate Balls with Chopped Filberts, and finish in the same way.

CHOCOLATE CREAMS FLAVOURED WITH PISTACHIOS

Blanch and peel some pistachios; pound them in a mortar, and rub them through a fine hair sieve ;

Mix the pounded pistachios with an equal quantity of Cream *Fondant* Paste, prepared as described in the preceding recipe ;

Roll the mixture into balls, dip them in chocolate, and finish the balls as directed for Chocolate Balls with Chopped Filberts.

REMARKS ON LIQUEUR BONBONS

For these bonbons always use the best *liqueurs*;

To colour them, use either green and yellow vegetable colouring, some prepared cochineal, or ultramarine blue;

When colouring the bonbons, the colours should be put in with great discretion, and only in small quantities at a time; for bonbons when too highly coloured have a very unpleasant appearance.

LIQUEUR BONBONS

Boil some sugar *to the blow*, and season it with any kind of *liqueur*, and colour it with any of the colours described above;

When it is half cold, pour the syrup into some designs, which you must have previously imprinted in starch *(vide* Remarks on the Moulding of Bonbons, page 252);

When all the impressions are filled with the syrup, sift some more starch over the bonbons to a $\frac{1}{4}$-inch thickness, and put the tray in the hot-closet at a temperature of 80° Fahr.;

The bonbons will require to remain about twenty-four hours in the hot-closet;

When you think they are done, take one of the bonbons out of the starch, and, if it is quite firm, take out all the others; brush them lightly to free them from any adhering starch powder, set the bonbons in a candy tin, and candy them as described in Remarks on the Candying of Bonbons *(vide* page 254).

Liqueur bonbons are sometimes moulded in the shape of raspberries; the sugar should then be flavoured with *Crême de Framboises*;

Bonbons moulded in such a way will be very full of *liqueur* and of a very pleasant taste.

BERLINGOTS DE ROUEN

Put in a sugar-boiler :

1 lb. of sugar,

$\frac{1}{2}$ pint of water,

$\frac{1}{16}$ oz. of cream of tartar ;

Put the sugar over a slow fire till it is melted ; then boil it up over a brisk fire; add a tablespoonful of cold water, and take off the scum ; clean the edges of the sugar-boiler with a damp sponge, and boil the sugar *to the hard crack*; add a teaspoonful of Lemon Flavouring, and take the sugar-boiler off the fire ;

When the sugar is partly cold, pour it on to a warmed and oiled marble slab ; put the sugar-boiler over the fire to melt any sugar that might adhere to it, and pour this also on the marble ;

As the sugar spreads out on the marble, bring it back to the centre, so that the whole may cool evenly ; then hold the sugar with the left hand, and with the right pull it apart, fold it over and pull and fold it over again, and continue working the sugar in the same way until it becomes of an opaque white ;

Pull the sugar into strips $\frac{3}{4}$ inch wide, and cut these across with some scissors into even-sized squares, turning the strip half round after each cut ;

The working of the sugar must be done quickly, as it would be impossible to cut it if it was too cold.

To prepare these bonbons successfully, the sugar must be boiled *to the hard crack* without colouring it.

ORANGE BERLINGOTS

Boil the sugar as described in the preceding recipe, flavouring it with Orange Flavouring, and adding a little prepared cochineal, and a little yellow vegetable colouring to give it an orange tint;

Work the sugar and cut the bonbons in the same manner.

VANILLA BERLINGOTS

Make the bonbons as directed for *Berlingots de Rouen*, flavouring the sugar with some Vanilla Flavouring, and adding a few drops of prepared cochineal.

COFFEE BERLINGOTS

Boil some sugar *to the hard crack*, add some Coffee Flavouring, and finish the bonbons as directed for *Berlingots de Rouen*.

These bonbons may also be flavoured with Peppermint or Orange Flower Water.

TWISTED BONBONS

Boil some sugar *to the hard crack*; let it assume a light yellow tinge, and pour it on to a warmed and oiled marble slab;

When partly cold, gather the sugar together with a knife, and, when it is set, divide it into portions the size of a large nut; roll these into lengths, flatten them slightly, and twist them round a stick $\frac{1}{2}$ inch in diameter, so as to give them the shape of short corkscrews;

The sugar may be flavoured with either Orange, Lemon, or Orange Flower Water.

ANOTHER KIND OF TWISTED BONBONS

Boil some sugar *to the crack* ;

Add the flavouring, and any colouring which may be desired ;

Work the sugar as directed for *Berlingots de Rouen*, without, however, making it opaque ;

Pull the sugar out into lengths $\frac{1}{8}$ inch in diameter, and twist them quickly round a stick, and put the bonbons to dry on a sieve.

CHOCOLATE CARAMEL TABLETS

Boil 1 lb. of sugar and $\frac{1}{4}$ lb. of unsweetened chocolate *to the crack* ;

Let the sugar cool, and pour it on to a warmed and oiled marble slab ;

When nearly cold, cut the sugar with a 1-inch square sugar-cutter, and put the tablets on a sieve to dry.

COFFEE CARAMEL TABLETS

Boil some sugar *to the crack*, add some Coffee Flavouring, and boil it again *to the crack* ;

When partly cold, pour the sugar on to a warmed and oiled marble slab, and cut it in the way described in the preceding recipe.

ORANGE FLOWER CARAMEL TABLETS

Boil some sugar *to the crack*, and add 1 oz. of Candied Orange Flowers to every pound of sugar ; stir over the fire until it assumes a reddish tinge ; cool, and finish the tablets as directed for Chocolate *Caramel* Tablets.

Observation.—All the above tablets may be glazed with *Fondant* Icing as follows :

Melt some *Fondant* Paste (*vide* page 257) ;

Dip the tablets into the paste, and put them on some baking sheets sprinkled with fine sugar ; sprinkle some more sugar on the tablets, and put them to dry in the hot-closet.

BOULES DE GOMME

Melt 1 ½ oz. of the best gum Arabic in 3 gills of water ;

Put in a sugar-boiler :

    1 lb. of sugar,

    a pinch of cream of tartar,

    the gum water, previously strained through a silk sieve ;

Boil the sugar *to the crack* ; let it cool, and pour it on to a warmed and slightly oiled marble slab ;

When the sugar is half cold, cut it into even-sized pieces, about the size of a large nut ; roll them to a ball and put them on a sieve, and continue shaking the balls about on the sieve, until they are cold and quite round.

Great attention must be paid to the proper cooking of the sugar, as the clearness and limpidity of the balls depends entirely on it.

RASPBERRY BALLS

Boil some sugar *to the crack* ; add some Raspberry Juice, boil it again *to the crack*, and finish the balls as directed in the preceding recipe.

ORANGE BALLS

Boil some sugar *to the crack*, and add some Orange Flavouring, strained through a silk sieve, and a little prepared cochineal and yellow vegetable colouring, to give it an orange tinge ;

Boil the sugar again *to the crack*, and finish the balls as directed for *Boules de Gomme.*

PEPPERMINT BALLS

Boil 1 lb. of sugar *to the crack*, add 3 drops of Essence of Peppermint, and a little green vegetable colouring to give the sugar a pale green tint ;

Boil the sugar again, and finish the balls as directed for *Boules de Gomme.*

CANDIED ALMOND PASTE FLAVOURED WITH MARASCHINO

Blanch and peel $\frac{1}{2}$ lb. of Jordan almonds ; steep them in cold water for two hours ; drain, and pound them in a mortar, moistening, by degrees, with the white of an egg; and rub the almonds through a fine hair sieve ;

Boil $\frac{1}{2}$ lb. of sugar *to the ball*;

Put the pounded almonds on to a marble slab ; add the boiled sugar ; mix, and let the paste cool a little ; then add 2 tablespoonfuls of Maraschino and a few drops of prepared cochineal, and work the paste, by folding it over and over, until it is very smooth ;

Divide the paste into portions about the size of an olive, give them the shape of one, and put them on a sieve for six hours ;

Set the portions of almond paste in a candy tin, and candy them as described at page 254.

CANDIED ALMOND PASTE FLAVOURED WITH VANILLA

Blanch, peel, and cool $\frac{1}{2}$ lb. of Jordan almonds, and pound them in a mortar, adding the white of an egg whilst pounding ;

Rub the pounded almonds through a fine hair sieve, and put them on a marble slab ;

Boil $\frac{1}{2}$ lb. of sugar *to the ball* ; add it to the pounded almonds ; flavour the paste with Vanilla Flavouring, and finish and candy the paste as directed in the preceding recipe.

CANDIED PISTACHIO PASTE

Blanch and peel $\frac{1}{4}$ lb. of Jordan almonds and $\frac{1}{4}$ lb. of pistachios ; pound both together in a mortar, moistening, by degrees, with the white of an egg ;

Rub the whole through a fine hair sieve, and put it on a marble slab ;

Boil $\frac{1}{2}$ lb. of sugar *to the ball*; add it to the pounded almonds, and finish and candy the paste as directed for Candied Almond Paste Flavoured with Maraschino (*vide* page 266).

CANDIED FILBERT PASTE

Roast $\frac{1}{2}$ lb. of filberts in a copper pan to remove the skins ;

When the filberts are cold, pound them in a mortar, moistening with a little white of egg, and rub them through a fine hair sieve on to a marble slab ;

Boil $\frac{1}{2}$ lb. of sugar *to the ball*; add it to the pounded filberts, together with one tablespoonful of Kirschenwasser and sufficient yellow colouring to give the paste a pale yellow tint ;

When the sugar is nearly cold, mix the whole to a smooth paste, roll it into balls $\frac{1}{2}$ inch in diameter, and candy the paste as described at page 254.

Observation.—Instead of being candied, all the foregoing pastes may be prepared as directed above and glazed with *Fondant* Icing :

Make some *Fondant* Paste (*vide* page 257) ;

Melt it with a little syrup registering 32°; dip the balls of paste into it; put them on some baking sheets sprinkled with fine sugar, and dry them in the hot-closet for ten minutes.

BURNT ALMONDS FLAVOURED WITH VANILLA

Spread 1 lb. of Jordan almonds on a cloth; rub them lightly in it, and pick out any that may be broken;

Put in a shallow copper bowl:

1 lb. of loaf sugar,

$\frac{1}{2}$ pint of water,

2 sticks of vanilla;

Boil the sugar *to the ball*, and pour the almonds into it, stirring with a wooden spatula;

Continue stirring over the fire until the sugar is boiled *to the crack* and the almonds begin to crack;

Take the bowl off the fire, and stir the almonds till all the sugar is set; then throw them into a very coarse wire or cane sieve, and sift off the loose sugar;

Put the almonds back into the bowl, and stir them over the fire until the sugar adhering to them begins to melt; then throw them back into the sieve, and cover it to keep the almonds warm;

Put all the sugar sifted from the almonds into the bowl, adding $\frac{1}{2}$ lb. of loaf sugar and 1 gill of water, and boil the sugar *to the crack*; add the almonds, stir them over the fire until all the sugar adheres to them, and throw them once more into the sieve;

Sift off the loose sugar and put it into the bowl, adding $\frac{1}{2}$ lb. of loaf sugar and 1 gill of water; boil the sugar *to the crack*, add the almonds, stir them over the fire until all the sugar adheres to them, and keep them warm so that they may glaze more easily;

To glaze the sugared almonds: clean the copper bowl and put in it 1 oz. of gum Arabic and $\frac{1}{2}$ oz. of sugar dissolved in $\frac{1}{2}$ gill of water;

Put the bowl over the fire, and, when the water boils, add the sugared almonds, toss them until they are glazed all over, and put them to dry in the hot-closet.

BURNT ALMONDS FLAVOURED WITH CHOCOLATE

Prepare and sugar the almonds as directed in the preceding recipe, merely adding $1\frac{1}{2}$ oz. of grated chocolate to the sugar each time it is boiled up; and glaze the almonds in the same way.

BURNT ALMONDS FLAVOURED WITH ROSE WATER

Prepare and sugar the almonds as directed for Burnt Almonds Flavoured with Vanilla, substituting some Rose Water for the vanilla;

Glaze them in the same manner, adding a little Rose Water and a few drops of prepared cochineal to the gum water;

A very little cochineal will be sufficient, as the sugar should be of a pale rose colour only.

BURNT FILBERTS

Choose some fine filberts, and roast them in a copper pan to remove the skins;

Sugar the filberts in the way described for Burnt Almonds Flavoured with Vanilla, flavouring the sugar with Kirschenwasser instead of vanilla, and glazing them with some gum dissolved in Kirschenwasser instead of water.

BURNT PISTACHIOS

Select some large pistachios of a violet tinge; reject all those with black spots;

Sugar the pistachios as directed for Burnt Almonds Flavoured with Vanilla, and glaze them in the same way.

PEPPERMINT DROPS

Pound some sugar and sift it through a coarse hair sieve; then sift it through a finer sieve, and use the coarse sugar which has not sifted through this last sieve to make the drops;

Put 1 lb. of this coarsely sifted sugar into a basin, and mix it to a stiff paste with some cold water; add some Essence of Peppermint, drop by drop; mix, and taste the sugar after each drop has been added;

Put part of the paste in a *pastille* sugar-boiler, and stir it over the fire until it boils; then hold the sugar-boiler in the left hand, inclining it over a baking sheet, and, with a wire held in the right hand, cut off the drops as they fall from the spout; they will then fall in even-sized drops on to the baking sheet;

Put the drops to dry in the hot-closet for twenty minutes, and put them on a sieve to cool.

RED CURRANT DROPS

Mix 1 lb. of coarsely sifted sugar to a stiff paste with equal quantities of Red Currant Juice and water, and make the drops as directed in the preceding recipe.

PINEAPPLE DROPS

Make the drops as described above, mixing the sugar to a stiff paste with some unsweetened Pineapple Juice.

STRAWBERRY DROPS

Steep some small Alpine strawberries in cold water for two hours, and rub them through a fine broth napkin;

Mix some coarsely sifted sugar to a stiff paste with the strawberry juice, add a few drops of lemon juice and a few drops of prepared cochineal, and make the drops as described above.

Strawberry drops are sometimes made by mixing the sugar to a paste with some strawberries rubbed through a hair sieve, but this preparation is not so likely to prove successful, the fruit being liable to prevent the drops drying properly.

All fruit drops are prepared in the same way, by mixing the sugar to a stiff paste with the juice.

ROSE DROPS

Mix some coarsely sifted sugar to a stiff paste with some Rose Water; add a few drops of prepared cochineal to give it a pink tinge, and finish the drops as directed for Peppermint Drops.

ORANGE FLOWER WATER DROPS

Make the drops as directed above, mixing the sugar to a paste with Orange Flower Water.

CHOCOLATE DROPS

Put some chocolate in a copper sugar-boiler and put it over the fire until it is partly melted; then divide the chocolate into portions about the size of a small nut, and roll these round to a ball shape;

Place the balls on a warm baking sheet; move it about until the balls have flattened down so as to form the drops, and, when they are cold, put them on a sieve to dry.

To candy the drops:

Place them on a baking sheet, cover them with syrup registering 36°, and let them remain thus for twenty hours;

Drain the drops on a sieve, and put them to dry in the hot-closet for five minutes.

ITALIAN PEPPERMINT DROPS

Put 1 oz. of gum tragacanth in a basin, and pour in sufficient Peppermint Water to come $\frac{1}{4}$ inch above the gum;

When the gum is dissolved, press it through a new cloth on to a marble slab; mix and work the gum with sufficient fine sugar, added by degrees, to make a smooth paste, and let it rest for two days;

Roll out the paste to $\frac{1}{8}$-inch thickness, and roll over it with a fluted rolling-pin;

Cut the paste with a $\frac{3}{4}$-inch plain round cutter, and put the drops on a sieve to dry in the hot-closet.

ITALIAN CINNAMON DROPS

Prepare the drops as directed in the preceding recipe, substituting some Cinnamon Water for the peppermint.

All Italian drops are prepared in the same way; varying the flavouring by using Aniseed, or Orange Flower Water, Essence of Bitter Almonds, Coffee, or Vanilla.

PÂTE DE GUIMAUVE

Put 1 oz. of gum tragacanth in a small basin, and pour in sufficient water to come $\frac{1}{4}$ inch above the gum;

Boil 2 oz. of marshmallow roots, previously scraped, washed, and cut in pieces, in half a pint of water; strain through a fine hair sieve, and reduce the water over a slow fire until only two tablespoonfuls are left;

When the gum is dissolved, press it through a new cloth on to a marble slab; add the two tablespoonfuls of marshmallow decoction and sufficient fine sugar, added by degrees, to form a smooth stiff paste;

Divide the paste and shape it into sticks $2\frac{1}{2}$ inches long, $\frac{1}{4}$ inch in diameter; or roll out the paste to a $\frac{1}{4}$-inch thickness and cut it with a $\frac{3}{4}$-inch round cutter.

Keep the *Pâte de Guimauve* in a cool place.

FRUIT GLAZED WITH FONDANT ICING

TANGERINE ORANGES

Peel some Tangerine oranges, divide them into their quarters, and stick a thin wooden skewer into the point of each quarter;

Make some *Fondant* Paste (*vide* page 257), flavouring it with some Tangerine orange juice and a little of the grated orange peel, and adding a few drops of prepared cochineal and a little yellow vegetable colouring to give the icing an orange tinge;

Melt the icing, and dip each piece of orange into it; stick the end of the skewers into a basinful of pounded sugar, as described for Oranges *Glacées au Caramel* (*vide* page 207), and put the glazed oranges to dry in the hot-closet.

GRAPES

Choose some fine white grapes, stick a thin wooden skewer into each grape, and dip them into some *Fondant* Paste flavoured with *Anisette*, and coloured with sufficient vegetable colouring to give it a pale green tinge ;

. Should the icing be too thick, add a little syrup registering 32° on the saccharometer ;

Stick the end of the skewers in a basinful of sugar, and put the grapes to dry in the hot-closet.

CHERRIES

Dry some brandy cherries in the hot-closet, and dip them in some *Fondant* Paste flavoured with Kirschenwasser, and finish them as described above.

Fresh cherries are prepared in the same way.

STRAWBERRIES

Choose some even-sized British Queens, dip them in some *Fondant* Paste (*vide* page 257) flavoured with strawberry juice, and dry them in the hot-closet as aforesaid.

ALMOND PASTE GLAZED WITH FONDANT ICING

Make some paste as directed for Candied Almond Paste (*vide* page 266), omitting the Maraschino, and adding 15 bitter almonds ;

Divide the paste into small portions, roll them round into balls, and dip them into some *Fondant* Paste (*vide* page 257), prepared with milk of almonds ; and finish as directed above.

CHESTNUT PURÉE GLAZED WITH FONDANT ICING

Make some chestnut *purée* as directed for Compote of Vermicelli Chestnuts (*vide* page 200).

Divide it into portions about the size of a cherry, and press each portion in the corner of a cloth so as to shape it like a chestnut ;

Dip the chestnuts in some *Fondant* Paste (*vide* page 257) flavoured with chocolate, and dry them in the hot-closet.

Observation.—All these fruit bonbons are put into small fancy paper cases, and are dressed on stands for dessert or for ball suppers.

PESTLE AND MORTAR.

CHAPTER XXV

FRUIT PRESERVED IN BRANDY

CHERRIES

CHOOSE some fine May-Duke or Morella cherries ; cut off all but ½ inch of the stalks ;

Put the cherries into glass jars ; fill them up with some strong pale brandy ; cork the jars carefully, tie some bladder over the top, and put the jars in a dry place for six weeks ;

At the end of that time uncork the jars, and put in some loaf sugar, adding ¼ lb. of sugar to every quart of spirit ; cork the jars up again, and tie some bladder over the top.

GREENGAGES

Prepare some greengages as directed for Preserved Greengages (*vide* page 245), merely boiling up the syrup four times, instead of eight ;

Drain, and put the greengages into glass jars ;

Boil the syrup until it registers 36° on the saccharometer, and mix it with an equal quantity of strong pale brandy, and pour it into the jars so as to cover the fruit entirely ;

Cork the jars, and tie some bladder over the top.

APRICOTS

Prepare some apricots as described for Preserved Apricots (*vide* page 246), only boiling up the syrup six times, instead of eight;

Drain, and put the apricots into glass jars;

Boil the syrup until it registers 36°; mix it with an equal quantity of strong pale brandy, and finish as directed in the preceding recipe.

PEACHES

Preserve some peaches as directed at page 246, boiling up the syrup only six times, instead of eight;

Drain the peaches, and put them into glass jars;

Boil the syrup until it registers 36°; mix it with an equal quantity of strong pale brandy;

Fill up the jars, cork them carefully, and tie some bladder over the top.

Pears, *Mirabelle* plums, and green almonds, are preserved in the same way.

CHESTNUTS

Prepare and preserve some chestnuts as directed for Preserved Chestnuts (*vide* page 250), boiling up the syrup only three times;

Drain the chestnuts, and put them into glass jars;

Boil the syrup until it registers 28° on the saccharometer, and mix it with an equal quantity of strong pale brandy;

Fill up the jars, cork them, and tie some bladder over the corks.

CHAPTER XXVI

LIQUEURS

REMARKS ON LIQUEURS

THE utensils required for preparing *Liqueurs* are the same as those used for Bonbons ;

The best spirit of wine is indispensable to obtain a good *liqueur* ;

All fruit should be perfectly sound and ripe ;

The herbs and seeds must be dried carefully, and of the year's growth in which they are used ;

The best loaf sugar should be used, so as to obtain a clear syrup ;

The filtering-bag should be perfectly clean, and the filtering-paper of the best kind ;

All the vessels should be thoroughly dried, as the least moïsture in any of the bottles would make the *liqueurs* dim.

The proportions I have indicated for the sweetening of *liqueurs* is that generally adopted, but it can be either increased or diminished to suit individual taste.

CASSIS

Take sufficient black currants to obtain 2 lbs. of fruit when picked ;

Put the currants into a stone jar, with 3 quarts of spirit

of wine registering 55° by Gay Lussac's alcoholometer; close the jar, and let them remain thus for three months;

Strain the whole through a filtering-bag, and, for 3 quarts of the currant spirit, add 1 quart of syrup registering 28° on the saccharometer;

Mix thoroughly, pour the *liqueur* into bottles, and cork and seal them carefully.

A refreshing drink may be prepared in the following manner with the currants which remain in the filtering-bag:

Put the currants into a basin; add a quart of cold water, crush and mash the currants, and pour the whole into a filtering-bag;

Add 1 gill of spirit of wine and 1 gill of syrup to the filtered juice; mix the whole thoroughly, and bottle it.

RATAFIA

Put in a stone jar:

    1 lb. of picked raspberries,

    1 lb. of picked wild cherries,

    1 lb. of picked red currants,

    $\frac{1}{2}$ oz. of cinnamon,

    $\frac{1}{4}$ oz. of cloves,

    3 quarts of spirit of wine registering 55° by Gay Lussac's alcoholometer;

Close the jar, and let the whole macerate for three months;

Pour the contents of the jar into a filtering-bag, and, when the spirit has strained through, add 1 quart of syrup, registering 28° on the saccharometer, to 3 quarts of the infusion; mix, and bottle the *liqueur*.

RATAFIA DE NEUILLY

Put in a stone jar :

    1 lb. of picked cherries,

    1 lb. of picked black currants,

    1 oz. of black currant leaves,

    $\frac{1}{2}$ oz. of flowering-clove petals,

    3 quarts of spirit of wine registering 55° by Gay
        Lussac's alcoholometer ;

Close the jar, and let the whole remain thus for three months ;

Filter the *ratafia*, sweeten, and bottle it as directed in the preceding recipe.

With the residue left in the filtering-bag, a refreshing drink may be prepared in the following way :

Put the fruit in a basin ; crush and mash it, and add 1 quart of cold water ; strain the whole through a filtering-bag ; add 1 gill of spirit of wine and 1 gill of syrup to the juice ; mix, and bottle it.

QUINCE LIQUEUR

Grate a sufficient quantity of quinces over a basin to obtain 2 lbs. of pulp ; add 1 quart of syrup registering 30° on the saccharometer ; cover the basin, and let it remain thus for one day ;

Pour the contents of the basin into a filtering-bag ; add 1 pint of spirit of wine, registering 35° by Gay Lussac's alcoholometer, to the strained syrup ; mix, and pour the whole again through a filtering-bag, and bottle the *liqueur*.

PINEAPPLE LIQUEUR

Take $\frac{1}{2}$ lb. of peeled pineapple, and cut it into slices ;

Boil 3 quarts of syrup until it registers 38° on the

saccharometer; add the slices of pineapple, the juice of
4 oranges, and the yellow peel of 2 oranges; let it boil up,
and pour the whole into a jar;

Close the jar carefully, and let the pineapple infuse thus
for two days;

Strain the syrup through a hair sieve, mix it with 1 quart
of spirit of wine registering 60° by Gay Lussac's alcoholometer, and filter the whole through a felt filtering-bag;

Bottle the *liqueur*, and keep it in a dry place.

WILD CHERRY AND RASPBERRY LIQUEUR

Take 2 lbs. of wild cherries; put them in a basin, and
crush and pound them, without removing the stones or
stalks;

Put the crushed cherries into a jar, with 1 lb. of picked
raspberries and 1 gallon of spirit of wine registering 50° by
Gay Lussac's alcoholometer;

Close the jar, put it in a warm place, and let it remain
there for three months;

Strain the spirit through a hair sieve, mix it with 1 quart
of syrup registering 30° on the saccharometer, pour it into
a filtering-bag, and bottle the liqueur when it is filtered.

STRAWBERRY LIQUEUR (CRÊME DE FRAISES)

Pick 2 lbs. of small Alpine strawberries; put them into a
jar, and pour over 3 quarts of cold syrup registering 38°
on the saccharometer; let the strawberries steep for three
days; then strain the syrup through a hair sieve, and add
1 quart of spirit of wine registering 50° by Gay Lussac's
alcoholometer;

Should the *liqueur* be too pale in colour, add a few drops
of prepared cochineal;

Strain through a felt filtering-bag, and bottle the *liqueur*.

RASPBERRY LIQUEUR (CRÈME DE FRAMBOISES)

Make the *liqueur* as directed in the preceding recipe, substituting an equal quantity of raspberries for the strawberries.

MINT LIQUEUR (CRÈME DE MENTHE)

Put 2 oz. of green mint into a jar, pour over 1 quart of spirit of wine registering 50° by Gay Lussac's alcoholometer, and let it steep for eight days; add 3 gills of syrup registering 30° on the saccharometer; mix it with some filtering-paper, and pour the whole into a filtering-bag;

When the *liqueur* is thus strained, it should be perfectly clear and limpid; bottle it, and keep the bottles in a dry place.

ANGELICA LIQUEUR (CRÈME D'ANGÉLIQUE)

Take ¾ lb. of angelica, previously blanched in hot water, and peeled; remove the thin skin round the stalk, and cut the angelica in small pieces;

Put them into a jar with 1 quart of spirit of wine registering 50° by Gay Lussac's alcoholometer, and let it remain therein for eight days; then filter, and finish the *liqueur* as directed in the preceding recipe.

VANILLA LIQUEUR (CRÈME DE VANILLE)

Cut 3 large sticks of vanilla, lengthwise, into halves, and cut each half across in two pieces;

Put the vanilla in a jar with 1 quart of spirit of wine registering 60° by Gay Lussac's alcoholometer, and let it steep for twenty-four hours;

Strain the vanilla spirit, and add to it 3 gills of syrup

registering 30° on the saccharometer, and a few drops of prepared cochineal;

Mix the *liqueur* with some filtering-paper, and pour it twice through a filtering-bag;

Bottle the *liqueur*, and keep it in a cool place.

NOYAU LIQUEUR

Blanch and peel $\frac{1}{4}$ lb. of apricot kernels; wash them in cold water, and dry them in a cloth;

Put the almonds into a jar with 1 quart of spirit of wine registering 50° by Gay Lussac's alcoholometer;

Close the jar, and let the almonds remain therein for eight days;

Pour off the spirit, and mix it with 3 gills of syrup registering 28° on the saccharometer;

Filter the *liqueur* twice with some paper through a filtering-bag, and bottle it.

BLACK CURRANT-BUD LIQUEUR

Take 1 lb. of the budding shoots of some black currant trees, and put them into a jar with 3 quarts of spirit of wine registering 50° by Gay Lussac's alcoholometer, and let them remain therein for a fortnight, keeping the jar closed;

Strain the spirit through a hair sieve; mix it with $2\frac{1}{2}$ pints of syrup registering 30° on the saccharometer, and some filering-paper, and pour the whole into a filtering-bag;

Bottle the *liqueur* and keep it in a cool place.

PEACH KERNEL LIQUEUR

Having had an opportunity of tasting this *liqueur*, I thought it so delicious that I must here give its recipe.

Break 50 peach stones, and put the kernels and wood into a jar, with ¼ oz. of pounded cochineal and 3 quarts of spirit of wine registering 50° by Gay Lussac's alcoholometer; and let them steep thus for a fortnight;

Strain the spirit through a hair sieve, and mix it with 2¼ pints of syrup registering 30° on the saccharometer;

Strain the *liqueur* through a filtering-bag, and bottle it.

EAU D'OR LIQUEUR

Put in a jar:

1 oz. of coriander seeds,
½ oz. of cinnamon,
½ oz. of cloves,
1 quart of spirit of wine registering 60° by Gay Lussac's alcoholometer;

Let the spices steep for twenty-four hours; then add 3 gills of syrup registering 24° on the saccharometer, and filter the whole three times through a felt filtering-bag;

Add 2 sheets of gold leaf to the *liqueur*; shake it to divide the gold, and bottle it.

CURAÇOA

Cut off the yellow peal of 6 Seville oranges, and put it in a jar with 1 quart of spirit of wine registering 45° by Gay Lussac's alcoholometer;

Let the orange infuse for eight days;

Boil 1 oz. of Brazil wood in 1 gill of water until it is reduced to ½ gill;

Add 3 gills of syrup, registering 28° on the saccharometer, to the orange spirit, and colour the *liqueur* with the wood decoction;

Mix the *liqueur* with some filtering-paper, and pour the whole into a filtering-bag.

Bottle the *liqueur*, and seal the corks.

DRY CURAÇOA

Make the *liqueur* as directed in the preceding recipe, merely sweetening it with 1 gill of syrup registering 20°, instead of the quantity indicated therein.

ABSINTHE LIQUEUR

Those who, liking the ordinary alcoholic absinthe, yet fear its effects, may partake of this *liqueur*, as a substitute, with perfect confidence ;

Take 1 lb. of picked wormwood leaves, and spread them out to dry for five days in a dry and shady place ; then put them into a jar with 1 gallon of spirit of wine registering 50° by Gay Lussac's alcoholometer, and let them steep therein for a fortnight ;

Strain the spirit through a hair sieve, and mix it with $\frac{1}{4}$ lb. of gum Arabic dissolved in $\frac{1}{2}$ pint of water, and 3 gills of syrup registering 30° on the saccharometer ;

Filter the whole, with some paper, through a felt filtering-bag, and bottle the *liqueur*.

This *liqueur*, mixed in very cold water, will make a pleasant and wholesome drink.

VERMUTH LIQUEUR

Scrape off the outside of some German horseradish ; cut 1 oz. of it into pieces, and put them into a jar, with :

> ¼ lb. of cochlearia,
> ¼ lb. of green walnuts, previously broken with a hammer,
> 2 oz. of pounded quinine,
> 1 oz. of juniper berries,
> 2 quarts of spirit of wine registering 80 by Gay Lussac's alcoholometer;

Let the whole macerate for a fortnight, and filter it with some paper through a felt bag;

Add 3 gallons of Châblis, and 1 quart of syrup registering 24° on the saccharometer;

Pour the whole through the filtering-bag, and continue pouring it back until the *liqueur* is perfectly clear and limpid; then bottle it.

DUTCH BITTERS

Put in a jar:
> 2 oz. of picked hyssop leaves,
> 2 oz. of St. John's wort,
> 1 oz. of badiana aniseed,
> ½ oz. of matricaria,
> the yellow peel of 2 oranges and 1 lemon,
> 3 quarts of spirit of wine registering 40° by Gay Lussac's alcoholometer;

Let the herbs macerate for eight days;

Put ½ oz. of quassia to infuse in a small jar with ½ pint of spirit of wine;

Boil 2 oz. of Brazil wood in 1 pint of water, and reduce it to half a pint by boiling gently over a slow fire;

Filter the herb spirit, with some paper, through a filtering-bag, and add 1½ pint of syrup registering 20° on the saccharometer;

Colour the *liqueur* with the Brazil wood decoction, and add some of the quassia infusion;

The quantity of quassia infusion cannot be indicated exactly, as the *liqueur* must be made more or less bitter, according to taste ;

Pour the *liqueur* through the filtering-bag until it is perfectly clear, and bottle it for use.

CUMMIN LIQUEUR

Put 1 oz. of cummin seeds in a jar with 1 quart of spirit of wine registering 80° by Gay Lussac's alcoholometer, and let them steep for two days ;

Pour off the spirit, and mix it with 3 gills of syrup registering 28° on the saccharometer ;

Filter the *liqueur*, with some paper, through a felt bag, and bottle it for use.

DIGESTIVE LIQUEUR

Put in a jar ;

    $\frac{1}{2}$ oz. of balm mint leaves,

    $\frac{1}{2}$ oz of pounded coriander seeds,

    $\frac{1}{4}$ oz. of green mint leaves,

    $\frac{1}{4}$ oz. of matricaria,

    3 quarts of spirit of wine registering 60° by Gay Lussac's alcoholometer ;

Macerate the whole for six days ;

Filter the spirit through a felt bag, and add one quart of syrup registering 28° on the saccharometer ;

Pour the whole in the filtering-bag, and pour it back again until the *liqueur* is perfectly clear, and bottle it for use.

A small quantity of the above *liqueur* taken after meals will be found to aid digestion.

ORANGE FLOWER LIQUEUR

Take a sufficient quantity of fresh orange blossoms to obtain 1 oz. of picked petals; put them into a jar with 1 quart of spirit of wine registering 40° by Gay Lussac's alcoholometer;

Let the orange blossoms steep for two days; add 1 pint of syrup registering 30° on the saccharometer, and filter the *liqueur*, with some paper, through a filtering-bag, and bottle it.

ACACIA BLOSSOM LIQUER

Pick a sufficient quantity of acacia blossoms to obtain $\frac{1}{2}$ lb. of petals, and put them to steep for four days in 2 quarts of spirit of wine registering 50° by Gay Lussac's alcoholometer;

Boil $1\frac{1}{2}$ lb. of loaf sugar with $1\frac{1}{2}$ pint of water, clarify the syrup with some whites of egg (*vide* Clarified Syrup, page 255), and boil it until it registers 30° on the saccharometer;

Strain the acacia spirit, and mix it with the cold syrup; filter the *liqueur*, with some paper, through a filtering-bag, and continue pouring it through until it is quite clear and bright;

Put the *liqueur* into bottles previously rinsed out with spirit of wine; cork and seal them carefully.

JESSAMINE LIQUEUR

Pick $\frac{1}{4}$ lb. of jessamine blossoms, and put them in a jar with 2 quarts of spirit of wine registering 50° by Gay Lussac's alcoholometer;

Let the blossoms steep for two days;

Prepare $1\frac{1}{2}$ pint of Clarified Syrup registering 30° on the saccharometer;

Strain the jessamine spirit, mix it with the cold syrup, and filter it, with some paper, through a filtering-bag; continue pouring the *liqueur* through and through until it is quite clear, and bottle it for use.

Before closing this chapter, I shall give a few recipes which, while they are beyond the range of my subject, may still be of a nature to be in frequent request.

QUININE WINE

Break into small pieces 1 oz. of Sulphate of Quinine, and put it in a glass jar with 2 oz. of rectified spirit of wine;

Let the quinine infuse for twenty-four hours; add 1 quart of Claret, and let it remain thus for twelve days; then filter the wine through a felt bag, and bottle it for use.

The above quantity of quinine may be dissolved, without the addition of spirit of wine, in any of the following wines: Madeira, Marsala, Malaga, Lunel, or Alicant.

ANTISCORBUTIC WINE

Put in a jar:

$\frac{1}{4}$ lb. of horseradish root, cut in small pieces,
2 oz. of scurvy-grass
2 oz. of watercress   }coarsely chopped,
2 oz. of buck-bean leaves
2 oz. of crushed mustard seeds,
1 oz. of Muriate of Ammonia,
2 quarts of Châblis;

Infuse the whole for a fortnight;

Strain the wine, filter it through a filtering-bag, and bottle it for use.

RHUBARB WINE

Cut 2 oz. of Turkey rhubarb roots in pieces, and put them in a glass jar with $1\frac{1}{2}$ oz. of rectified spirit of wine ; let it infuse for four days, and add 2 quarts of Dry Sauterne or Châblis, and let it infuse for eight days more ;

Filter the wine through a filtering-bag, and bottle it for use.

EAU DE COLOGNE

Put the following essences in a glass jar :

$\frac{1}{2}$ oz. of essence of lemon,

$\frac{1}{2}$ oz. of essence of bergamot,

$\frac{1}{2}$ oz. of essence of citron,

$\frac{1}{4}$ oz. of essence of rosemary,

$\frac{1}{8}$ oz. of essence of neroli,

1 quart of spirit of wine registering 80° by Gay Lussac's alcoholometer ;

Let the whole infuse for eight days, and pour it into a paper filter placed in a glass funnel (*vide* Modes of Filtering, page 137);

When the *Eau de Cologne* is filtered, bottle it for use.

EAU DE BOTOT

Infuse the following for eight days in 1 quart of spirit of wine registering 50° by Gay Lussac's alcoholometer :

$\frac{1}{2}$ oz. of green aniseed,

$\frac{1}{8}$ oz. of cinnamon,

$\frac{1}{8}$ oz. of cloves,

$\frac{1}{8}$ oz. of quinine wood,

$\frac{1}{8}$ oz. of cochineal,

$\frac{1}{8}$ oz. of essence of peppermint,

$\frac{1}{16}$ oz. of essence of cloves ;

Pour the spirit in a paper filter placed in a glass funnel, and bottle it for use.

CHAPTER XXVII

RECIPES FOR INVALIDS

IN putting together a number of recipes of light food and drinks especially adapted for the use of the sick, I have endeavoured to make them as simple as possible, and have selected none but the least expensive, so as to allow of their being prepared in any home.

I have indicated, at the same time, the special virtue which these preparations are generally held to possess; the use of them, although it may not be of great benefit to the patient, is quite free from any risk, and in some cases may be attended with great success in warding off disease.

To convalescents, particularly, my recipes will offer a welcome variety of light and palatable food.

TAR WATER

Put in a glass or china jar:

$\frac{1}{4}$ lb. of Stockholm tar,

3 pints of water;

Let the tar infuse for twenty-four hours, stirring it occasionally, and pour off this first water; then pour 3 pints of fresh water on to the tar, and let it infuse for twelve hours;

The jar should be replenished with water as it is used, renewing the tar every month only.

Tar Water may be drank alone or mixed with Claret; it is considered a good blood purifier.

IRON WATER

Put ¾ lb. of new iron nails in a large glass bottle with
½ pint of water ; let them remain thus for 8 days, and pour in
1 quart more water ;

Replenish the bottle with water as it is used ;

Iron Water is taken at meals with a little Claret added,
and is recommended for delicate children.

RHUBARB WATER

Put 1 oz. of Turkey rhubarb roots into a quart bottle ; fill
it up with water, and let it infuse for two days.

A glassful of this water mixed with a little Claret should
be taken at meals, to facilitate digestion.

HOP WATER

Infuse ½ oz. of hops in 1 quart of boiling water for an
hour, and strain the infusion through a hair sieve.

This water is taken at meals, adding one-third of Claret
to two-thirds of the water ; it purifies the blood, and is, at
the same time, a tonic.

GENTIAN AND QUININE WATER

Infuse in 1 quart of cold water for five hours :

¼ oz. of gentian,

¼ oz. of quinine.

Drink the water as directed for Hop Water ; it is also of a
tonic and strengthening nature.

LETTUCE WATER

Pour 1 quart of boiling water over ¼ lb. of lettuce leaves; let them infuse for an hour, and strain the water through a fine hair sieve.

The water should be taken three times a day, an hour before meals;

Dose : a small teacupful of the water lukewarm.

It is recommended for persons of weak digestion.

BOUILLIE FOR INFANTS

Bouillie is made either with wheaten flour, arrowroot, maizena, or potato flour;

Wheaten flour is, however, the best for infants.

For delicate children, the *bouillie* should be made thin.

It is unfortunately the case that this, one of the earliest foods of infancy, is in most instances carelessly prepared; it is often made too thick or lumpy, or not sufficiently cooked; and this last is the worst fault, as *bouillie* only becomes easily digestible when thoroughly cooked;

It often happens that a baby will cry and scream because it suffers from a sluggish digestion, and, as the child cannot express the nature of its pain, it is rocked and soothed in order to allay it; but this will not cure it, and its suffering will last until the heavy *bouillie* has been digested.

Flour for preparing the *bouillie* is sometimes dried or baked in the oven; I do not think it advisable; a better way is to mix the flour with the water or milk, and to put the mixture at once on the fire.

PREPARATION OF THE BOUILLIE

Put in a stewpan 1 oz. of flour (best Whites); add 1 pint of good milk or water, and mix it very smooth; should there be any lumps, strain the mixture through a fine strainer ;

Add a small pinch of salt and $\frac{1}{4}$ oz. of loaf sugar, and put the *bouillie* on the fire for twenty minutes, stirring all the time, to prevent its adhering to the stewpan ;

If the *bouillie* is too thick, add a little milk ; it should be of about the thickness of melted butter ;

Let the *bouillie* cool, for it should only be taken lukewarm ; I have often noticed that nurses are in too great a hurry to make their infant charges eat the hot *bouillie* ; this is a very foolish and reprehensible habit.

BROTH FOR INVALIDS

CHICKEN BROTH

Take half a chicken ; remove all fat and skin, and break up and pound the meat and bones in a mortar ;

Put the pounded chicken in a stewpan, and stir in, by degrees, 1 quart of water ; add :

> 1 oz. of leeks, previously blanched and cut in pieces,
> 20 blanched and peeled Jordan almonds,
> a very small pinch of salt ;

Continue stirring the broth over the fire until it boils ; then simmer for twenty minutes, and strain the broth through a silk sieve, or through a broth napkin previously rinsed in hot water.

PARTRIDGE BROTH

Pick, draw, and singe a partridge ; remove all the fat and skin, and pound the bones and meat in a mortar ;

Put the pounded partridge into a stewpan, and stir in 1 quart of cold water ; add :

 1 oz. of sliced carrots,

 1 oz. of sliced onions, previously blanched,

 a small pinch of salt ;

Boil, and finish the broth as directed in the preceding recipe.

BEEF BROTH

Take 1 lb. of leg of beef ; trim off all fat and gristle, and pound the meat in a mortar ;

 Put the pounded meat in a stewpan, with :

 1 oz. of carrots, cut in slices,

 $\frac{3}{4}$ oz. of blanched onions, also cut in slices,

 $\frac{3}{4}$ oz. of blanched leeks, cut in pieces,

 a small pinch of salt,

 1 quart of water;

Boil, and finish the broth as directed for Chicken Broth.

The above broths will be of much service in long illnesses, as they will furnish a variety of wholesome and nourishing diet.

CHICKEN JELLY

Put in a small stockpot :

 a chicken,

 2 blanched and boned calf's feet,

 1 lb. of boned knuckle of veal,

 3 quarts of water,

 a small pinch of salt ;

Boil, skim, and add :

 4 oz. of carrots,

 4 oz. of onions, previously blanched,

 4 oz. of leeks, also blanched,

 1 oz. of blanched and peeled Jordan almonds ;

Simmer till the calf's feet are done; remove all the fat carefully, and strain the broth through a broth napkin into a basin ;

The broth should be sufficiently reduced to set to a jelly.

Clarify the jelly as follows :

Put 3 whites of egg in a stewpan with 1 pint of the jelly; whip it with a wire whisk, and, when the egg and jelly are mixed, add the remainder of the jelly ;

Put the stewpan on the fire, and continue stirring the jelly with the whisk until it boils up ;

Strain the whole through a jelly-bag or through a broth napkin ; continue pouring it back until it is perfectly clear, and keep the jelly in a basin on the ice or in a cold place.

SWEET JELLIES

RED CURRANT JELLY

Take a sufficient quantity of red currants to obtain 7 oz. of fruit when picked ;

Make 3 gills of syrup registering 30° on the saccharometer ; put the currants into the boiling syrup ; let them remain thus for an hour, and strain the whole through a filtering-bag ;

Steep $\frac{1}{2}$ oz. of the best gelatine in a little cold water for twenty minutes ; drain, and put the gelatine in a copper sugar-boiler with 1 gill of water, and melt it *au bain-marie*, stirring with a silver spoon ;

When the gelatine is dissolved, pour it into a basin ; let it cool a little, and add the filtered currant syrup ;

Mix, and pour the jelly into custard cups, and set them on the ice.

For all coloured jellies, I would recommend the exclusive use of copper sugar-boilers and silver spoons ; for if tinned utensils are used, the colour of the jellies will be impaired.

STRAWBERRY, RASPBERRY, AND CHERRY JELLIES

Make the jellies as directed in the preceding recipe, using the same proportion of fruit, syrup and gelatine as there indicated.

ORANGE JELLY

Press some oranges to obtain 1 gill of juice, and filter it through a paper filter (*vide* Modes of Filtering, page 136);

When this jelly is prepared between March and January, add a third part of lemon juice to the orange juice before filtering it;

Make $\frac{1}{2}$ pint of syrup, registering 30°, and add the filtered orange juice to it;

Dissolve $\frac{1}{2}$ oz. of gelatine, as described for Red Currant Jelly;

When the gelatine is partly cold, mix it with the syrup;

Pour the jelly into custard cups and set them on the ice.

LEMON JELLY

Filter 1 gill of lemon juice; mix it with $\frac{1}{2}$ pint of syrup registering 30°; add $\frac{1}{2}$ oz. of dissolved gelatine, and finish as directed in the preceding recipe.

BROTH CUSTARDS

Put the yolks of 4 new laid eggs in a basin, beat them with a spoon, and pour in 3 custard-cupfuls of broth freed from all fat; strain the custard through a hair sieve;

Fill 4 cups with the custard, and set them in a stewpan with sufficient boiling water to come up to within $\frac{1}{2}$ inch of the top of the cups;

Put the stewpan over a slow fire, put on the cover with some live coals on the top, and let the custards remain thus until they are set, being careful that the water does not boil;

Let the custards cool in the water, take them out and wipe the cups:

These broth custards may be eaten hot or cold.

COFFEE CUSTARDS

Break 4 yolks of egg in a basin, beat them up with 2 oz. of pounded sugar; add 1 cupful of strong coffee, and 2 cupfuls of milk, previously boiled, and set the custards as directed in the preceding recipe.

CHOCOLATE CUSTARDS

Dissolve 2 oz. of vanilla chocolate in 3 cupfuls of boiled milk;

Break 4 yolks of egg in a basin, beat them up with $1\frac{1}{2}$ oz. of pounded sugar, and add the chocolate; mix, and strain the custard mixture through a fine strainer;

Fill 4 cups and set them *au bain-marie* as described for Broth Custards.

VANILLA CUSTARDS

Boil 3 cupfuls of milk, and put half a stick of vanilla, cut in small pieces, to steep in it for an hour;

Beat up 4 yolks of egg with $1\frac{1}{2}$ oz. of pounded sugar, add the milk, and finish the custards as directed in the preceding recipe.

ORANGE AND LEMON CUSTARDS

Make the custards as directed in the preceding recipe, substituting some grated orange or lemon peel for the vanilla.

ORANGE FLOWER WATER CUSTARDS

Make the custards as directed for Vanilla Custards, flavouring the milk with Orange Flower Water instead of the vanilla.

ALMOND BLANC-MANGER

Blanch, peel, and wash 2 oz. of Jordan almonds;

Pound the almonds in a mortar, adding ½ pint of water;

Press the whole through a broth napkin, and put the almond milk into a basin; add ½ pint of cold syrup registering 32°, and a teaspoonful of Orange Flower Water;

Dissolve ½ oz. of gelatine in the way described for Red Currant Jelly (*vide* page 296);

When the gelatine is cold, mix it with the almond milk, pour the whole into a mould, and set it on the ice.

LAIT DE POULE

Put the yolks of 2 new laid eggs in a basin;

Beat them up with 1 oz. of pounded sugar and a teaspoonful of Orange Flower Water, and stir in ½ pint of boiling water or milk.

Lait de Poule should be taken very hot, and will be found very soothing for coughs and colds.

HERB BROTH

Take 2 oz. of fillet of veal, trim off all fat and skin, cut the meat in small pieces, and put it in a stewpan with 2 quarts of water;

Boil, skim, add a little salt, and simmer for twenty minutes; then put the stewpan over a brisk fire, boil up the broth, and put in :

4 oz. of picked lettuce leaves,

4 oz. of picked sorrel,

4 oz. of picked chervil;

Close the stewpan, take it off the fire, and let the herbs steep for an hour;

Strain the broth through a fine hair sieve, or through a broth napkin.

The broth may be prepared in the same way, substituting an equal quantity of chicken for the veal, and omitting the sorrel.

JUJUBE PASTE

Take $\frac{1}{2}$ lb. of jujube fruit, cut each jujube in two, remove the stones, and put the fruit in a jar with 4 oz. of water, and let it macerate for twelve hours;

Wash 3 lbs. of gum arabic in several waters, drain, and put it in a sugar-boiler with $3\frac{1}{2}$ lbs. of water, add the jujube water, previously strained through a hair sieve, and place the sugar-boiler in a stewpan of boiling water, and put the whole over a slow fire, so that the water in the stewpan shall only simmer;

When the gum is dissolved, strain the water, and put it back into the sugar-boiler, add 2 lbs. of loaf sugar, and 4 oz. of Orange Flower Water;

Put the sugar-boiler back into the stewpan in some more boiling water; put the stewpan on the fire, and let the water contained therein *boil* for twelve hours, replenishing with boiling water as it evaporates;

Remove the scum and skin from the top, and pour the contents of the sugar-boiler, to a $\frac{1}{4}$ inch thickness, on to some slightly oiled tin baking-sheets;

Put the paste to dry in the hot closet, turning it over when one side is dry;

Cut the jujube paste into small diamond-shaped pieces, and keep them in a tin in a dry place.

LICHEN PASTE

Put 1 lb. of Iceland lichen in a copper stewpan, and cover it entirely with water; boil for five minutes and drain the lichen on a sieve; wash it three times in cold water, drain, and put it back in the stewpan with 5 quarts of water;

Boil until the water is reduced to 3 quarts, and strain the decoction through a broth napkin into a sugar-boiler;

Wash 3 lbs. of gum arabic, add it to the decoction, and dissolve it *au bain-marie* as directed in the preceding recipe;

Strain the dissolved gum through a hair sieve, or through a broth napkin into a sugar-boiler, add 2 lbs. of loaf sugar, and stir the whole over the fire until it is reduced to a proper consistence;

Pour the paste on to a slightly oiled marble slab, and when cold, wipe it and cut it into $\frac{3}{4}$ inch square pieces.

LIQUORICE PASTE

Wash 2 lbs. of gum arabic, and dissolve it *au bain-marie* with 2 quarts of water;

Dissolve 4 oz. of Spanish liquorice in 1 quart of water;

When the gum and liquorice are dissolved, strain both through a silk sieve into a sugar-boiler; add 2 lbs. of loaf-sugar, and stir the whole over the fire until it is reduced to a proper consistence;

Slightly oil some tin baking-sheets, and pour the paste on to them to a $\frac{3}{4}$-inch thickness;

Put the paste to dry in the hot-closet, turning it over when one side is dry;

Keep the liquorice paste in tins, and cut it as it is required.

WHEY

Boil 1 quart of milk, and throw into it $\frac{1}{4}$ oz. of Citric Acid dissolved in a tablespoonful of water; when the milk is curdled strain it through a fine hair sieve, and clarify it as follows;

Put the white of an egg in a stewpan, whip it with a wire whisk, and mix in the whey when nearly cold;

Put the stewpan on the fire, and stir the whey until it boils, simmer for two minutes, strain through a filtering-bag and keep the whey in a cool place;

The clarifying process is not necessary as it does not improve the quality of the whey, but merely gives it a more pleasing appearance.

EXTRACT OF HERBS

Pick :

 1 oz. of succory,

 1 oz. of water cresses,

 1 oz. of lettuce leaves ;

 1 oz of fumitory ;

Pound the herbs in a mortar, and press them through a coarse broth napkin, previously rinsed in boiling water;

Filter the herb juice through a paper-filter placed in a glass funnel (*vide* Modes of Filtering, page 136), and bottle it for use.

REMARKS ON THE PREPARATION OF ALL HERBS AND FLOWERS USED FOR INFUSIONS

When preparing these teas and decoctions, none but utensils reserved for this one purpose, should be used.

As a general rule, no infusion or decoction should extend over one hour.

The different beverages should not be made too strong.

It is usual to boil all roots, and to put all flowers to infuse in water.

The teas will be found easier of digestion if taken tepid, rather than cold.

In summer, an agreeable and refreshing drink can be made by putting some picked currants, or bruised cherries, to steep in boiling water, and, when cool, straining the water, and sweetening it according to taste ;

When strawberries are used in this way, they should be steeped in cold water ;

Oranges or lemons are cut into slices, put to steep in hot or cold water, strained, and sweetened in the same way.

MULLEIN FLOWERS

As this plant continues blossoming for some time, the flowers should be gathered as they open ; they should be spread out on a wooden table in a shady place ; moved about twice a day till they are quite dry ; put in a paper bag, or in tins, and kept in a dark place.

WHITE NETTLE BLOSSOMS

Gather the blossoms when quite free from moisture, pick, and spread them out to dry in the shade, and keep them in a dark cupboard in tins, or paper bags.

LINDEN BLOSSOMS

Gather the blossoms before sunrise, pick them, spread them out to dry in the shade, and keep the dried blossoms in tins, or in paper bags.

ELDER FLOWERS

Elder flowers should, like Linden blossoms, and similar flowers, be gathered before sunrise ;

Put the blossoms all together in a wooden bucket, cover them with a thick cloth, and let them remain thus until their own heat has ripened and opened every blossom; then sift them through a cane sieve ;

Spread out the sifted flowers on a table in a shady place, until they are dry, and keep them in tins or in paper bags ;

The blossoms should not be left too long in the bucket, or they would redden, and lose their aroma.

HOLLYHOCK BLOSSOMS

Pick off the flowers as they open, spread them out in a shady place, until they are perfectly dry ; and keep them in paper bags or in tins.

CAMOMILE FLOWERS

Gather the flowers, and pick off all the stalks ;

Spread the flowers out on a table, placed in the shade, and move them about twice a day until they are quite dry, and keep the dried flowers in tins or in paper bags.

VIOLET BLOSSOMS

Pick the blossoms off the stalks, spread them out to dry in the shade, moving them about occasionally ;

When quite dry pick the flowers again, and keep them in paper bags, or in tins, in a dry place.

MALLOW FLOWERS

Pick the blossoms off the stalks, spread out the flowers to dry in a shady place, and keep them in paper bags, or in tins, in a dry place.

ROSES

Pick the roses to pieces, and spread out the leaves on a table, in a shady place;

When quite dry, keep the rose-leaves in tins, or in paper bags.

POPPIES

Pick some poppies to pieces as directed in the preceding recipe; spread them out to dry on a table, placed in the shade;

Detach the petals, if they adhere to one another, and keep the dried poppies in tins, or in paper bags.

ORANGE FLOWERS

Pick the blossoms to pieces, spread them out to dry in the shade, and keep them in paper bags or in tins.

ORANGE LEAVES

Gather some middle-sized leaves off some orange trees before sunrise;

Spread them out to dry in the shade and keep them in tins or in paper bags.

BORAGE FLOWERS

Cut off the blossoming tops of the plants; dry the flowers on a table placed in the shade, and keep them in tins or in paper bags.

MARSH-MALLOW FLOWERS

Gather the flowers before sunrise ;

Pick them off the stalks, and spread them out on a table in a shady place.

When the flowers are perfectly dry put them into tins or in paper bags, and keep them in a dry place.

COMMON CENTAURY AND OTHER HERBS

Tie the centaury into small bundles, about ten sprigs in each bundle, and tie them to a string across a warm, airy and dark place; when quite dry keep the bundles in tins or in paper bags.

Hyssop, Mint, Thyme, Bayleaves, Rosemary, Sage, Fennel, Marjoram and Basil are tied in bundles and dried in the same way.

CHAPTER XXVIII

THE PRESERVING OF EGGS AND MILK

PRESERVED EGGS

Many means have been tried for preserving eggs : by using either salt, bran, sawdust, straw, ashes, &c.

Appert's plan was to subject the egg to a determined degree of heat, but this means was not successful, because an egg that has already been partly cooked is no longer suitable for the more delicate culinary operations; Finger Biscuits, *Meringues* and Creams prepared with such eggs would not possess the required lightness; this is self-evident, for when the white of an egg is partly set, it will be found impossible to whip it.

Lime water has also been employed, with a somewhat better result, but it has been found most difficult to regulate the proper quantity of lime which should be added to the water; moreover, the slightest crack in the shell would give access to the lime water, which would harden the egg and make it unfit for anything but hard-boiling.

I consider salt water the best preserving medium; it should be used as follows:

Boil some water and salt to a density of 18° by the saccharometer;

Set a layer of eggs at the bottom of a barrel, cover it with 3 inches of salt water; place a second layer of eggs on the first, and pour in some more salt water; and continue in the same way till the barrel is full ; close it up, and each time any of the eggs are taken out for use, see that those remaining in the barrel be covered entirely with salt water.

Eggs which are intended for preserving thus, should be chosen as fresh as possible ; but in case they should be quite new-laid, they must be allowed to get cold.

This mode of preserving eggs, which I have long seen applied with the best results, appears to me the simplest and best.

PRESERVED MILK

As with eggs, many attempts have been made to preserve milk.

Appert tried boiling the milk by steam, after enclosing it in air-tight tins.

This did not answer because the fatty part of the milk separated from the more liquid part, and it was found difficult to re-unite them.

By adding the yolk of eggs to the milk he met with a better result, but this method also, on account of its difficulties, had to be abandoned ;

Gay Lussac, the celebrated chemist, boiled the milk with Bi-Carbonate of Soda ; this boiling he would repeat every other day in cold weather, and daily in summer ; the drawback to this process was, that some 15 to 20 quarts of milk were used to obtain about 5 quarts at the end of two months daily boilings.

M. de Lignac was rather more successful :

He put the milk to evaporate over a slow fire, adding $\frac{1}{4}$ lb. of sifted sugar to every quart of milk ; he thus obtained a thick extract of milk of about the consistence of honey ;

This extract he would enclose in soldered air-tight tins, which he then boiled in water for an hour.

A tablespoonful of this extract, diluted with five table-spoonfuls of water, is a capital substitute for fresh milk.

This process therefore is the one I would recommend.

BUTTER MAKING

Besides having good milk, the following directions should be observed in order to ensure making good butter :

All the utensils should be kept scrupulously clean ;

For the several washings of the butter in summer, very cold water should be used ;

The temperature of the dairy in which the butter is churned should not in summer exceed 50° Fahrenheit, nor fall below that point in winter ;

The milking-pails should be well scalded and rinsed in cold water ;

Before milking, the cows' teats should be washed ;

The milk, as soon as milked, should be poured out into clean and dry earthenware pans, and allowed to stand from fifteen to eighteen hours.

Skim off the cream and put it into a churn, and work it with a very regular action ; to churn it either too fast or too slowly would be prejudicial to the quantity and the quality of the butter produced ;

Take the butter out of the churn, and put it in a wooden trough filled with cold water; press and work the butter in the water with the hands ; changing the water several times, and adding a little salt ; and continue thus until all the butter-milk is expelled ;

Then take the butter out and lay it on some clean coarse cloths, cover it over with some more cloths, and press it well to expel entirely any remaining butter-milk or water ;

Shape the butter into equal sized rolls or pats and keep it in a cool place wrapped in cloths.

SALT BUTTER

To preserve butter so that its flavour be retained, no better way has yet been discovered than to salt it;

To clarify it by melting, cannot be considered a kindred process, for in the melting the butter loses all its flavour and most of its other qualities.

Butter is generally salted by adding 1 lb. of salt to every 20 lbs. of butter, but this proportion I consider somewhat excessive.

When the butter has been made as just directed, put it in the salting-bin and add 1 lb. of salt to every 25 lbs. of butter; mix in the salt with some wooden spatulas;

Put the salted butter into earthenware jars, with a layer of salt half an inch thick on the top;

I cannot impress sufficiently on my readers, that the careful washing of the butter is the point on which its quality entirely depends; and I am convinced that butters which now sell at inferior prices, would fetch the highest price if this important matter was properly attended to.

CLARIFIED BUTTER

Clarified butter is generally prepared with inferior qualities of butter; it is used for frying and for all other preparations where fresh butter is not necessary.

Half fill a large stewpan with butter and put it to boil in another stewpan containing some water;

Skim off the scum as it rises to the surface, and keep stirring the butter with the skimmer, to prevent its overflowing ; butter so melted rises as suddenly as boiling milk, and requires watching accordingly ;

When the butter becomes quite clear and transparent, take it off the fire and skim it carefully ;

Strain the butter through a broth napkin, and pour it into earthenware jars ;

When cold, cover the jars, and keep the butter in a cool place.

It is important that the butter should be skimmed carefully, and that the sediment at the bottom of the stewpan should not be poured into the jars with the butter, as it would spoil its clearness, and might give it an unpleasant taste.

PREPARATION OF CAKE CHOCOLATE

Take :

2 lbs. of Maravilla cocoa berries,

2 lbs. of Caraccas cocoa berries,

4 lbs. of pounded sugar ;

Pick the berries to remove all foreign substances, and use only those which are perfectly sound ;

Roast the berries in a copper pan over a slow fire to remove the skins ; crush the berries and shake them in a pan so that all the skins and husks may blow away ;

Put the berries in an iron mortar, previously warmed, and pound them until they form a soft paste ; add the sugar, and continue pounding until the whole is well mixed together ;

Take the paste out of the mortar and grind it, in small quantities, with a rolling-pin, on a stone kept constantly warm ;

Press the chocolate into $\frac{1}{4}$ or $\frac{1}{2}$ lb. tin moulds, place the

moulds on a baking-sheet, shake them to make the paste
fall well into the shape, and let the chocolate get cold;

Unmould the chocolate and wrap it up, first in tin foil
and then in paper.

VANILLA CHOCOLATE

Proceed as above; and whilst grinding the paste on the
stone, add 6 sticks of vanilla and 2 oz. of sugar previously
pounded together and sifted through a silk sieve.

CINNAMON CHOCOLATE

For 2 lbs. of chocolate paste prepared as above, add $\frac{1}{8}$
oz. of ground and sifted cinnamon.

FERRUGINOUS CHOCOLATE

Add $\frac{3}{4}$ oz. of pulverised iron filings to 2 lbs. of the
chocolate paste prepared as directed above.

As this chocolate does not keep well, it should only be prepared in small quantities.

SALEP CHOCOLATE

Mix 1 oz. of pounded and sifted salep to every 2 lbs. of
the chocolate paste.

REMARKS ON CHOCOLATE

In establishments where large quantities of chocolate are
used, and where there are plenty of hands to assist, I should
advise its being manufactured on the premises, as it will be
found much more economical.

The first cost of the several utensils will soon be covered by the difference in the price, and by the superior quality of the chocolate.

I have specified in the above recipe a lesser quantity of sugar than that generally adopted by chocolate manufacturers; but it must be remembered that the quantity of sugar, far from improving the quality of the chocolate, merely tends to reduce its cost price.

REMARKS ON WINES

I shall close this book with a few remarks on the use of wine, its influence on health, and the proper mode and time of serving it.

Wine has so important an influence on health that great judgment and discernment should be exercised in using it.

Thus to children of a weak and languid constitution it will be best, at meals, to give a full bodied Burgundy in small quantities, and diluted with three parts of water to one of wine ; after meals a very small quantity of wine, without water, may be allowed them without injury.

Whilst for strong healthy children, light Claret, diluted with, at least, three parts of water, will be preferable, and wine without water should very seldom be given to them.

For persons far advanced in years, old wine, in small quantities, is always to be preferred ; taken in such a way, it is a valuable tonic, but when taken in anything approaching excess, it loses all its beneficial effects.

To those fortunate individuals in the prime of life who are gifted with a powerful constitution, I would recommend but a very sparing use of wine, and only of the lighter kinds.

The following remarks on the subject, taken from a work

by Dr. P. Gaubert, ' On the Stimulating Effect of Wine,' are
to the point :

' The strength or weakness of a constitution depending
upon that of the main organs of the circulation of the blood,
whenever any of these, particularly the heart, show any
symptoms of weakness, I would recommend the greatest
caution in the use of wine.

' When wine is taken by persons in such an unsatisfactory
state of health, the stimulating power, which all good wine
possesses, and which is proportionate to its body, puts upon
the diseased organ a sudden strain which exceeds what it
can bear.

' What is true of the heart, and other organs of the circulation of the blood, applies with the same force to the
brain ; whenever the cerebral machinery is out of its proper
equilibrium with that of the other organs, it will be better
to abstain from wine; the least excess will produce con-
gestion, which, in its mildest form, we so often see painfully
illustrated by headache.

' In a lesser degree, it can be said of all the minor organs
that, where there is a chronic tendency to weakness, there
will wine first manifest its injurious effects; thus, in the
same way as a weak sight suffers from too much light or
wind, so will it suffer from the use of alcoholic stimulants,
and manifest the fact by inflamed and blood-shot eyes.

' My object is not to recommend in all such cases the total
abstinence from wine, but merely to advise its discreet use
and judicious selection.'

In a general way, wine may be said to have the following
influence on our frame. A light clear wine, with but little
colour and alcohol, gives a wholesome fillip to the circulation ; a full-bodied and alcoholic wine, on the contrary, is
rather calculated to make it sluggish.

THE SERVING OF WINE

Having had many opportunities of testing the most pleasant mode of serving wine at dinner, and its most successful order of precedence, I think it well to give a few hints on this subject.

After the soup and fish, Sherry, Madeira, or Marsala, are frequently served ; but I would advise selecting lighter wines, such as Sauterne, Grâves, Châblis, Pouilly, Meursault, or Montrachet; all these wines, as well as light Champagnes, which can with advantage be served at this stage of a dinner, should be very cool ;

Such wines do not clog the appetite, as stronger wines would do, but, on the contrary, they give it a gentle fillip, and endow it with new vigour.

Comparing a dinner to a brilliant orchestral composition, it strikes me very forcibly that, if, at the very first bars, I am deafened by the big drum, the double bass, and the trombone, I shall no longer be able to appreciate the sweet melodies which are about to follow.

Similarly if, at the beginning of a meal, my host is too persistent in helping me to full-bodied wines, he will deaden my palate, take off the edge of my appetite, and prevent my appreciating the delicacy of the cookery.

At the beginning of a dinner, therefore, have only the lighter kinds of wine; with the roast serve those which have more body ; they will prepare the palate for the more delicate wines, which should follow, namely, such Burgundies as Corton, Clos-Vougeot, Romanée-Conti, and Pomard; or such as some of the undermentioned Clarets : St. Julien, Gruau-Laroze, Léoville, Lafite, and Château-Margaux.

With dessert, serve the following sweet wines : Malaga, Alicant, Rivesaltes, Malmsy, Lacryma-Christi, Constance, Tokay, and the higher brands of Champagne (iced).

Following these remarks, will be found a long list of wines, amongst which the reader will be able to make his own selection.

My directions for serving wine will probably be criticised; but I would beg of those who differ from me to judge the question on its own merits : if the art of the cook is to provoke appetite without overtaxing the digestive organs, surely that of he who boasts of a good cellar is to induce his friends to drink without endangering their sobriety ?

I consider it bad taste to serve too many different wines ; variety without profusion should be the aim ; and quality should be the very first consideration, not only for the Higher Class Wines, but principally for the more common descriptions of *vins ordinaires*, which, as they are most used during the meal, should be selected with proportionate care.

Lastly, the following directions should be attended to before serving the different wines :

Vin ordinaire should be served in claret jugs, and very cool ; in winter it will be sufficient to bring it direct from the cellar, when wanted ; in summer it should be very slightly iced, or put to cool in spring water.

Claret of a choice vintage should be brought from the cellar a few hours before it is required, so that it may become of the same temperature as the dining-room ; it is a mistake to imagine that putting it before the fire improves it.

Burgundy is best when cool, by which I do not mean *cold* ; for, should the weather be very cold, it will be improved by being kept in the dining-room some little time before it is served.

Champagne, on the contrary, is never so good as when it is iced ; icing brings out all its latent qualities ; and your guests, when they drink it, will find therein the necessary eloquence to praise worthily the efforts made to please them.

HIGHER CLASS FRENCH WINES

The GIRONDE district produces : Château-Lafite, Château-Margaux, Château-Latour, Château-Haut-Brion, Rozan, Gorse, Léoville, Château-Larose, Brane-Mouton, Pichon-Longueville, Calon, Pauillac, Pessac, Saint-Estèphe, Saint-Julien, Reignac, Castelnau, Médoc.

White wines: Sauterne, Château-Yquem, Pontac, Sauterne-Saluce, Carbonieux, Sainte-Croix, Pujol, Langon, Grâves.

The DROME district produces several growths of Red Hermitage ;

White wines : White Hermitage, Mercurol, Dié.

The RHONE district produces : Côte-Rôtie, Vérinay, Condrieu.

The VAUCLUSE district produces the following red wines : Côteaux-Brûlés, Clos de la Nerthe, Saint-Patrice.

The GARD district produces such first-class wines as : Thuzelan, Tavel, Saint-Geris, Lirac, Lenedon.

. The ARDÈCHE district produces: Cornac, Saint-Joseph, red wines ; and Saint-Péray, Saint-Jean, white wines.

The CÔTE D'OR, queen of wine-growing districts, produces: Romanée-Conti, Chambertin, Clos-Vougeot, Laperrière, Richebourg, Musigny, Latache, Romanée-Saint-Vivant, Saint-George, Prémeau, Du Tart, Saint-Jacques, Mazi, Morjot, Nuits, Chambolle, Volnay, Pomard, Beaune, Savigny, Meursault, Chassagne, Santenay.

The white wines grown in this district are less in number, but are quite equal to the red in delicacy and aroma ;

amongst them I will mention: Montrachet, Chevalier-Mont-rachet, Bâtard-Montrachet, Perrière, Combette, Goutte-d'Or, Santenot, Charmes, Meursault, Rougeot.

The MARNE district produces most of the best growths of Champagne, such as : Verzenay, Bouzi, Mailly, Verzy, Clos-Saint, Thierry, Sillery, Clozet, Aï, Pierry, Cramant, Avise, Oger, Lemeuil, Epernay, Cumière.

There are also a few red wines, which are very agreeable, and possess a delicate aroma, but they do not keep well.

The YONNE district produces : Côtes-Olivotte, Migraine, Préaux, Chainette, Clairion, Quétard, Chapotte, Rosoir, Francy, Coulange.

White wines : Vaumorillon, Grisées, Clos de Val-Mur, Grenouille, Vaudésir, Bourguereaux, Châblis.

The SAÔNE-ET-LOIRE district produces: Moulin-à-vent, Thorins, Chenac, Fleury, Romanèche, Chapelle-Guinchey, Mercurey, Gevry.

White wines : Pouilly, Fuissey, Solutré, Chaintré.

The JURA district is celebrated for such white wines as : Arbois, Château-Châlon, Étoile de Quintigel.

The HIGHER AND LOWER RHINE districts produce the following white wines: Molsheim, Volxheim, Guebwiller, Turckheim, Riquewihr, and the sparkling and delicate fla-voured Ribeauvillés.

FRENCH VINS ORDINAIRES

After giving a list of the choicer wines I think it well to mention a few good sound *vins ordinaires*.

The wines most generally used for mixing with lighter wines to give them more body and colour are: Roussillon, Narbonne, Gaillac, Marseille and Cahors.

The BOUCHES-DU-RHONE district produces some full-bodied and highly coloured wines, which will be found useful as *vins ordinaires*, diluted with water, for they are too strong to be taken undiluted in any considerable quantity; amongst these wines I will mention: Château-Gomber, Quartier des Olives, Léon Kint, Henry Cuque.

The GARD district produces the following, which will also bear diluting with water: Saint-André, La Casagne, Laube, Petit-Casagne, Pérouse.

The TARN district produces: Cunac, Caisequet, Saint-Juéry, Saint-Amarans.

The HÉRAULT district produces: Langlade, Saint-Drezery, Saint-Georges.
Lunel and Frontignan produce some good sweet wines.

The HAUTE GARONNE district produces: Villandric, Fronton-Montesquieu, Volvestre, Buzet, Cugnaux.
All these wines are very good diluted with water, and may also be mixed with lighter wines.

The BASSES-PYRÉNÉES district produces strong and generous wines much valued for exporting, such as: Côteaux de Moneins, Aubertin, Luc, Lasseube, Jurançon.

The VAR district produces: Baudot, Castelet, Saint-Cyr, Bauset; which are all good *vins ordinaires*.

The SAÔNE-ET-LOIRE district produces: Mercurey, Touche, Estroy, Bourgneuf.

These are all light wines, with a fine aroma, which will improve by keeping; they should be classed as superior *vins ordinaires*.

The YONNE district produces the best and most general *vins ordinaires*, such as: Auxerre, Tonnerre, Cheney, Molosem, Vermanton, Vezinnes, Juniac, Saint-Martin-sur-Armançon, Saint-Julien-du-Saut, Joigny.

The RHONE district produces: Villiers, Durette, Etoux, Reigner, Cercie, Jasseron, Vadoux.
All these wines may be drunk when they are. two years old.

The DROME district produces: Saillan, Verchemy, Dié, Dozère, Roussai, Montélimar, Mont-Ségur, Géry.
These wines will require four years' keeping before they are drunk.

The GIRONDE district produces: Médoc, Red Grâves, Blaye, Palus, Queyries, Côte-d'entre-deux-mers.
These wines, and those grown in the YONNE district, are the most general *vins ordinaires*.

The LOIRET district produces some very good and agreeable red wines; and some white wines, grown about Vouvray, which are appreciated by many, notwithstanding their strong earthy flavour.

PRINCIPAL FOREIGN WINES

To buy these wines, and to know what one is buying, is so difficult a matter, that I would really advise relying rather upon the recommendation of a respectable wine-merchant, than endeavouring to select them unaided.

I will mention among Italian wines: Acqui, Valenza, Tortona, Alessandria, Casali, Turin, Pignerol, Saluzzo, Alba, Barotto, Alzona.

Rhenish wines, such as: Johannisberg, Rüdesheim, Steinberg, Grafenberg, Kidrich, Liebfrauenmilch (Our Lady's Milk), Assmannshaüser, Bacharacher.

Unadulterated Paraxite Sherry, of a good quality, is very seldom to be obtained; amongst other sherries of a somewhat inferior quality, I will mention: Rancio, Peralta, Amontillado, Manzanilla.

Portugal produces some good dry wines, such as: Celleiros, St. Ubes, Termo, Bucellas, Carcavellos.

Hungary produces the following red wines : Buda, Erlau, Sirmien, Lutz.
White wines : Schirarker, Calemberg, Luttenberg, Styria.

I would also class Dry Marsala and Castel-Veterano amongst good Italian white wines.

I consider Dry Madeira, when of a good quality and unadulterated, one of the most agreeable Foreign Wines.

SWEET WINES

Among sweet wines, none are to be compared to Tokay, Lacryma-Christi, Red and White Muscatel, Alicant, Rosa, Malaga, Malmsy, Pedro-Ximenes, Constance, and Madeira-Malmsy.

AGES OF DIFFERENT WINES WHEN AT THEIR PRIME

The age named below for each wine will be found to be that at which it possesses its fullest flavour and when it will be best to drink it.

Port, 20 years. Madeira, 10 years. Sherry, 10 years. Red Madeira, 6 years. Madeira-Malmsy, 5 years. Callavella, 4 years. Malaga, 3 years. Muscatel, 3 years.

Red Hermitage, 20 years. White Hermitage, 20 years. Roussillon, 20 years. Rivesaltes, 20 years. Banyuls, 20 years. Collioure, 15 years. Salces, 10 years. La Palme, 10 years. Sigean, 8 years. Carcassone, 8 years. Beziers, 8 years. Lunel, 8 years. Champagne, 6 years. Montpellier, 5 years. Frontignan, 5 years.

The best wines are far from being those which contain the most alcohol; as the superiority of Champagne, Bordeaux, and Burgundy growths over those of Narbonne, Beziers, and Montpellier, tends to show.

The wines of the South of France are very rich in alcohol, but are unpleasant taken alone; they are very valuable for mixing with lighter wines.

Wine as it grows older will, if it be well corked, increase the quantity of alcohol which it contains; this explains the greater strength of the older of two wines made from grapes grown in the self-same district.

All the wine exported from Spain is mixed, and it is next to an impossibility to get it genuine.

INDEX

INDEX TO WOODCUTS

LONDON: PRINTED BY
SPOTTISWOODE AND CO., NEW-STREET SQUARE
AND PARLIAMENT STREET